# BAPTISM IN THE HOLY SPIRIT

JAMES D. G. DUNN

# BAPTISM
## IN THE
# HOLY SPIRIT

*A Re-examination of the New Testament Teaching
on the Gift of the Spirit
in relation to Pentecostalism today*

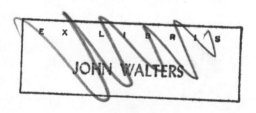

The Westminster Press
Philadelphia

Copyright © SCM Press Ltd 1970

Published by The Westminster Press ®

Philadelphia, Pennsylvania

PRINTED IN THE UNITED STATES OF AMERICA

Library of Congress Cataloging in Publication Data

Dunn, James D    G    1939–
    Baptism in the Holy Spirit.

    Includes bibliographical references and indexes.
    1. Baptism in the Holy Spirit — Biblical teaching.
I. Title.
BS680.H56D86 1977       234'.1       77-3995
ISBN 0-664-24140-9

# CONTENTS

# ABBREVIATIONS

| | |
|---|---|
| Arndt and Gingrich | W. F. Arndt and F. W. Gingrich, *A Greek-English Lexicon of the New Testament* (ET 1957) |
| AV | Authorized (King James) Version |
| *Bib.Sac.* | *Bibliotheca Sacra* |
| Blass-Debrunner-Funk | F. Blass and A. Debrunner, *A Greek Grammar of the New Testament and Other Early Christian Literature* (ET and ed. R. W. Funk, 1961) |
| BNT | *Baptism in the New Testament* – A Symposium by A. George and others (ET 1964) (originally a special study in two numbers of *Lumière et Vie,* 1956) |
| BNTE | *The Background of the New Testament and its Eschatology – Studies in Honour of C. H. Dodd* (ed. W. D. Davies and D. Daube, 1954) |
| BQ | *The Baptist Quarterly* |
| BZAW | Beihefte zur *Zeitschrift für die alttestamentliche Wissenschaft* |
| CBQ | *Catholic Biblical Quarterly* |
| ed. | Editor |
| EQ | *Evangelical Quarterly* |
| ET | English translation |
| EvTh | *Evangelische Theologie* |
| ExpT | *Expository Times* |
| HNT | Handbuch zum Neuen Testament |
| IB | *The Interpreter's Bible* |
| ICC | The International Critical Commentary |
| JB | The Jerusalem Bible |
| JBL | *Journal of Biblical Literature* |
| JTS | *Journal of Theological Studies* |
| Liddell and Scott | H. G. Liddell and R. Scott, *A Greek-English Lexicon* (revised by H. S. Jones, 1940) |
| LXX | Septuagint |
| Moffatt | The Moffatt New Testament Commentary (based on the translation of the NT by J. Moffatt) |
| Moulton and Milligan | J. H. Moulton and G. Milligan, *The Vocabulary of the Greek Testament* (1930) |

| | |
|---|---|
| n.d. | No date given |
| NEB | The New English Bible |
| *NovTest* | *Novum Testamentum* |
| NTD | Das Neue Testament Deutsch |
| *NTS* | *New Testament Studies* |
| *Peake* | *Peake's Commentary on the Bible* [2](ed. M. Black 1963) |
| *RB* | *Revue Biblique* |
| *RGG*[3] | *Die Religion in Geschichte und Gegenwart* [3](1957ff.) |
| RSV | Revised Standard Version |
| *SJT* | *Scottish Journal of Theology* |
| Strack-Billerbeck | H. L. Strack and P. Billerbeck, *Kommentar zum Neuen Testament aus Talmud und Midrasch* (1922ff.) |
| *TDNT* | *Theological Dictionary of the New Testament* (ET of *TWNT*) (trans. and ed. G. W. Bromiley 1964ff.) |
| TEV | *Good News for Modern Man: The New Testament: Today's English Version* |
| *TLZ* | *Theologische Literaturzeitung* |
| *TWBB* | *A Theological Word Book of the Bible* (ed. A. Richardson 1950) |
| *TWNT* | *Theologisches Wörterbuch zum Neuen Testament* (ed. G. Kittel; now G. Friedrich, 1933ff.) |
| *TZ* | *Theologische Zeitschrift* |
| *VocB* | *Vocabulary of the Bible* (ed. J.-J. von Allmen, ET 1958) |
| *ZNW* | *Zeitschrift für die neutestamentliche Wissenschaft* |

# PREFACE

This monograph is primarily a New Testament study. But it is occasioned by the increasing interest in and influence of Pentecostalism over the past ten years, and therefore has several subsidiary purposes. It is my hope that these chapters will help to introduce scholars, students and ministers to the most distinctive aspect of Pentecostal theology – baptism in the Holy Spirit. It will become evident that this doctrine cannot escape heavy criticism from a New Testament standpoint, but I would hope also that the importance and value of the Pentecostal emphasis will not be lost sight of or ignored. In particular, the Pentecostal contribution should cause Christians in the 'main-line' denominations to look afresh with critical eyes at the place they give to the Holy Spirit in doctrine and experience and in their various theologies of conversion, initiation and baptism. And any voice which bids us test familiar traditions by the yardstick of the New Testament is to be welcomed.

I wish to take this opportunity of expressing my thanks: to the Rev. Michael Harper for his interest, information and fellowship at various stages of my research; to Dr G. R. Beasley-Murray and the Rev. J. P. M. Sweet for their comments on an earlier draft (my thesis); and to the Rev. John Bowden and Miss Jean Cunningham of SCM Press for their advice and skill in the preparation of the manuscript for publication. I cannot sufficiently express my gratitude to Professor C. F. D. Moule, that most gracious Christian gentleman and scholar, whose acute and constructive criticism at all times during my research was invaluable. Above all comes my debt to my mother, whose years of sacrifice on her family's behalf is I hope rewarded in some small measure by this volume, and to Meta, my wife and 'true yokefellow', whose love and patience have been a constant inspiration and support in all the hours spent on this book.

*Edinburgh, March 1970*                    JAMES D. G. DUNN

# I

# INTRODUCTION

WITHIN more radical and pietistic Protestantism there has grown up a tradition which holds that salvation, so far as it may be known in this life, is experienced in two stages: first, the experience of becoming a Christian; then, as a later and distinct event, a second experience of the Holy Spirit. For many Puritans the second experience was one of assurance.[1] For Wesley the first stage was justification and partial sanctification, the second the divine gift of entire sanctification or Christian perfection.[2]

A direct line can be drawn from Puritan teaching on the Spirit through early Methodism to the nineteenth-century Holiness Movement with its 'Higher Life' message, in which justification by faith (deliverance from the penalty of sin) was distinguished from the second divine work of sanctification, also received by faith (deliverance from the power of sin). One of the Holiness Movement's most vigorous offspring, the Keswick Convention, used to be notable for its 'second blessing' teaching,[3] and such metaphors as the one which characterizes some Christians as living between Calvary and Pentecost still have currency at the Convention.

Within this whole tradition the idea of Spirit-baptism has often been associated with the second stage. Thomas Goodwin equated the experience of assurance with the 'seal of the Spirit' in Eph. 1.13f. and with the baptism with the Holy Ghost; he even called it 'a new conversion'.[4] John Fletcher, the saintly Methodist, quite

[1] See J. I. Packer, *The Wisdom of our Fathers* (Puritan Conference, 1956) 14-25; J. K. Parratt, *EQ* 41 (1969) 163; cf. *The Westminster Confession* XVIII.
[2] J. Wesley, *A Plain Account of Christian Perfection* (reprinted 1952).
[3] S. Barabas, *So Great Salvation – the History and Message of the Keswick Convention* (1952); see also B. B. Warfield, *Perfectionism* (1958) 3-215.
[4] Goodwin, *Works* I, Sermon XV, XVI, especially 237f., 247f., 251.

often used the phrase 'baptism with the Spirit' and understood it to describe the sudden receiving of entire sanctification.[5] And among the earlier 'Higher Life' teachers the second experience of sanctification was commonly called 'the baptism of the Holy Ghost'.

However, towards the close of the nineteenth century, particularly in America, the emphasis in the use of the phrase gradually shifted from the idea of sanctification and holiness (a purifying baptism of fire cleansing from sin) to that of empowering for service (principally on the basis of Luke 24.49; Acts 1.5, 8). At the same time in the United States there was a growing interest in spiritual gifts, and several prominent Holiness leaders taught that these could, and should still be in operation within the Church.

It was directly from this context that Pentecostalism sprang, the latest and most flourishing branch of Christianity. As a full-scale movement it dates from the remarkable series of meetings in Azusa Street, Los Angeles, which began in 1906. But its beginnings may be traced back to Topeka Bible College where what was to become the distinctive belief of Pentecostals was first fully formulated at the end of 1900 – namely, 'that in apostolic times, the speaking in tongues was considered to be the initial physical evidence of a person's having received the baptism in the Holy Spirit'. According to J. R. Flower, a leading figure in the American Assemblies of God from 1914 to 1959, 'It was this decision which has made the Pentecostal Movement of the Twentieth Century'.[6]

As a result of their own experience the early pioneers of this movement came to believe that the baptism in the Holy Spirit is a second (Pentecostal) experience distinct from and subsequent to conversion which gives power for witness (Acts 1.8), that speaking in tongues, as in Acts 2.4, is the necessary and inevitable evidence of the 'baptism', and that the spiritual gifts listed in I Cor. 12.8–10 may and should be manifested when Pentecostal Christians meet for worship. As so often happens in such cases, succeeding generations have hardened these early less rigid beliefs into the dogmas of Pentecostal tradition.

Pentecostalism has now become a movement of world-wide importance, reckoned as 'a third force in Christendom' (alongside Catholicism and Protestantism) by not a few leading churchmen. Moreover, since 1960 Pentecostal teaching has been making a

[5] N. Bloch-Hoell, *The Pentecostal Movement* (ET 1964) 141.
[6] C. Brumback, *Suddenly . . . From Heaven* (1961) 23.

significant penetration into older denominations.[7] Taken together these facts make imperative a close study of the distinctive Pentecostal doctrines.

Of particular interest to the NT scholar is the Pentecostal's teaching about the baptism in the Spirit, for in it he claims to have discovered the NT pattern of conversion-initiation – the only pattern which makes sense of the data in Acts – and also the principal explanation for the amazing growth of the early Church. But does the NT mean by baptism in the Holy Spirit what the Pentecostal understands the phrase to mean? Is baptism in the Holy Spirit to be separated from conversion-initiation, and is the beginning of the Christian life to be thus divided up into distinct stages? Is Spirit-baptism something essentially different from becoming a Christian, so that even a Christian of many years' standing may never have been baptized in the Spirit?

These are some of the important questions which Pentecostal teaching raises, and it will be the primary task of this book to re-examine the NT in the light of this teaching with a view to answering these questions. Put in a nutshell, we hope to discover what is the place of the gift of the Spirit in the total complex event of becoming a Christian. This will inevitably involve us in a wider debate than merely with Pentecostals. For many outside Pentecostalism make a straightforward identification between baptism in the Spirit and the Christian sacrament of water-baptism,[8] while others distinguish two gifts or comings of the Spirit, the first at conversion-initiation and the second at a later date, in Confirmation[9] or in the bestowal of charismata.[10] I shall therefore be

[7] See e.g. H. Berkhof, *The Doctrine of the Holy Spirit* (1964) 85–90; A. Walker, *Breakthrough: Rediscovering the Spirit* (1969) 40–54. For a fuller treatment see my forthcoming article in *SJT*.

[8] See p. 98 n. 17 below. For want of a better or more convenient label I shall use the word 'sacramentalist' to describe the view which regards water-baptism as the focus of conversion-initiation, so that forgiveness, the gift of the Spirit, membership of Christ, etc., become a function of the rite, and can be said to be mediated or conveyed through it (cf. C. Gore, *The Holy Spirit and the Church* [1924] 124 n. 1). The title does not describe a theological position as such, but in different passages different commentators will adopt a sacramentalist interpretation.

[9] For a high doctrine of Confirmation see especially A. J. Mason, *The Relation of Confirmation to Baptism* (1891); G. Dix, *Confirmation or the Laying on of Hands* (1936), also *The Theology of Confirmation in Relation to Baptism* (1946); L. S. Thornton, *Confirmation and its Place in the Baptismal Mystery* (1954).

[10] See p. 55 n. 1, p. 94 below.

defining my position over against two and sometimes three or four different standpoints.

This whole subject has often been treated in the past, but the Pentecostal doctrine of Spirit-baptism makes a new and important contribution to an old debate, and by focusing attention on the gift of the Spirit and separating the gift of the Spirit from conversion-initiation, it both revitalizes the debate and calls in question many of the traditionally accepted views of Christian baptism. A complete re-examination of the NT teaching on the gift of the Spirit and its relation to belief and baptism is therefore necessary.[11]

I hope to show that for the writers of the NT the baptism in or gift of the Spirit was part of the event (or process) of becoming a Christian, together with the effective proclamation of the Gospel, belief in *(εἰς)* Jesus as Lord, and water-baptism in the name of the Lord Jesus; that it was the chief element in conversion-initiation so that only those who had thus received the Spirit could be called Christians; that the reception of the Spirit was a very definite and often dramatic *experience*, the decisive and climactic experience in conversion-initiation, to which the Christian was usually recalled when reminded of the beginning of his Christian faith and experience.[12] We shall see that while the Pentecostal's belief in the dynamic and experiential nature of Spirit-baptism is well founded, his separation of it from conversion-initiation is wholly unjustified; and that, conversely, while water-baptism is an important element in the complex of conversion-initiation, it is neither to be equated or confused with Spirit-baptism nor to be given the most prominent part in that complex event. The high point in conversion-initiation is the gift of the Spirit, and the beginning of the Christian life is to be reckoned from the experience of Spirit-baptism.

We shall see that the baptism in the Spirit from the start was

[11] Cf. J. Weiss, *Earliest Christianity* (ET 1937) 623.

[12] J. Denney: 'In Acts, as elsewhere in the NT, the reception of the Spirit is the whole of Christianity' (*Dictionary of Christ and the Gospels* [1906] I 738); cf. R. C. Moberly, *Atonement and Personality* (1901) 90; *Doctrine in the Church of England* (1938). See also E. Schweizer, *TWNT* VI 394; L. Newbigin, *The Household of God* (1953) 89. The *experience* of the Spirit has been rightly emphasized by most writers on the Spirit; e.g. E. F. Scott, *The Spirit in the New Testament* (1923); H. W. Robinson, *The Christian Experience of the Holy Spirit* (1928); H. P. Van Dusen, *Spirit, Son and Father* (1960); G. S. Hendry, *The Holy Spirit in Christian Theology* [2](1965).

understood as an initiatory experience (chapter II), that even with Jesus himself the anointing of the Spirit at Jordan was essentially initiatory, and that the water-baptism of John was only preparatory for and not conflated with the bestowal of the Spirit (chapter III). The Pentecostal doctrine is built chiefly on Acts, but a detailed study will reveal that for the writer of Acts in the last analysis it is only by receiving the Spirit that one becomes a Christian; water-baptism is clearly distinct from and even antithetical to Spirit-baptism, and is best understood as the expression of the faith which receives the Spirit (Part Two). In the Pauline literature the story is much the same, although the distinction between water-baptism and Spirit-baptism is not so sharp (Part Three). With John both Pentecostalist and sacramentalist have firmer ground to stand on, but not firm enough to bear the weight of their respective theologies (Part Four). A final examination of Hebrews and I Peter confirms the negative conclusions and more restricted role we have had to give to the sacrament of baptism (Part Five).

Before turning to the detailed exegesis and exposition I should perhaps explain why I describe the event of becoming a Christian by the inelegant title 'conversion-initiation'. 'Baptism' is the usual shorthand description. But the trouble with 'baptism' is that it is a 'concertina' word: it may be used simply for the actual act of immersion in water, or its meaning may be expanded to take in more and more of the rites and constituent parts of conversion-initiation until it embraces the whole.[13]

Two difficulties arise: first, we are never quite sure just how broadly or how narrowly it is being used; second, however broad its use, at its centre always stands the rite of immersion. The inevitable happens: no matter how whole-hearted the initial protest that 'baptism' is being used for the whole event of becoming a Christian, sooner or later the reader becomes aware that the wind has been squeezed out of the concertina and we are really talking about the rite of immersion, and it is to the water-rite that all the blessings (forgiveness, union with Christ, the gift of the Spirit, etc.) of the whole event are being ascribed. It will become apparent in this study that the confusion of water-baptism with Spirit-baptism inevitably involves the confusion of water with Spirit, so

[13] E.g. R. Allen, *Missionary Methods – St Paul's or Ours?* [5](1960) 73 n. 1; N. Clark in *Crisis for Baptism* (ed. B. S. Moss 1965) 71.

that the administration of water becomes nothing other than the bestowal of the Spirit.[14]

In Reformed theology a 'sacrament' has been classically defined as having two parts: 'an outward and sensible sign' and 'an inward and spiritual grace thereby signified' (*The Westminster Larger Catechism* 163). 'Neither of these, the sign or the "grace", is by itself the Sacrament; a Sacrament exists where sign and grace are brought together into one operation and constitute a single action.' The 'outward part (the sign) . . . actually conveys and confers its spiritual part' (H. J. Wotherspoon and J. M. Kirkpatrick, *A Manual of Church Doctrine According to the Church of Scotland* [1920], revised and enlarged by T. F. Torrance and R. S. Wright [1965] 17–19; see also 19–25; cf. Wotherspoon, *Religious Values in the Sacraments* [1928] 123–6 and *passim*; R. S. Wallace, *Calvin's Doctrine of the Word and Sacrament* [1953] 159–71; Church of Scotland, Special Commission on Baptism, *The Biblical Doctrine of Baptism* [1958] 62–64, 67–69; also *The Doctrine of Baptism* [1962] 11; T. F. Torrance, *TZ* 14 [1958] 243f.; E. J. F. Arndt, *The Font and the Table* [1967] 14f., 17). In my opinion this definition misinterprets the teaching of the NT. The Oxford Dictionary shows that both in traditional and modern usage 'sacrament' refers primarily to the ceremony or rite seen as somehow a means of grace.

Even more important is the fact that although βάπτισμα and βαπτίζειν are used in the NT either literally or metaphorically, these uses are quite distinct, as we shall see; no single occurrence of either word embraces both meanings simultaneously. The NT never uses 'baptism' as a description of the total event of becoming a Christian (including repentance, confession, water-baptism, forgiveness, etc). In the NT βάπτισμα and βαπτίζειν are never concertina words; their meanings are always clear cut.

I am thus in fundamental disagreement at this point with the Church of Scotland's Special Commission: 'Baptisma never refers to the rite of Baptism alone; it refers also to the salvation events which give the rite its meaning and which are operative in the rite through the work of the Holy Spirit (*Biblical Doctrine* 17f.; see also their *Interim Report* [1955] 8–10; Torrance 248f.).

An alternative to 'baptism' is not easy to find. For the sake of precision we want to distinguish water-baptism from the other ritual acts like oral confession and laying on of hands. There are

[14] See p. 98 n. 17 below.

also the more inward, subjective (even mystical) aspects of the whole event like repentance, forgiveness, union with Christ. I shall therefore use 'initiation' to describe the ritual, external acts as distinct from these latter,[15] and 'conversion' when we are thinking of that inner transformation as distinct from, or rather without including the ritual acts. The total event of becoming a Christian embraces both 'conversion' and 'initiation', and so we shall call it 'conversion-initiation'.

My sole purpose here is clarity of thought. The terms chosen do not pre-judge the relation between 'conversion' and 'initiation', whether they are distinct, or simultaneous, or synonymous. The terms themselves are far from adequate,[16] and impart an element of rigidity which is regrettable, but in a discussion which has been obscured by lack of precise definitions with terms often too fluid to be grasped adequately, it is of the utmost importance that we enter the debate with the meaning of such central concepts clear and unambiguous.

[15] This restriction of the meaning to the ritual act refers only to the noun 'initiation'.

[16] 'Initiation' has overtones of pagan cults and secret societies, and 'conversion' tends to be popularly linked with an emotional (and too often shallow) 'decision for Christ'. More serious is the fact that 'conversion' properly describes man's act of turning to God (cf. F. Field, *Notes on the Translation of the New Testament* [1899] 246–51; W. Barclay, *Turning to God: Conversion in the New Testament* [1963] 21–25); but there is no other suitable word, and its use in a broader, less literal sense, of something which happens to and in a man ('to be converted') rather than or including something he himself does ('to convert') is quite common and respectable. See e.g. W. James, *The Varieties of Religious Experience* (1960 edition) 194; A. C. Underwood, *Conversion: Christian and Non-Christian* (1925); O. Brandon, *Christianity from Within* (1965) 23–25. In my use 'conversion' embraces both the human and the divine action in the whole (non-ritual) event of becoming a Christian.

## PART ONE

## II

## THE EXPECTATION OF JOHN THE BAPTIST

A STUDY of the 'baptism in the Holy Spirit' naturally begins with the words of John the Baptist: in Mark's version (1.8):

ἐγὼ ἐβάπτισα ὑμᾶς ὕδατι,
αὐτὸς δὲ βαπτίσει ὑμᾶς πνεύματι ἁγίῳ.

We will confine ourselves initially to the second half of the logion – a clause which has caused commentators much perplexity. Two questions pose themselves: 'What was its original form (Matthew and Luke add καὶ πυρί)?' and 'What did it originally mean?' Since the end of the last century two reconstructions have gained approval, so that today most scholars would deny that John mentioned the Holy Spirit, at least in this connection: either he spoke of baptism in fire alone,[1] or else he spoke of baptism with wind (πνεῦμα) and fire,[2] in both cases the metaphor of baptism being equivalent to the metaphor of winnowing and destruction by fire which immediately follows (Matt. 3.12; Luke 3.17).

---

[1] C. A. Briggs, *The Messiah of the Gospels* (1894) 67, cited in H. G. Marsh, *Origin and Significance of New Testament Baptism* (1941) 29; J. Wellhausen, *Das Evangelium Matthaei* (1904) 6; M. Dibelius, *Die urchristliche Überlieferung von Johannes dem Täufer* (1911) 56; H. von Baer, *Der heilige Geist in den Lukasschriften* (1926) 161–3; R. Bultmann, *The History of the Synoptic Tradition* (ET 1963) 246; J. M. Creed, *The Gospel According to St Luke* (1930) 54; T. W. Manson, *The Sayings of Jesus* (1949) 40f.; W. F. Flemington, *The New Testament Doctrine of Baptism* (1948); P. Vielhauer, RGG³ III (1959) 804f.; W. C. Robinson Jr., *The Way of the Lord* (1962) 89; E. Haenchen, *Der Weg Jesu* (1966) 43, 50. See also V. Taylor, *The Gospel According to St Mark* (1952) 157.

[2] A. B. Bruce, *Expositor's Greek Testament* (1897) I 84; H. M. Treen, *ExpT* 35 (1923–24) 521; R. Eisler, *The Messiah Jesus and John the Baptist* (1931) 274–9; C. K. Barrett, *The Holy Spirit and the Gospel Tradition* (1947) 126; C. H. Kraeling, *John the Baptist* (1951) 59–63; H. J. Flowers, *ExpT* 64 (1952–53) 155f.; E. Schweizer, *ExpT* 65 (1953–54) 29; also TWNT VI 397; M.-A. Chevallier, *L'Esprit et le Messie dans le Bas-Judaisme et le Nouveau Testament* (1958) 55f.;

8

Two factors, however, make it quite probable that John foretold a baptism in Spirit (even Holy Spirit) and fire. First, the Baptist was not simply a prophet of wrath. For all the Synoptic Gospels his ministry is one of good news. For Mark it is 'the beginning of the gospel of Jesus Christ' (1.1), and the note of judgment and wrath is altogether missing from John's message (even the Coming One's baptism is with Holy Spirit alone). In Matthew John preaches the same Gospel as Jesus: 'Repent, for the Kingdom of God is at hand' (3.2; 4.17) which can otherwise be expressed as 'the gospel of the Kingdom' (4.23; 9.35). Luke continues the quotation from Isaiah to conclude with the words, 'and all flesh shall see the salvation of God' (3.6), and sums up John's preaching in terms of εὐαγγελίζεσθαι (3.18;[3] see also 1.16f., 76f.). Nor can the remission of sins be described as anything other than good news (Mark 1.4; Luke 3.3; 1.77). Destruction is certainly threatened, but the trees about to be axed are those which do not bring forth good fruit (Matt. 3.10; Luke 3.9). Those who produce fruit that befits or proves their repentance (Matt. 3.8; Luke 3.8) – presumably exemplified for Luke in John's replies to his questioners (3.10–14), but certainly initially signified and expressed by submission to John's baptism (Mark 1.4; Luke 3.3) – will escape the coming wrath. Again, the picture of winnowing has its 'gospel' side also: the gathering of the wheat into the granary, as well as the burning up of the chaff. There is more room in John's preaching for a gracious Spirit than one would think at first glance.

Second, and more important, is the fact that the Qumran sect talked freely of a, or God's holy spirit (or spirit of holiness) as a cleansing, purifying power (1QS 3.7–9; 4.21; 1QH 16.12; cf. 7.6; 17.26; frag. 2.9, 13). John almost certainly had some contact with the sect, even if only peripheral – sufficient at least for him to adopt

---

E. Best, *NovTest* 4 (1960) 236–43; W. Grundmann, *Das Evangelium nach Lukas* (1961) 105; F. W. Beare, *The Earliest Records of Jesus* (1964) 39f.; W. Bieder, *Die Verheissung der Taufe* (1966) 41, 53. See also Taylor 157; E. Schweizer, *Das Evangelium nach Markus* (NTD 1967) 17; R. Schütz, *Johannes der Täufer* (1967) 85.

[3] H. Conzelmann argues that εὐαγγελίζεσθαι here means simply 'to preach' (*The Theology of St Luke* [ET 1961] 23 n. 1). This is special pleading. The stages in salvation-history can still be distinguished even when we allow the note of Gospel in John's preaching (cf. Acts 1.24–26; 19.4). See also Schütz 70f.; W. Wink, *John the Baptist in the Gospel Tradition* (1968) 51–53.

(and adapt) some of their ideas.[4] And if, as some believe, 1QS 4.21 recalls the words of Mal. 3.2f.,[5] we shall be hard pressed to find in Jewish sources a closer parallel to Matt. 3.11, Luke 3.16. Thus, while the suggestion that John spoke only of wind and fire is attractive, there is no really decisive reason for denying the originality of the Q version of the logion.[6] As we shall see below, the fuller saying makes excellent sense when interpreted in the context of John's ministry and against the background of Jewish thought prior to John.

What did John mean when he foretold an imminent baptism in Spirit and fire? The two traditional interpretations understood it either of an inflaming, purifying baptism – a purely gracious outpouring of the Holy Spirit[7] – or of a twofold baptism, of the righteous with the Holy Spirit and of the wicked with fire.[8] Neither of these is adequate. In Q the characteristic note of John's preaching is imminent judgment and wrath (Matt. 3.7, 10, 12; Luke 3.7, 9, 17). 'Fire' is a prominent word (its threefold repetition in Matt. 3.10–12 is particularly striking), and standing on either side of the baptism logion it signifies the fire of punitive destruction. The 'baptism with . . . fire' therefore cannot be solely gracious, and must at least include an act of judgment and destruction.

[4] See H. Braun, *Qumran und das Neue Testament* (1966) II 2f., 10f., for those who see a more or less close relationship between Qumran and the Baptist. Braun himself accepts that the Baptist was quite possibly influenced by Qumran in his expectation of the nearness of the End-time (11f., 22).

[5] A. R. C. Leaney, *The Rule of Qumran and its Meaning* (1966) 159; M. Black, *The Scrolls and Christian Origins* (1961) 135.

[6] Cf. J. Delorme in *BNT* 54–57; D. Hill, *Greek Words and Hebrew Meanings* (1967) 244–7. For a fuller treatment of this point see my forthcoming article in *NovTest*.

[7] This derives from Chrysostom, and is still found in the Roman Catholic commentators, M.-J. Lagrange, *Evangile selon Saint Matthieu* [7](1948) 53; B. Leeming, *Principles of Sacramental Theology* (1956) 35; and P. Gaechter, *Das Matthäus Evangelium* (1963) 97.

[8] This derives from Origen. In this century it has been maintained by F. Büchsel, *Der Geist Gottes im Neuen Testament* (1926) 143f.; B. S. Easton, *The Gospel According to St Luke* (1926) 40; W. Michaelis, *Täufer, Jesus, Urgemeinde* (1928) 32f.; E. Lohmeyer, *Das Urchristentum I – Johannes der Täufer* (1932) 84–86; F. Lang, *TWNT* VI 943; W. F. Arndt, *St Luke* (1956) 116f.; W. H. Brownlee in *The Scrolls and the New Testament* (ed. K. Stendahl, 1957) 43; G. Delling, *NovTest* 2 (1957) 107; J. Schmid, *Das Evangelium nach Matthäus* (1959) 58f.; F. V. Filson, *The Gospel According to St Matthew* (1960) 66; F. J. Leenhardt, *Le Saint-Esprit* (1963) 37; C. H. Scobie, *John the Baptist* (1964) 71; also *The Scrolls and Christianity* (ed. M. Black 1969) 59–61; R. E. Brown, *New Testament Essays* (1965) 135f. See also C. E. B. Cranfield, *St Mark* (1959) 51; Schweizer, *Markus* 17.

Against the view of Origen it is important to realize that John regarded the Coming One's baptism as the complement and fulfilment of his own:

ἐγὼ ὑμᾶς βαπτίζω (ἐν) ὕδατι
αὐτὸς ὑμᾶς βαπτίσει ἐν πνεύματι ἁγίῳ.

Two things should be noted. First, the future baptism is a single baptism in Holy Spirit and fire, the ἐν embracing both elements. There are not two baptisms envisaged, one with Spirit and one with fire, only one baptism in Spirit-and-fire.[9] Second, the two baptisms (John's and the Coming One's) are to be administered to the same people – ὑμᾶς. That is to say, Spirit-and-fire baptism is not offered as an alternative to John's water-baptism, nor does one accept John's baptism in order to escape the messianic baptism. Rather one undergoes John's water-baptism with a view to and in preparation for the messianic Spirit-and-fire baptism. In which case, the Coming One's baptism cannot be solely retributive and destructive. Those who repent and are baptized by John must receive a baptism which is ultimately gracious. In short, if John spoke of a future baptism at all there was both gospel and judgment in it.

The most probable interpretation is that Spirit-and-fire together describe the one purgative act of messianic judgment which both repentant and unrepentant would experience, the former as a blessing, the latter as destruction.[10] The idea of immersion in the river Jordan was itself one which was able to convey the ideas of both judgment and redemption, and the baptismal metaphor to describe the Coming One's ministry is obviously taken from the rite which most characterized John's ministry.

In the OT the river and the flood are used as metaphors for being overwhelmed by calamities (Ps. 42.7; 69.2, 15; Isa. 43.2). It is this figure which probably stands behind Mark 10.38, Luke 12.50. The Evangelists

---

[9] Cf. P. Bonnard, *L'Évangile selon Saint Matthieu* (1963) 38.

[10] ὑμᾶς could be confined to those baptized by John (J. M. Robinson, *The Problem of History in Mark* [1957] 26; E. E. Ellis, *The Gospel of Luke* [1966] 90), but it is more probable that it covers all those addressed (ὁ λαός – Luke 3. 15f.), both the impenitent who refused baptism (as Matt. 3.7–10, Luke 3.7–9 imply), and those whose baptism had little or no repentance in it, as well as the truly repentant baptisands. It would be odd if John did not understand the Coming One's judgment to apply to all (cf. G. R. Beasley-Murray, *Baptism in the New Testament* [1963] 38), and it is certainly implied by the immediately following metaphor, which represents the Coming One's ministry as comprehensively as the baptism metaphor.

would probably understand this implication since βαπτίζεσθαι (sometimes even βαπτίζειν) was popularly used in extra-biblical Greek for tribulation and calamity overwhelming someone. But a river can also signify messianic blessing (Ezek. 47.3 – ὕδωρ ἀφέσεως), and Naaman was healed of his leprosy by immersing himself in the Jordan (II Kings 5.14). Moreover, John certainly understood his baptism as in some sense a way of escape from the coming wrath, and it prefigured the means the Coming One would use to bless those who truly repented at John's preaching. See also n. 19.

That fire means judgment is certain,[11] but in Jewish eschatology fire not only symbolized the destruction of the wicked, it could also indicate the purification of the righteous (that is, judgment but not destruction).[12] Just as Malachi spoke both of refining fire and of destructive fire (3.2–3; 4.1), so it is quite likely that John himself understood the baptism in . . . fire as both refining and destructive.[13]

If Malachi illuminates the meaning of fire in the baptism logion, the other prophet who chiefly features in the Baptist narratives illuminates the meaning of πνεῦμα. For Isaiah, rūaḥ is often a spirit of purification and judgment (4.4; 30.28), for some purely retributive (29.10) and destructive (11.15), but for God's people the bringer of blessing, prosperity and righteousness (32.15–17; 44.3). It may well be that Isa. 4.4 was in the Baptist's mind[14] – cleansing Jerusalem 'by a spirit of judgment and by a spirit of burning' is no far cry from a messianic baptism in Spirit and fire. Moreover, the fact that 'liquid' verbs are one of the standard ways of describing

[11] See, e.g., Isa. 31.9; Amos 7.4; Mal. 4.1; Jub. 9.15; 36.10; Enoch 10.6, 12f.; 54.6; 90.24–27; Sib. III.53–54; 4 Ezra 7.36–38; Ps. Sol. 15.6f.; in Qumran it is the same, e.g., 1QH 6.18–19. See also above, p. 10. That John could picture judgment as a stream of fire is quite possible (Dan. 7.10; 4 Ezra 13.10f.; 1QH 3.29[?]; in Enoch 67.13 the waters of judgment 'change and become a fire which burns for ever'). See also n. 19.

[12] Isa. 1.25; Zech. 13.9; Mal. 3.2f.; 1QH 5.16. See also L. W. Barnard, *JTS* 8 (1957) 107. On the dual role of fire in the thought of the first Christian centuries see C.-M. Edsman, *Le Baptême de Feu* (1940) 1–133.

[13] See further I. Abrahams, *Studies in Pharisaism and the Gospels I* (1917) 44f.; N. A. Dahl in *Interpretationes ad Vetus Testamentum Pertinentes S. Mowinckel* (1955) 45; and on ὑμᾶς above. This would be even clearer to the first three Evangelists since they all describe John in the language of Mal. 3.1 (Mark 1.2; Matt. 11.10 and Luke 7.27, both Q). Mal. 4.5 is also referred to John in Mark 9.12 and Matt. 17.11, and Luke 1.17 combines Mal. 3.1 with 4.5–6 in describing John (see also Luke 1.76).

[14] As G. W. H. Lampe suggests (in *Studies in the Gospels: Essays in Memory of R. H. Lightfoot* [ed. D. E. Nineham, 1955] 162).

the gift of the Spirit in the last days[15] would make it very easy for John to speak of the messianic gift of the Spirit in a metaphor drawn from the rite which was his own hall-mark. It is quite conceivable, therefore, that John spoke of such a baptism – in which the 'spirit' neither was merely gracious nor bore the sense of storm wind, but was God's holy spirit, purgative and refining for those who had repented, destructive (like the πνεῦμα of II Thess. 2.8 and the slighted Spirit of Acts 5.1–10) for those who remained impenitent.[16]

John clearly regarded himself as a herald of the End; he probably saw himself in the role of Elijah, the precursor of 'the great and terrible day of the Lord' (Mal. 4.5).[17] The frightening urgency of his tone was due to his belief not only that his generation stood on the threshold of the messianic age, but also that the end could not be introduced without great suffering and judgment[18] which, for the unrepentant, would mean destruction. Even the repentant would not escape judgment, for their deliverance would only come through a process of refining and winnowing and that would mean suffering enough, but it would afford them entry into the blessings of the new age.[19] Therefore repent, cried John, that the coming wrath might mean redemption and not utter destruction.

In short then, the baptism in Spirit-and-fire was not to be something gentle and gracious, but something which burned and consumed, not something experienced by only Jew or only Gentile, only repentant or only unrepentant, but by all. It was the fiery πνεῦμα in which all must be immersed, as it were, and which like a smelting furnace would burn up all impurity. For the unrepentant

---

[15] Isa. 32.15; 44.3; Ezek. 39.29; Joel. 2.28f.; Zech. 12.10; cf. Ezek. 36.25–27; and see the Qumran references above.

[16] Cf. Kraeling 61–63; Dahl 45.

[17] Contra J. A. T. Robinson, *Twelve New Testament Studies* (1962) 28–52.

[18] The belief in a period of 'messianic woes' immediately prior to the establishment of the messianic kingdom, in which the people of God suffer great tribulation and which culminates in the destruction of the wicked, can be traced back to Dan. 7.19–28, and is probably best expressed in I Enoch 90.13–27 and II Baruch 24–29.

[19] Kraeling is probably right in his suggestion that John's water-baptism symbolized the 'fiery torrent of judgment' and that submission to John's baptism was 'symbolic of acceptance of the judgment which he proclaimed' (117f.; cf. Barnard 107). See also Dahl 45. M. G. Kline has also pointed out that the idea of John's baptism portraying the coming judicial ordeal is supported by the water ordeals of ancient court procedure (*The Westminster Theological Journal* 27 [1964–65] 131–4).

it would mean total destruction. For the repentant it would mean a refining and purging away of all evil and sin which would result in salvation and qualify to enjoy the blessings of the messianic kingdom. These were the sufferings which would bring in the messianic kingdom; it was through them that the repentant would be initiated into that kingdom.

A second important issue is the role of John's water-baptism in all this. In particular, what was its relation to the expected baptism in Spirit-and-fire? It is important to recognize that John's ministry was essentially preparatory. John himself did not bring in the End. It was the Coming One who would do that. With John the messianic Kingdom has drawn near but it has not yet come. The note of the unfulfilled 'not yet' predominates. John is only the messenger who makes ready the way, the herald who goes before arousing attention and calling for adequate preparation.[20] His baptism is thus preparatory also. It does *not* mark the beginning of the eschatological event;[21] it does *not* initiate into the new age;[22] it is the answer to John's call for preparedness: by receiving the Preparer's baptism the penitent prepares himself to receive the Coming One's baptism.[23] It is the latter alone which initiates the Kingdom and initiates into the Kingdom. The baptism in Spirit-and-fire is the tribulation through which all must pass before the Kingdom can be established and before the penitent can share in the blessings of the Kingdom – the purifying transition from the old aeon to the new. The repentant therefore submits to John's baptism in order that when the greater one has come he may receive the greater baptism, for only thus and then will he be initiated into the messianic Kingdom.[24]

Beyond this we may say that John's baptism was the concrete

[20] A. H. McNeile, *The Gospel According to St Matthew* (1915) 25; G. Bornkamm, *Theologische Blätter* 17 (1938) 43; J. M. Robinson 24f.; C. F. D. Moule, *St Mark* (1965) 10. S. Talmon has reminded us that in the OT and the Qumran literature the desert comes to be viewed as the place of preparation (in *Biblical Motifs: Origins and Transformations* [ed. A. Altmann, 1966] 31–63).

[21] Contra Lohmeyer, *Das Evangelium des Markus* [16](1963) 19; Beasley-Murray 32.

[22] Contra A. Gilmore in *Christian Baptism* (ed. Gilmore, 1959) 73.

[23] See J. J. von Allmen, 'Baptism' in *VocB*. In Mark the only point that John really makes about his own baptism is that it is no more than a preparatory rite (D. E. Nineham, *St Mark* [1963] 57).

[24] See also Dahl 45.

and necessary expression of repentance, even that it constituted the ✻ act of turning (μετάνοια/*šūb*). Mark and Luke describe it as a βάπτισμα μετανοίας; Matthew and Mark tell how all were baptized in Jordan 'confessing their sins'; and Matthew has the peculiar phrase about John baptizing εἰς μετάνοιαν, which is best understood to mean that the actual acting out of the resolve to be baptized helped to crystallize repentance and to stir it up to full expression.[25]

We may not however say that John or the Evangelists considered his baptism to be the instrument of God in effecting forgiveness – as though εἰς ἄφεσιν ἁμαρτιῶν depended on βάπτισμα and not μετάνοια.[26] This is hardly how Luke understood the phrase when he took it over from Mark, and since Mark nowhere else speaks of forgiveness (except the irrelevant 3.29) or repentance, Luke must be our guide as to the meaning here. Luke 24.47 shows that μετάνοια εἰς ἄφεσιν ἁμαρτιῶν is a compact phrase and unitary concept – repentance bringing or resulting in forgiveness of sins. In 3.3, therefore, it is better to take the *whole* phrase as a description of βάπτισμα, with εἰς dependent only on μετανοίας. In other words, it is not a repentance *baptism* which results in the forgiveness of sins, but John's baptism is the expression of the *repentance* which results in the forgiveness of sins. This is confirmed by a comparison with such passages as Acts 3.19; 5.31; 10.43; 11.18; 13.38; 26.18.[27]

Moreover, the very idea of a rite which effected forgiveness was wholly foreign to the prophetic genius of the OT.[28] The Qumran sect certainly rejected any idea that sprinkled water could be efficacious to cleanse from sins and restricted the cleansing effects of water to the flesh, distinguishing that cleansing from the cleansing from sin which is effected by the holy spirit of the community

---

[25] Cf. Kraeling 71; Taylor 155; Moule, *Mark* 9. Despite Matt. 3.11 J. Schneider argues that conversion is distinct from and the presupposition of baptism (*Die Taufe im Neuen Testament* [1952] 23; cf. TEV; see also p. 94). On Lohmeyer's view that repentance was *received* rather than expressed in baptism (*Täufer* 67–73, 75–78; followed by Behm, *TDNT* IV 1001), see Beasley-Murray 34f.

[26] So argue Büchsel 139f.; E. Klostermann, *Das Markusevangelium* 4(HNT 1950); O. Cullmann, *Baptism in the New Testament* (ET 1950) 11; G. Delling, *Die Taufe im Neuen Testament* (1963) 43.

[27] See also W. Wilkens, *TZ* 23 (1967) 33f.; cf. Mark 16.16 (often taken as an addition to Mark patterned on Luke's narrative of the Gospel's expansion in Acts), where again the decisive element is belief, and baptism can be seen only as an expression of belief. See further in ch. IX.

[28] See Kraeling 121; also Barrett, *Tradition* 30f.; Schweizer, *Markus* 16; cf. C. G. Montefiore, *The Synoptic Gospels* 2(1927) I 7.

(1QS 3.3–9). According to Josephus, John's baptism was 'not to beg for pardon for sins committed, but for the purification of the body, when the soul had previously been cleansed by right behaviour'.[29] The unanimity of this witness makes it virtually certain that John would have been the first to reject the idea that his baptism effected or was the means by which God bestowed forgiveness.

It has become customary in recent years to meet these arguments by an appeal to the idea of prophetic symbolism: John's baptism not only expressed God's will but also in some small degree effected it.[30] The resemblance of some prophetic action to mimetic magic is unquestionable (particularly II Kings 13.18f.), and it is probable that John's baptism falls into this category. However, it should be noted that the great majority of examples cited by Wheeler Robinson are prospective, foretelling acts – which symbolize events which will take place some time in the future. Indeed it is difficult to find examples of a prophetic act which symbolizes something present to the prophet at the time of his action. This confirms what is already obvious from the Baptist's own preaching: that John's baptism is a prophetic symbol not of present forgiveness, but of the future Spirit-and-fire baptism. John's baptism was a prophetic act in the sense that it was necessary for this baptism to be administered before the Coming One could appear to administer his own baptism (indeed John 1.31–34 implies as much). In *that* sense John's baptism helped to bring about the baptism in Spirit-and-fire. But we certainly cannot say that John's baptism effected the messianic baptism in the sense in which those who bring up this point speak of baptism effecting forgiveness.

The fact is that in relation to repentance and forgiveness John's baptism was a rite rather than a prophetic action,[31] and we must look for its meaning at this point within the context of OT ritual.[32] The principal purpose of the OT rites and ceremonies was to

---

[29] *Ant.* 18.117. See again Kraeling 121.

[30] H. W. Robinson in *Old Testament Essays* (ed. D. C. Simpson 1927) 15, *JTS* 43 (1942) 129–39, and *Spirit* 192ff. See further Flemington 20–22; N. Clark, *Approach to the Theology of the Sacraments* (1957) 11; Gilmore 75–83; Beasley-Murray 43. R. E. O. White, *The Biblical Doctrine of Initiation* (1960) recognizes some of the difficulties of this argument (81–83).

[31] Cf. G. W. H. Lampe, *The Seal of the Spirit* 2(1967) 22f.; H. Kraft, *TZ* 17 (1961) 400, 402f.

[32] See p. 21; also Dahl 37–45.

enable men to 'draw near' to God. They cleansed the body and thus removed the ceremonial defilement which prevented access, but they did not cleanse the heart or take away sins.[33] They were therefore symbols of the cleansing which God himself immediately effected apart from this ritual (e.g. Deut. 30.6; Ps. 51; Isa. 1.10–18; Joel 2.12–14); but, more than symbols, they were also the means God used to encourage the humble and give confidence to the repentant to approach him, by indicating his gracious will to forgive and receive such. Indeed we may truly characterize them by saying that they were the means God gave to the worshipper to express his repentance and to indicate openly his desire for God's forgiveness. It was only when they were divorced from that true repentance and genuine desire that the prophets attacked them and called for the repentance without the ritual (e.g. Deut. 10.16; I Sam. 15.22; Jer. 4.4; 7.3–4; Ezek. 18.30–31; Hos. 6.6; Amos 5.21–24), for even then it was evident that it is the repentance which receives the forgiveness, not the ritual, and not even the repentance necessarily expressed in the ritual. But God's intention was that both ritual and repentance should be united, the former giving vital expression to the latter, and the latter giving meaning to the former, so that the ritual act in fact would be the *occasion*, though *not* the *means* of cleansing. *In this sense* John's baptism was a 'sacrament', an 'effective sign', but not in the sense that it effected what it signified.

To sum up, John's baptism was essentially preparatory, not initiatory, a prophetic symbol of the messianic baptism, in that it symbolized and prepared the way for the action and experience of the messianic judgment. In its immediate application as a rite it proclaimed God's willingness to cleanse the penitent there and then and to bring him safely through the coming wrath. Like the rites of the OT it enabled the repentant to draw near to God by giving him a visible expression of his repentance and itself expressing symbolically God's forgiveness. By helping forward the repentance and bringing it to full flower the rite would provide the occasion for the divine-human encounter in which the forgiveness was received. Otherwise the forgiveness was mediated directly and independently of the rite, for in prophetic theology it is the repentance alone which results in and receives the forgiveness, even when it is expressed in the rite (cf. 1QS 3.6–9).

[33] The writer to the Hebrews denied that this was even possible (9.9–14; 10.1–4).

A third important question is, What light do the Gospel records
at this point shed on the Christian understanding of John's prophecy of a future Spirit-and-fire baptism? Many answer by taking
the talk of baptism literally: the prophecy, they say, was referred
to Christian baptism.[34] But this will hardly do. βαπτίζειν in and of
itself does not specify water.[35] Like the baptism of Mark 10.38f.,
Luke 12.50, the baptism in Spirit(-and-fire) is obviously a metaphor. It was originated as a rhetorical device to bring out the
contrast between John's ministry and that of the Coming One
most sharply. As such it was suitable only because the rite most
characteristic of John served as a vivid and expressive figure of the
coming judgment.[36] The word 'baptize' was not an essential part
of the description of the messianic Spirit-and-fire ministry; other
metaphors might just as well have been used. The Christian fulfilment was, of course, different from the Baptist's expectation,[37] but
even with the Christian modification the Baptist's central contrast
between water-baptism and Spirit(-and-fire) baptism holds good.
This is most obvious in Luke for whom the baptism in the Spirit
continues to be a metaphorical use of 'baptism' and does not refer
to a rite at all.[38]

With Matthew it is in all probability the same, for he seems to
share Luke's view of the dispensational divide at the death and
resurrection of Jesus,[39] and he shares also the same Q tradition of
John's words with the same contrast between John's water-

[34] See e.g. Bultmann, *History* 247; Cullmann, *Baptism* 10.

[35] G. Kittel, *Theologische Studien und Kritiken* 87 (1914) 31. See also Delling,
*NovTest* 2 (1957) 97–102, and p. 129 below.

[36] So Wellhausen, *Matthaei* 6, *Das Evangelium Marci* (1903) 5. See also
Michaelis, *Täufer* 23; C. F. D. Moule, *Theology* 48 (1945) 246; A. E. J. Rawlin-
son, *Christian Initiation* (1947) 25; Best 242; J. Guillet in *BNT* 93; M. C.
Harper, *The Baptism of Fire* (1968) 10f.

[37] See ch. III. This meant that the metaphor became less appropriate, and
is probably the reason why its useful life as a description of the gift of the
Spirit soon came to an end (it is found only once without distinct reference to
Pentecost – I Cor. 12.13).

[38] Acts 1.5; 11.16. It is especially striking that the two receptions of the
Spirit in Acts specifically described as baptisms with Spirit (Pentecost and
Caesarea) are the ones most clearly separated from and independent of
Christian water-baptism (or any rite). See Part Two.

[39] Matthew probably regarded forgiveness as something which John's
baptism only foreshadowed, and which could not be given or received until
the completion of Jesus' mission, for he omits the phrase εἰς ἄφεσιν ἁμαρτιῶν
in his description of John's baptism and stands alone in including the same
phrase in the words of institution at the Last Supper (26.28).

baptism and the Coming One's Spirit-and-fire baptism. He certainly gives no indication that he thought the latter was a form of water-baptism, or involved such. The assumption must be that he too took it merely as a metaphor.

If Mark has consciously shaped the tradition of the Baptist's prophecy to exclude the 'and fire', as indeed all talk of judgment, it implies that he ignored John's own understanding of the future baptism and preserved the saying in the form most familiar to Christian experience, in which case he is almost certainly thinking of Pentecost.[40] Moreover, in Mark the contrast between the two baptisms is exceedingly sharp (far more so than in Q):

$$\text{ἐγὼ ἐβάπτισα ὕδατι}$$
$$\text{αὐτὸς βαπτίσει πνεύματι ἁγίῳ.}$$

Here the emphasized words are 'I' and 'He', 'water' and 'Holy Spirit'. Water is set over against Spirit as that which distinguishes John's baptism from the future baptism. It would seriously distort the sense of the logion if Spirit-baptism was equated or conflated with water-baptism.

In John, the Baptist three times insists that his baptism is ἐν ὕδατι. In replying to his questioners, who have assumed rightly or wrongly that baptism has an eschatological significance (1.25),[41] he does not deny that there is an eschatological baptism, but by disclaiming to be an eschatological figure, and by stressing that his baptism is in water, he implies that the Coming One's baptism will be of a different order (1.26). The purpose of John's baptism is to reveal Jesus to Israel, and presumably therefore it is only preparatory to the mission of the Christ (1.31); the Christ's baptism will not be ἐν ὕδατι but ἐν πνεύματι ἁγίῳ (1.33). The implication is that John's water-baptism is only a shadow and symbol of the Christ's Spirit-baptism.[42] The contrast between the two baptisms is the contrast between John and Jesus – the antithesis of preparation and fulfilment, of shadow and substance.

This contrast is probably resumed in 3.31–36. John seems to be ὁ ὢν ἐκ τῆς γῆς (v. 31 – W. Bauer, *Johannesevangelium* [HNT 1912] 40; E.

[40] Schweizer, *TWNT* VI 396.

[41] See R. E. Brown, *The Gospel According to John* (i–xii) (Anchor Bible, 1966) 46–54.

[42] J. H. Bernard, *St John* (ICC 1928) 51f.; G. H. C. Macgregor, *The Gospel of John* (Moffatt 1928) 25; R. Schnackenburg, *Das Johannesevangelium I* (1965) 304.

Hoskyns, *The Fourth Gospel* [2][1947] 224; C. K. Barrett, *The Gospel According to St John* [1955] 187; Brown, *John* 16of.; J. N. Sanders and B. A. Mastin, *The Gospel According to St John* [1968] 135; Wink 94; cf. M.-J. Lagrange, *Évangile selon Saint Jean* [5][1936] 97; M. Black, *An Aramaic Approach to the Gospels and Acts* [3][1967] 147f.), and v. 34 most likely includes a reference to Jesus' gift of the Spirit to his disciples (p. 32). Not only John and Jesus are set in antithesis (v. 31), but also their respective ministries: baptism with ὕδατα πολλά is set against a giving of the Spirit οὐκ ἐκ μέτρου.

We may not therefore reach the Christian sacrament by equating it with Spirit-baptism or by fusing the two limbs of the Baptist's antithesis. On the contrary, since, as most agree, Christian water-baptism derives directly from the Johannine rite, it is more likely that, in so far as the antithesis carries over into the Christian era, Christian water-baptism takes the place of John's water-baptism as a symbol of and contrast with Christ's Spirit-baptism.[43] As we shall see (pp. 99f. below), this is certainly nearer the truth so far as Luke is concerned.

It has sometimes been argued that the Baptist's prophecy was fulfilled during Jesus' ministry, whether in the baptism which Jesus is said to have administered in John 3.22 – a water-baptism which is also the Spirit-baptism foretold in 1.33[44] – or in the fact that Jesus' ministry constituted a sifting and judging of Israel.[45] With regard to the former, while such a theological overtone would not be out of place in the Fourth Evangelist, we have also to remember that he does write with at least some semblance of history, and particularly with regard to the Spirit he has set himself a historical 'not yet' in 7.39, which must take precedence over any theological deduction such as the one drawn here by his interpreters. In 3.22–24 he is relating a piece of the history of the incarnate Christ – v. 24 leaves us in no doubt on that score – and as such it falls within the Evangelist's self-imposed framework of history. 7.39 therefore rules out any attempt to see in 3.22 the fulfilment of 1.33.

[43] See also Cranfield, *Mark* 49.

[44] C. H. Dodd, *The Interpretation of the Fourth Gospel* (1953) 31of.; Bauer 39; Macgregor 89; R. H. Lightfoot, *St John's Gospel* (1956) 119; Cullmann, *Baptism* 79f.; Bieder 5of., 53. Schütz suggests that the activity ascribed to Jesus in 3.22, 26 is baptism in the Holy Spirit, *not* water-baptism (94–96).

[45] This is the thesis which J. E. Yates has argued in connection with Mark (*The Spirit and the Kingdom* [1963]). C. H. Dodd has supported the basic thrust of his argument (in a private communication dated 28 October 1966).

It is no doubt precisely because of these two facts (Jesus' baptism is Spirit-baptism, and the Spirit was not yet [given]) that the correction of 4.2 was added, whether by the Evangelist or by an editor.

The baptism administered by Jesus' disciples was probably a continuation of John's baptism (Bernard 128; Macgregor 90; Lagrange, *Jean* 91f.; Hoskyns 222, 227; Brown, *John* 151; M. Barth, *Die Taufe – Ein Sakrament?* [1951] 393; Guillet in *BNT* 100; contra R. Bultmann, *Das Evangelium des Johannes* [1950] 122 n. 3; Schütz 94–96). If we are to understand that the dispute of v. 25 was occasioned by a Jew who had been baptized by Jesus and was concerned with the relative merits of John's and Jesus' baptism (H. Strathmann, *Das Evangelium nach Johannes* [10][NTD 1963] 77; Schnackenburg 451) then we should note that the description of the discussion as περὶ καθαρισμοῦ sets *both* baptisms 'within the Jewish system of purifications' (Barrett, *John* 182); cf. 2.6 – κατὰ τὸν καθαρισμόν.

With regard to the latter, while Jesus' ministry certainly had a κρίσις-effect, proof is quite lacking that the Evangelists regarded these reactions to Jesus as a fulfilment of the saying about baptism in Spirit-and-fire. On the contrary, in John the two themes are quite distinct, Jesus' ministry as Baptizer in the Spirit being expressly postponed until he has been glorified (7.39). Again, the baptism in Spirit(-and-fire) is something which Jesus does, not merely a reaction to his presence. The Synoptic writers do not use the Johannine κρίσις-theme in the construction of their Gospels. In Mark it is absent even from the Baptist's preaching, and Mark 1.8 most clearly reflects the Christian understanding of Spirit-baptism.[46] So far as Matthew is concerned, the separation of good from evil and the destruction of the latter by fire still lies in the future in relation to the ministry of Jesus, ἐν τῇ συντελείᾳ τοῦ αἰῶνος (Matt. 13.40–43; 25.41, 46).

We have yet to examine the most important instance of John's baptism and the way in which Luke and John treat the theme of Spirit-baptism, but we can pause at this point to summarize our findings so far as they bear on our debate with Pentecostal and sacramentalist. The former must note that in the initial formulation of his favourite metaphor any idea of a baptism in the Spirit as something which those already in the Kingdom might yet be

---

[46] Had we Mark alone it would be impossible to link 'baptism in Spirit' with the various reactions to Jesus' ministry – which makes Yates's thesis all the more surprising. I suspect that Dodd is attracted to it by his desire to find Synoptic parallels to Johannine themes.

without is totally excluded. The baptism in the Spirit was not something distinct from and subsequent to entry into the Kingdom; it was only by means of the baptism in Spirit that one could enter at all.

To the sacramentalist we must make two points. First, the baptism in Spirit does not refer to water-baptism. It is simply a metaphor which was drawn from John's water-rite and which was chosen primarily with a view to bringing out the contrast with the water-rite most sharply. In the preaching of the Baptist water-baptism had no part in the future messianic baptism beyond symbolizing it and preparing for it. Second, it is a mistake to say that John's baptism gave or conveyed forgiveness. It is even imprecise and misleading to say that John's baptism resulted in forgiveness. It is the repentance expressed in the baptism which resulted in forgiveness, and it was God who himself conveyed the forgiveness directly to the heart of the repentant. Baptism was the means John used to stimulate repentance and to give it occasion for full and public expression – he may even have regarded baptism as the necessary form for expressing repentance – but that God conveyed the forgiveness through baptism we cannot say on either grammatical or theological grounds.

# III

## THE EXPERIENCE OF JESUS AT JORDAN

THIS event in the life of Jesus is of peculiar importance both for those who speak of baptism in the Spirit as a second experience for Christians, and for those who think of the Spirit as given through water-baptism. For both Pentecostal and sacramentalist the events at Jordan establish an invaluable precedent and pattern, which has a formative and even normative significance for later Christian doctrine and experience. If Jesus was baptized in the Spirit at Jordan, an additional blessing to equip him with power for his mission some thirty years after his supernatural birth through the Spirit, how much more should Christians receive the baptism in the Spirit after their birth from above in order to equip them for service, say the Pentecostals.[1] Sacramentalists, on the other hand, see in Jesus' baptism by John the connecting link between John's baptism and Christian baptism: it was Jesus' baptism which united John's water-baptism with the promised Spirit-baptism to form the Christian baptism in water-and-Spirit.[2] We shall examine these two views in turn.

On the face of it the Pentecostal has a good case. In view of the birth narratives of Matthew and Luke one can speak of Jesus' anointing with the Spirit at Jordan (Acts 10.38) as a second

[1] See e.g. M. C. Harper, *Power for the Body of Christ* (1964) 18–20; *Fire* 15; B. Allen, *New Life and New Power* (1965) 5; G. Lindsay, *Baptism of the Holy Spirit* (1964) 10f.; L. Christenson, *Speaking in Tongues and its Significance for the Church* (1968) 36f.; and earlier, R. M. Riggs, *The Spirit Himself* (1949) 38f. For a similar argument used on behalf of Confirmation see Thornton 96–100, 110–18, 128–32, 139f., 160f.

[2] A. E. J. Rawlinson, *The Gospel According to St Mark* (1925) 11; von Baer 163–9; H. W. Robinson, *BQ* 9 (1938–39) 389; Bornkamm 46; Lampe, *Seal* 34; Cullmann, *Baptism* 21; Gilmore 91; Conzelmann 23; Grundmann, *Lukas* 108; Church of Scotland Commission, *Biblical Doctrine* 18; Guillet in *BNT* 94f.; White 98, 108.

'experience' of the Spirit. It is quite probable, though not certain, that Luke means us to understand that Jesus was every bit as full of the Holy Spirit as John was (1.15), and that Jesus' growth in wisdom and grace was due to his possession of the Spirit (2.40, 52);[3] the link between the Spirit and divine sonship (and filial consciousness) would also be a pointer in this direction (1.35; 2.49; 3.22; cf. Rom. 8.15–16; Gal. 4.6).[4] Again we may legitimately speak of the descent of the Spirit on Jesus at Jordan as a baptism in the Spirit;[5] and we certainly cannot deny that it was this anointing with the Spirit which equipped Jesus with power and authority for his mission to follow (Acts 10.38).[6] It would even be possible to argue that the theme of *imitatio Christi*, which we find here and there in the NT (e.g. Mark 10.39; I Cor. 11.1; I Thess. 1.6; Heb. 2.10; I John 2.6) by implication covers this part of Jesus' life as well, although there is no real exegetical basis for this inference.

Where the Pentecostalist thesis breaks down is in its failure to grasp the fact that we are dealing here with events whose significance, at least for those who record them, lies almost totally in the part they play in salvation-history. There are only a handful of events in all this history which can be called pivotal. Jesus' reception of the Spirit at Jordan is one of them: on this pivot the whole of salvation-history swings round into a new course. In other words, we are dealing not so much with stages in the life of Jesus, which belong to the same dispensation of salvation-history and so can be appealed to as the pattern for all who belong to the same dispensation; we are dealing rather with stages in salvation-history itself. The experience of Jesus at Jordan is far more than something merely personal – it is a unique moment in history: the beginning of a new epoch in salvation-history – the beginning, albeit in a restricted sense, of the End-time, the messianic age, the new covenant. This means that although Jesus' anointing with the Spirit may possibly be described as a second experience of the

[3] Cf. H. B. Swete, *The Holy Spirit in the New Testament* (1909) 35; Marsh 103, 105; J. N. Geldenhuys, *The Gospel of Luke* (1950) 146f.

[4] Cf. Lampe in *Studies* 167f.

[5] See below pp. 31, 34f.; and J. M. Robinson 26; Barth, *Taufe* 74; P. Carrington, *According to Mark* (1960) 38; in addition to those cited in n. 2.

[6] Rawlinson, *Mark* 11, 254; Lampe in *Studies* 171; K. H. Rengstorf, *Das Evangelium nach Lukas* (NTD 1958) 59–60; Filson, *Matthew* 68; Grundmann, *Lukas* 108. See also p. 32 below.

Spirit for Jesus, it is not a second experience of the new covenant, or of Jesus within the new covenant. It is in fact the event which begins the new covenant for Jesus – it initiates the messianic age and initiates Jesus into the messianic age.[7] Let me demonstrate this more fully.

(*a*) Notice first the difference between the preaching of John and that of Jesus. For John, as we have seen, the End-time was still wholly future – imminent, but future; the majestic, messianic figure who would bring in the eschaton and the Kingdom through his baptism of judgment had not yet come, though he was almost on them. So too for the Evangelists John is only the forerunner, the way-preparer, the one who rushes ahead to announce the Coming One's approach. For Luke, in particular, John belongs very definitely to the old age of the law and the prophets (cf. Luke 16.16 with Matt. 11.11), for the fact that Luke relates the close of the Baptist's ministry before turning to his encounter with Jesus (3.18–20; cf. Acts 10.37; 13.24–25), even though the climax of his ministry lay in this encounter, implies that Luke wants to make precisely this point – John belongs in his whole ministry to the old epoch of salvation.[8]

Mark also seems to distinguish John's ministry from Jesus' fairly clearly (Mark 1.14 – J. M. Robinson 22f.; cf. Wink 6). ἐβάπτισα of 1.8 may indicate that the ministry of the Baptist ends when that of Jesus begins (so most); but it could also be a gnomic aorist = 'I baptize' (Rawlinson, *Mark* 8; Klostermann, *Markus*; Black, *Aramaic Approach* 128f.; Taylor 64, 157; Cranfield, *Mark* 48f.).

With Jesus, however, it is different. There is still talk of a Coming One (the Son of Man), still talk of a future judgment (e.g. Mark 13.24–26; Matt. 13.30; Luke 21.34–35). But there is also the

---

[7] Cf. von Baer 166f.; F. J. Leenhardt, *Le Baptême Chrétien* (1944) 27; Kraeling 154f.; Lohmeyer, *Markus* 25; Schweizer, *TWNT* VI 398; Conzelmann 22–27; J. M. Robinson 27f.; H. J. Wotherspoon, *What Happened at Pentecost?* (1937) 16; Hill 244.

[8] See Conzelmann 22–27; U. Wilckens, *Die Missionsreden der Apostelgeschichte* (1961) 101–5; H. Flender, *St Luke: Theologian of Redemptive History* (ET 1967) 122–4 – though Conzelmann overstates his case (see e.g. above p. 9 n. 3, and his treatment of Luke 7.27 – 167 n. 1). For a more thorough-going criticism of Conzelmann see W. C. Robinson 5–42, also Wink 46–57, who, however, both here and in his treatment of Matthew (27–41) does not give enough weight to the descent of the Spirit on Jesus as the decisive mark of the Kingdom and beginning of the age of fulfilment.

note of fulfilment. The time of the End expected by the prophets has come in some sense at least (Matt. 11.4–6; Luke 10.23f.). The Kingdom which for John was wholly future has come upon them and is in the midst of them (Matt. 12.28; Luke 17.20f.). Satan has already been bound and his goods are being plundered (Mark 3.27).[9] In short, a decisive 'shift in the aeons' has taken place. And if we inquire, At what point? the answer is clearly, At Jordan, when Jesus was anointed with the Spirit. It is after this event that the note of fulfilment enters: Jesus' first words in Mark's Gospel are, 'The time (καιρός – the eschatological time) is fulfilled . . .' (1.15) – fulfilled because the eschatological Spirit has come; the year of the Lord's favour has arrived because the Lord has anointed him with the Spirit (Luke 4.18f.). It is by the compulsion of the Spirit that Jesus goes to meet Satan, and in the power of the Spirit that Jesus defeats Satan (Mark 1.12f.; 3.22–30). It is this manifestation of power which demonstrates the Kingdom's presence – indeed it is only because the Spirit is present and active in Jesus that the Kingdom can be said to be present (Matt. 12.28).

This point is important: the fulfilment and Kingdom came not with Jesus alone or Jesus in himself (he was already about thirty years of age and the new age had not so far broken in through him), nor with the Spirit alone (who according to Luke was very active at the period of Jesus' birth and filled the Baptist from his birth); the decisive change in the ages was effected by the Spirit coming down upon Jesus. It is this unique anointing of this unique person which brings in the End.

That Luke uses the same language (πίμπλημι) to describe both John's experience of the Spirit and that of the Christians in Acts does not make the dispensational divide any narrower. John's experience can be described in terms of 'the spirit and power of Elijah' (Luke 1.17), whereas in the post-Pentecost situation Christians experience 'the Spirit of Jesus' (Acts 16.7). There is a content in Christian experience which was wholly lacking in John's. Cf. e.g. Swete 21f.; see also pp. 31f. below.

(b) Then there is the actual narrative of the Spirit-anointing of Jesus. There are several eschatological features here. The rending of the heavens, a common feature of apocalyptic writing, indicates a breaking through from the heavenly realm to the earthly.[10] But

---

[9] See E. Best, *The Temptation and the Passion* (1965) 11–15.
[10] Lohmeyer, *Markus* 21; Bornkamm 45; Taylor 160; H. Schlier, *Besinnung und das Neue Testament* (1964) 213; C. Maurer, *TWNT* VII 962; Bieder 81, 83.

in this instance it is not merely a vision which Jesus sees or a voice which he hears, but the Spirit himself comes upon him.

To link the voice with the Bath qol is to miss the whole point. For the 'daughter of the voice' was believed to have taken the place of the direct inspiration of the prophets by the Holy Spirit. And it is in this moment above all that the long drought of knowing the Spirit comes to an end. It is not simply that the age of prophecy returns (according to Luke that had already happened), but rather that the age of the Spirit has now come.

In this moment the eschatological hopes of the prophets for a Spirit-anointed Messiah were fulfilled (Isa. 11.2; 61.1). The dove also should probably be given eschatological significance.[11] Quite possibly it is intended to recall Gen. 1.2,[12] or even the dove sent out by Noah after the Flood.[13] Either way the dove would mean a new beginning, a new epoch in God's dealings with creation, even a new covenant – in the eschatological circumstances, *the* new covenant.

Finally, there is the heavenly voice. If indeed the words are intended as a combination of Ps. 2.7 and Isa. 42.1 (as most still maintain)[14] then we have to say that the Evangelists regard this as the moment when Jesus is anointed with the Spirit as Messiah.[15] It is only then that he can properly be called Messiah (the Anointed One), only then that he takes up the function of Messiah, and only then that the messianic age can be said to have begun.

(*c*) We have been touching here on the vexed question of the

[11] Beasley-Murray 61.

[12] The Rabbis sometimes took the dove as a picture of the Spirit 'brooding' over chaos (Lohmeyer, *Markus* 21, 25; Barrett, *Tradition* 39; Taylor 161).

[13] Von Baer 58, 169; J. Kosnetter *Die Taufe Jesu* (1936) 127f.; Leenhardt, *Baptême* 20; Lampe, *Seal* 36; also *SJT* 5 (1952) 167; Grundmann, *Das Evangelium nach Markus* (1959) 32. This suggestion gains in plausibility if John's baptism was intended to symbolize the coming flood of judgment (see above p. 12 n. 11, p. 13 n. 19), so recalling the Flood of Noah (cf. I Pet. 3.20–21); for then the dove would signify the end of judgment and the beginning of a new era of grace. This is perhaps another reason why Luke emphasizes the reality of the dove so much.

[14] M. Hooker disputes the allusion to Isa. 42.1 on the grounds of divergence from the LXX (*Jesus and the Servant* [1959] 68–73), a questionable argument in view of Matt. 12.18; cf. Acts 1.8 where the coming of the Spirit on the disciples equips them to fulfil what is in fact the Servant's mission ἕως ἐσχάτου τῆς γῆς (Isa. 49.6; cf. Acts 13.47).

[15] The voice refers to the gift of the Spirit: 'The word of God to Jesus explains the act of God on Jesus' (Büchsel 162).

messiahship of Jesus and the bearing of this event on it. The
question is often posed thus: Was the descent of the Spirit the
moment of Jesus' adoption as Son of God and appointment as
Messiah?[16] or merely the climax and confirmation of a growing
conviction that he was Son and Messiah?[17] It is not for us to
speculate about or defend the messianic self-consciousness of Jesus,
but it is important to call attention to the danger of discussing
those questions as though their primary importance related to the
person of Jesus, or even the personal self-consciousness of Jesus –
the same mistake as the Pentecostals make. The concern of the
Evangelists is much broader than that, important though it may
be; for them the importance of the whole event lies in its significance for the history of redemption. The descent of the Spirit on
Jesus effects not so much a change in Jesus, his person or his
status, as the beginning of a new stage in salvation-history. The
thought is not so much of Jesus becoming what he was not before,
but of Jesus entering where he was not before – a new epoch in
God's plan of redemption – and thus, by virtue of his unique
personality, assuming a role which was not his before because it
could not be his by reason of the καιρός being yet unfulfilled.

It is only when we grasp this point that we can give full significance both to the birth narratives in Matthew and Luke and to the
events at Jordan. Thus, for example, when the adoption formula
from Ps. 2.7 is quoted in part at least by Luke, his principal thought
is that the new age brings Jesus a new role. He does not intend to
deny what he has already written in chs. 1 and 2, nor does he
naïvely contradict himself; there is a sense in which Jesus is
Messiah and Son of God from his birth (1.35, 43, 76; 2.11, 26, 49);
but there is also a sense in which he only becomes Messiah and
Son at Jordan, since he does not in fact become the Anointed One
(Messiah) till then (Isa. 61.1–2; Luke 4.18; Acts 10.38),[18] and only
then does the heavenly voice hail him as Son; just as there is a
sense in which he does not become Messiah and Son till his resur-

---

16 An affirmative answer is given with varying degrees of conviction e.g.
by Dibelius 59, 63; Creed 56; D. Plooij in *Amicitiae Corolla: Essays presented
to J. R. Harris* (ed. H. G. Wood 1933) 241, 252; B. H. Branscomb, *The Gospel
of Mark* (Moffatt 1937) 16; Barrett, *Tradition* 41–44; Klostermann, *Markus* 7;
Nineham 62f.

17 Likewise e.g. Rawlinson, *Mark* 10, 254; Taylor 162; Cranfield, *Mark* 55;
G. B. Caird, *St Luke* (1963) 77; Moule, *Mark* 11.

18 W. C. van Unnik, *NTS* 8 (1961–62) 101–16.

rection and ascension (Acts 2.36; 13.33). The answer to these apparent contradictions is not to be found in different Christologies, as though Luke did not recognize the import of what he was writing, but in the movement of salvation-history. At each new phase of salvation-history Jesus enters upon a new and fuller phase of his messiahship and sonship. It is not so much that Jesus became what he was not before, but that history became what it was not before; and Jesus as the one who effects these changes of history from within history, is himself affected by them.

Thus, while giving full weight to the events at Jordan and their meaning for the Evangelists, one can still find plenty of room for a messianic self-consciousness and a conviction of divine sonship even before Jordan. We can even say, although we cannot prove, that it was as a result of this self-awareness that Jesus submitted to John's baptism, thereby committing himself to the fuller messiahship and sonship which followed with the descent of the Spirit and the inbreaking of the End-time thus brought by the Spirit.

(*d*) What was this new role, this fuller messiahship, which came to Jesus through the anointing with the Spirit, and to which he committed himself in his baptism? The first three Evangelists[19] would reply: The descent of the Spirit made Jesus the representative of Israel, the new Adam. This follows from the words spoken by the heavenly voice, for both the king (of Ps. 2) and the Servant (of Isa. 42) were representative figures,[20] and the three key words (of Mark) – υἱός, ἀγαπητός and εὐδόκησα – 'together form a concept which in the OT is applied only to Israel'.[21]

Each of the Evangelists enlarges on this idea in his own way. Mark has it that the Spirit descended like a dove εἰς αὐτόν;[22] since

[19] The salvation-history significance of the Spirit's descent on Jesus is not so clearly marked in John, who wishes to focus attention on the actual salvation-effecting events at the close of Jesus' earthly ministry (see ch. XIV), but it is implied in such passages as 1.33; 3.34 (see p. 32 below); 6.27; cf. 1.16f., where we might easily substitute πνεῦμα for χάρις (see p. 116 below).

[20] 'The king represents the people to Yahweh' (H. W. Robinson, 'The Hebrew Conception of Corporate Personality', BZAW 66 [1936] 56, reprinted as *Corporate Personality in Ancient Israel* [1964] 11); that the Servant of Isa. 42 was seen as a corporate personality = Israel is based on the assumption that the Servant there was equated with the Servant of Isa. 44.1f. See further H. H. Rowley, *The Servant of the Lord* (1952) 33–58.

[21] Hooker 73.

[22] In the light of Markan usage elsewhere this almost certainly means '*into* him', with εἰς deliberately preferred to ἐπί.

in Jewish tradition the dove is usually a symbol for Israel,[23] Mark may intend us to understand that with his reception of the Spirit Jesus became the representative of Israel. If the echoes of Isa. 63, particularly vv. 11f., suggested by S. I. Buse[24] could be established, it would suggest that Mark saw the events at Jordan as parallel in significance to the passing through the Red Sea.[25] The gift of the Spirit would then parallel the giving of the law at Sinai,[26] and the Temptations the wilderness period of Israel (see below). But perhaps more prominent in the immediately following narrative of the Temptations is the idea of Jesus as the new Adam: whereas at the beginning of the old creation the first Adam was tempted and fell, at the beginning of the new creation the second Adam is tempted but conquers (Mark 3.27).[27]

In Matthew the most striking feature is the Temptation narrative which again follows immediately on the reception of the Spirit. This passage has recently been justly classified as an early Christian midrash on Deut. 6–8.[28] As Yahweh led Israel his Son (cf. Ex. 4.22–23; Jer. 31.9; Hos. 11.1) in the wilderness for forty years to humble, to test ($\pi\epsilon\iota\rho\acute{a}\zeta\epsilon\iota\nu$) and to discipline him (Deut. 8.2–5), so Jesus is led into the wilderness by the Spirit[29] for forty days to be tested ($\pi\epsilon\iota\rho\acute{a}\zeta\epsilon\sigma\theta\alpha\iota$). Yahweh disciplined Israel, because that is what a father does with his son (Deut. 8.5); so Jesus, newly hailed as God's Son, is tested vigorously at just this point (Matt. 4.3, 6). God had made his covenant with Israel and tested him to see if he would be faithful, but Israel failed the test again and again. Now

---

[23] Strack-Billerbeck I 123–5.

[24] *JTS* 7 (1956) 74f.; cf. Lohmeyer, *Markus* 21; A. Feuillet, *RB* 71 (1964) 324.

[25] Cf. D. Daube, *The New Testament and Rabbinic Judaism* (1956) 111f. and A. R. C. Leaney, *The Gospel According to St Luke* (1958) 109.

[26] Cf. the outpouring of the Spirit at Pentecost (see pp. 47ff. below).

[27] Cf. Jeremias, *TDNT* I, 141; also *ZNW* 54 (1963) 278f.; Taylor 164; J. C. Fenton in *Studies in the Gospels* (ed. Nineham) 106; Nineham 64; Best, *Temptation* 6–10; Schweizer, *Markus* 22f.

[28] B. Gerhardsson, *The Testing of God's Son* (1966). The central links are at the three decisive points in the narrative – the replies of Jesus – from Deut. 8.3; 6.16 and 6.13 respectively. See also G. H. P. Thomson, *JTS* 11 (1960) 1–12; P. Doble, *ExpT* 72 (1960–61) 91–93; J. A. T. Robinson, *Twelve New Testament Studies* (1962) 53–60. J. C. Fenton, *St Matthew* (1963), sees Exodus typology in the baptism of Jesus and reminds us of Matt. 2.15, 20 (58f.).

[29] 'According to the late Jewish expositors, the Spirit of God was particularly active among the people of God at the time of the exodus and wandering in the wilderness' (Gerhardsson 37). See Isa. 63.8–14; Num. 9.20; 11.10–29.

the new covenant has been introduced and the new Israel is tested to see if he will be faithful. Only when he has been thus tested, proved and found obedient, and the covenant thus affirmed in himself and for himself, only then can he go forth in his work as Son and Servant for others (cf. Heb. 5.8f.). We need hardly inquire at what point the new covenant was established: the close connection between the descent of the Spirit and the πειράζειν into which Jesus was led by the Spirit indicates that the former incident is the decisive moment.

In Luke similar conclusions could be drawn from the temptation narrative. But perhaps even more striking is the Adam-christology which Luke employs. It can hardly be an accident that Luke inserts the genealogy of Jesus between his anointing with the Spirit and his temptation, nor that he traces Jesus' family tree back to 'Adam, the son of God'. Here is the race of Adam, the son of God, a race, which, by implication, suffered through his fall.[30] But here now is the second Adam, the 'Adam of the End-time',[31] newly hailed as Son of God, who is led forth into the wilderness to do battle with the same Satan, and to reverse the tragic results of the Fall, first by refusing to succumb himself, and then by acting on fallen man's behalf. The point at which this 'Saga of Man, Part Two' begins is the moment at which Jesus is anointed with the Spirit and hears the heavenly voice.

We see then that the Pentecostals cannot build their case on the experience of Jesus at Jordan. For this anointing with the Spirit was essentially an initiatory experience: it initiated the End-time and initiated Jesus into it. This anointing may well be called a baptism in the Spirit, for John had expected a baptism in the Spirit to be the means of bringing in the End, and the descent of the Spirit on Jesus did in fact bring in the End; but the only thing which this proves is that the baptism in the Spirit is initiatory. It is not something which merely accompanies the beginning of the new age, it is that which effects it. Even if it was right for Pentecostals to parallel Jesus' supernatural birth with that of Christians, it would be of no avail. Jesus' birth belongs entirely to the old covenant, the epoch of Israel.

Luke makes this very plain: the first two chapters are entirely OT in character and even in thought and phraseology; OT ritual and piety is prominent throughout, and the Spirit is pre-eminently the Spirit of

[30] Thompson 7f.   [31] E. Hirsch quoted in Rengstorf 61.

prophecy. See H. H. Oliver, *NTS* 10 (1964) 202–26; W. B. Tatum, *NTS* 13 (1967) 184–95; cf. Wink 81. P. S. Minear overlooks this point when he argues that 'the mood, resonance, and thrust of the birth narratives are such as to discourage the neat assignment of John and Jesus to separate epochs' (in *Essays in honor of Paul Schubert: Studies in Luke – Acts* [ed. L. E. Keck and J. L. Martyn 1966] 120–3).

Only with the descent of the Spirit does the new covenant and new epoch enter, and only thus does Jesus himself enter the new covenant and epoch. He enters as representative man – representing in himself Israel and even mankind. As such, this first baptism in the Spirit could well be taken as typical of all later Spirit-baptisms – the means by which God brings each to follow in Jesus' footsteps. Jesus as representative of the people (ὁ λαός – cf. Luke 2.10, 32; 3.21) is the first to enter the promise made to the people.

At the same time, Pentecostals are right to recognize that Jesus' anointing with the Spirit was what equipped him for his messianic ministry of healing and teaching (Acts 10.38). This 'empowering for service' should not however be taken as the primary purpose of the anointing – it is only a corollary to it. The baptism in the Spirit, in other words, is not primarily to equip the (already) Christian for service; rather its function is to initiate the individual into the new age and covenant, to 'Christ' (= anoint) him, and in so doing to equip him for life and service in that new age and covenant. In this Jesus' entry into the new age and covenant is the type of every initiate's entry into the new age and covenant.

For us the most important ministry for which the descent of the Spirit equipped Jesus was his messianic task of baptizing in the Spirit (cf. Grundmann, *Markus* 31; J. M. Robinson 29; Beasley-Murray 61). This is most clearly brought out by John 1.33 (Bauer 23; Dodd 311). It is also implied in 3.34 where the primary reference is no doubt to the Father's gift of the Spirit to Jesus (οὐκ ἐκ μέτρου), but where by careful ambiguity John may also refer to Jesus' administration of the Spirit (δίδωσιν–present, cf. 1.33) (Brown, *John* 158, 161f.; Schnackenburg 399f.; Hoskyns 224, 230f.; cf. Sanders and Mastin 136). The addition of καὶ μένον in John 1.33 also implies that Jesus is empowered for his whole mission (both as Lamb of God and Baptizer in the Spirit) by the gift of the Spirit (cf. Barrett, *John* 148).

We turn now to those who talk of Jesus being given the Spirit in, or even through his baptism, and of this baptism in water-and-Spirit as the prototype of Christian baptism. This interpretation must be firmly rejected. I have deliberately refrained from entitling this chapter 'The Baptism of Jesus', for an examination of each of the four Gospels makes it quite plain that Jesus' baptism at the hands of John was not the principal interest. Nor can the concertina be expanded to make 'baptism' embrace the whole event. The Fourth Gospel does not even mention the baptism, and the three Synoptics speak of the baptism as a completed act (all aorists) which preceded the main action of the pericope. As elsewhere 'baptism' means no more than the act or rite of immersion. To entitle this paragraph 'The Baptism of Jesus' is therefore a misnomer. It reflects the interest of later ecclesiastics rather than the emphasis of the Evangelists.

For the Fourth Evangelist the important thing about the encounter between the Baptist and Jesus was the descent of the Spirit on Jesus. Far from implying that this was effected through or by water-baptism John focuses attention exclusively on the operation of the Spirit. It cannot be that the author either wished us to understand that Jesus received the Spirit in and through John's baptism or wanted to make Jesus' experience at Jordan a type of 'Christian baptism in water-and-Spirit' for, if he did, his failure to mention Jesus' baptism at 1.32f. (or 3.34 and 6.27) is incomprehensible.

In Luke it is quite evident that the supreme experience for Jesus was the descent of the Spirit, not the water-rite. In Acts 10.38 the baptism does not come into the picture, and in Luke 3.21f. it is passed over in an aorist participle ($\beta\alpha\pi\tau\iota\sigma\theta\acute{\epsilon}\nu\tau\sigma\varsigma$).[32] The aorist participle, of course, often signifies coincident action, but here the action of $\beta\alpha\pi\tau\iota\sigma\theta\acute{\epsilon}\nu\tau\sigma\varsigma$ obviously precedes in time the action of the *present* participle $\pi\rho\sigma\sigma\epsilon\upsilon\chi\sigma\mu\acute{\epsilon}\nu\sigma\upsilon$. Had Luke wished to link the descent of the Spirit directly with the baptism he would have said $\beta\alpha\pi\tau\iota\zeta\sigma\mu\acute{\epsilon}\nu\sigma\upsilon$. As it is, he evidently intends us to understand that the descent of the Spirit coincided with the praying of Jesus, not with his baptism, which had already been completed.[33] For Luke the Spirit is given in response to prayer,[34] and neither in nor

[32] 'In consequence of the construction used the performance of baptism on Jesus is not actually related by Luke' (Klostermann, *Lukasevangelium* [2][HNT 1929] 55). Dibelius calls Jesus' baptism in Luke 'an accessory circumstance' (Nebenumstand) (60).

[33] Creed 57; cf. Lampe, *Seal* 42f.; Ellis 91; W. C. Robinson 8f.; Feuillet 333; Haenchen, *Weg* 56; Flender 51; Wilkens, *TZ* 23 (1967) 29.

[34] Luke 3.21; 11.2 (Marcion); 11.13; Acts 1.14 with 2.1–4; 2.21 with 2.39; 4.23–31; 8.15–17; cf. 22.16.

through baptism. The whole sentence moves cumbrously forward through three participles to focus attention on the principal action – the experience of the heaven opening, the Spirit descending, and the voice speaking.

In Matthew the descent of the Spirit is more closely associated with the baptism, and in Mark even more closely – καὶ ἐβαπτίσθη . . . καὶ εὐθὺς ἀναβαίνων . . . εἶδεν . . . τὸ πνεῦμα . . . καταβαῖνον . . . The two words which link the descent of the Spirit to the baptism most closely are εὐθύς and ἀναβαίνων. But too much weight should not be laid on these.[35] εὐθύς is one of Mark's favourite words, and, as usually happens when a conjunction or adverb is overworked, it is often used loosely and in the weakened sense of 'then' or 'so then' (e.g. Mark 1.21, 23, 28).[36] ἀναβαίνων does not describe the emergence above the surface of the water which follows the complete immersion; it describes rather the climbing out of the river on to the bank after the rite has been completed. This is implied by Matthew's ἀνέβη ἀπὸ τοῦ ὕδατος, which could be translated simply, 'he left the water', and is shown most clearly by Acts 8.39, where *both* Philip and the eunuch came up out of the water (ἀνέβησαν ἐκ τοῦ ὕδατος), and certainly Philip had not been immersing himself (see also Mark 6.51). Matthew and Mark are therefore not really so different from Luke. Matthew indeed seems to set the events in sequence – baptized, left the water, experienced the Spirit. Mark's picture is of the heaven opening and the Spirit descending actually while Jesus was climbing out of the water on to the bank, with his baptism completed. The two events are more or less juxtaposed.

Three points more should be made. First, it is striking that Mark, the one who transmits John's words about the messianic baptism in the form of their actual fulfilment, is also the one who most sharply opposes the water-baptism of John to the Spirit-baptism of the new covenant. Indeed we might well say that he simplifies the Baptist's saying in order to sharpen the antithesis. If then he saw the descent of the Spirit on Jesus as the beginning of

---

[35] Contra, e.g., Lagrange, who concludes: 'The movement of the Spirit depends on baptism' (*Évangile selon Saint Marc* [4][1947] 9).

[36] See G. D. Kilpatrick, *The Bible Translator* 7 (1956) 3f.; cf. D. Daube, *The Sudden in the Scriptures* (1964) 60. Even if εὐθύς should here be translated 'immediately' it qualifies the main verb εἶδεν rather than the participle (RSV; Daube 46f.).

the promised baptism in the Spirit,[37] it confirms that he saw the two events – water-baptism and Spirit-baptism of Jesus – as fundamentally distinct.

Second, in Mark this passage is the second member of a sequence of three sections which are bound together by the theme of the Spirit (vv. 4–8, 9–11, 12–13)[38] – a fact all the more striking in view of the infrequent mention of the Spirit in Mark (only three times more). Clearly then the action of the Spirit is the central feature of this experience of Jesus, and that on which attention should focus.[39]

Third, in all three Synoptics the eschatological features appear after the baptism. It was what happened *after* the baptism which brought in the new age. The baptism is not part of the eschaton or of its inbreaking. It is still the baptism of John, still the preparatory rite whose fulfilment lies not in itself but awaits the future. That the fulfilment follows the performance of the rite in the case of Jesus is due not to the rite but to the person involved in it (see below).

It is quite evident, therefore, that much theologizing about the relation between baptism and the Spirit has been based on a fundamental mistake. Indeed, the false conclusions drawn from 'the baptism of Jesus' have been the chief source of the unscriptural views about Christian baptism which for far too long have distorted the Church's understanding of the Holy Spirit. It must be stated emphatically, that the baptism of Jesus and the descent of the Spirit are two distinct events – closely related, but distinct. Moreover, the emphasis in any theologizing on these events should fall on the descent of the Spirit: the baptism is only a preliminary to it – a necessary preliminary perhaps, but a preliminary. John's baptism remains in the role and with the significance John himself gave it – essentially preparatory for and antithetical to the imminent Spirit-baptism. It was not water-baptism which initiated into the messianic office,[40] but only the baptism in Spirit.

The precise relation between the two events in Jesus' case is

---

[37] This is altogether likely since τὸ πνεῦμα of v. 10 naturally looks back to the πνεῦμα ἅγιον of v. 8 (von Baer 59). See also p. 31 above.

[38] J. M. Robinson 29; S. E. Johnson, *The Gospel According to St Mark* (1957) 35.

[39] See also Büchsel 149; Haenchen, *Weg* 52. J. M. Robinson 27, and Nineham 58, note the disappearance of all human agents from the narrative.

[40] Contra Kosnetter 115–17.

fairly straightforward. The baptism of Jesus was initially understood as an expression of repentance (like that of the prophets,
identifying themselves with the people and the people's sins), of
submission to God's will (cf. Matt. 3.15), and commitment to the
work to which he had been called.[41] It was in response to and as a
result of this repentance, submission and commitment that the
Spirit was given and the new era was begun with the apocalyptic
roll of drums and the heavenly proclamation. If there is a causal
connection between the two events, in other words, it is between
the attitude of the person who was baptized and the Spirit, not
between the rite and the Spirit. It was not the rite which made the
difference, since many others were baptized by John and heard and
saw nothing;[42] it was the person who made the difference. And
not merely the person, for he had been living about thirty years,
but the attitude with which he came. The rite played a role, and
an important role at that, but not the decisive role which most
sacramentalists like to give it. It was the occasion of Jesus' commitment and the means by which he expressed his submission to his
Father's will. But it was only that. It was not the baptism at which
the Father expressed his pleasure; it was his Son with whom he
was well pleased, because he had shown his willingness for his
divine mission. It was this attitude which God commended, and it
was this attitude which resulted in the gift of the Spirit.

If then the events at Jordan are intended to be a type of
Christian conversion-initiation,[43] we should note what it means. It
certainly does *not* mean that the ritual act and experience *coincides*
and is *identical* with the spiritual act and experience it 'symbolizes',
as Plooij so rashly expressed it. What it does mean is that water-
baptism and Spirit-baptism are distinct events, that any connection

[41] Cf. Taylor 618; Cranfield, *SJT* 9 (1955) 54; C. F. D. Moule, *The Phenomenon of the New Testament* (1967) 74; K. Barth, *Die kirchliche Dogmatik* IV/4
66–73. Note also Rowley's description of proselyte baptism as 'an act of self-
dedication to the God of Israel' (*From Moses to Qumran* [1963] 226). If ὁ ἀμνὸς
τοῦ θεοῦ implies Jesus' death as Suffering Servant (J. Jeremias, *TDNT* I
338–40; Cullmann, *Early Christian Worship* [ET 1953] 63–65) or as paschal
lamb (Barrett, *John* 147), and it truly derives from the Baptist, it would
strengthen the view that Jesus saw his baptism from the first as a dedication
to and symbol of his death.

[42] Cf. Barrett, *Tradition* 25.

[43] Schweitzer, *The Mysticism of St Paul* (ET 1931) 234 and Beasley-Murray
64 rightly point out that in the NT the baptism of Jesus is never brought into
any kind of connection with Christian baptism. But our discussion is not in
terms of baptism. See p. 99 below.

between them is to be found solely in the repentance, submission and commitment expressed in the former, and that all the emphasis and attention is to be focused almost entirely on the latter.

It might appear to some of the more Catholic tradition that the considerations advanced here favour those who have argued for a high view of Confirmation as distinct from baptism.[44] It must be made clear, therefore, that we are dealing here not with two ritual actions but only one – baptism; that the bestowal of the Spirit is entirely the action of the Father; that the latter alone can properly be said to bring in and into the new age and covenant; that the ritual action, while distinct from and subordinate in significance to what follows, nevertheless leads to and results in the bestowal of the Spirit, though not because of any virtue or sacramental efficacy in the rite itself, but rather because of the submission and commitment it expresses. As a type of Christian conversion-initiation, we see that entry into the new age and covenant is a single complex event, involving distinct actions of man (baptism) and God (gift of Spirit), bound together by the repentance and commitment which is expressed in the former and results in the latter.

[44] Cf. Mason 14–16; A. T. Wirgman, *Doctrine of Confirmation* (1897) 40–53; F. H. Chase, *Confirmation in the Apostolic Age* (1909) 14f.; W. K. Lowther Clarke, *Confirmation or the Laying on of Hands* (1926) 15, 19; Dix, *Laying on of Hands* 15; also *Theology* 30.

# PART TWO

# IV

## THE MIRACLE OF PENTECOST

PENTECOST is a word which lies close to the heart of every Pentecostal. Not only does it give him his 'brand' name, but it also provides him with his distinctive (and sometimes most precious) doctrine, it affords to him the key to a full Christian life and witness, it speaks to him of his most treasured experiences of Christ, and it enables him to express his deepest devotion and praise. Pentecost is the message of the Pentecostal and epitomizes the particular contribution and emphasis he makes to and in the Christian faith. Ernest Williams puts it thus: 'To be Pentecostal is to identify oneself with the experience that came to Christ's followers on the Day of Pentecost; that is, to be filled with the Holy Spirit in the same manner as those who were filled with the Holy Spirit on that occasion.'[1] Pentecostals argue that those who were baptized in the Spirit on the Day of Pentecost were already 'saved' and 'regenerate'. Their reception of the Spirit on that day was not their conversion; it was not the beginning of their Christian life. In other words, Pentecost was a second experience subsequent to and distinct from their earlier 'new birth'. As such it gives the pattern for all Christian experience thereafter. As the disciples were baptized in the Spirit at Pentecost, an experience subsequent to their 'regeneration', so may (and should) all Christians be baptized in the Spirit after their conversion.

The proof adduced for the claim that Pentecost was a second experience is drawn from the Gospels, principally John. The

---

[1] The Pentecostal Movement's systematic theologian, writing in *The Pentecostal Evangel* (15 January 1961) 11 – cited by F. D. Bruner, *The Doctrine and Experience of the Holy Spirit in the Pentecostal Movement and Correspondingly in the New Testament* (Hamburg dissertation 1963) 36; cf. K. Hutton, RGG[3] II (1958) 1303 f.; O. Eggenberger, TZ 11 (1955) 272, 292; J. T. Nichol, *Pentecostalism* (1966) 1f., 8f.

passages usually cited include John 13.10f.; 15.3; 20.22 and the single Lukan reference Luke 10.20.[2] The arguments are the same as those used by the old Holiness teachers,[3] and closely parallel the teaching of some Catholics that Pentecost was the apostles' Confirmation.[4]

The appeal to John's Gospel raises a basic methodological issue: Are we to approach the NT material as systematic theologians or as biblical theologians and exegetes? The common error into which too many of the former fall, is to treat the NT (and even the Bible) as a homogeneous whole, from any part of which texts can be drawn on a chosen subject and fitted into a framework and system which is often basically extra-biblical, though it may be constructed from the thought of a single biblical author like Paul. The method of the latter is to take each author and book separately and to (attempt to) outline his or its particular theological emphases; only when he has set a text in the context of its author's thought and intention (as expressed in his writing), only then can the biblical-theologian feel free to let that text interact with other texts from other books. The latter method is obviously the sounder, and though it involves more work, it is always liable to give the truer picture of the biblical thought than the former. This means, in our case, that we cannot simply assume that the Gospels and Acts are all bare historical narratives which complement each other in a direct 1:1 ratio; nor can we assume that Luke and John have the same emphases and aims. They may, of course, but we cannot assume it without proof. At any rate, we cannot start by relating John 20.22 to Acts 2: we must first understand the former in the

[2] See Riggs 50; Harper, *Power* 19 n. 4; also *Fire* 13; D. Prince, *From Jordan to Pentecost* (1965) 66; Christenson 37; H. M. Ervin, *These are not Drunken as ye Suppose* (1968) 89; cf. M. Pearlman, *Knowing the Doctrines of the Bible* (1937); H. Horton, *The Baptism in the Holy Spirit* (1961) 4; Lindsay 34.

[3] See especially R. A. Torrey, *The Baptism with the Holy Spirit* (1896) 11–16; A. Murray, *The Full Blessing of Pentecost* (1908); also *The Spirit of Christ* (1888) 24–32, 313–25.

[4] N. Adler, *Das erste christliche Pfingstfest* (1938) 135. The third-century work *On Rebaptism* takes the view that Peter's baptism was in two parts: the first linked with his confession of faith recorded in Matt. 16.16, the second taking place at Pentecost (cited in J. Crehan, *Early Christian Baptism and the Creed* [1950] 42f). Alternatively, John 20.22 is concerned with the apostles' 'interior consecration', while Luke deals only with 'the outward manifestation of the Spirit' (X. Léon-Dufour, *The Gospels and the Jesus of History* [ET 1968] 261); cf. J. H. E. Hull, *The Holy Spirit in the Acts of the Apostles* (1967), who argues that at Pentecost the apostles only became aware of the gift of the Spirit they had already received (50, 86).

context of the Fourth Gospel and the latter in the context of Luke's thought, and *only then* can we correlate the individual texts themselves. John we leave aside for the time being; to clarify Luke's understanding of Pentecost is our present task.

When we look at Pentecost in the context of Luke–Acts it becomes evident that Pentecostal and Catholic alike have again missed the principal significance of the story. For once again we stand at a watershed in salvation-history, the beginning of the new age and new covenant, not for Jesus this time, but now for his disciples. What Jordan was to Jesus, Pentecost was to the disciples.[5] As Jesus entered the new age and covenant by being baptized in the Spirit at Jordan, so the disciples followed him in like manner at Pentecost.[6] With the wider enjoyment of the messianic age made possible by Jesus' representative death, so at Pentecost the new covenant, hitherto confined to the one representative man, was extended to embrace all those who remained faithful to him and tarried at Jerusalem in obedience to his command.

The 'all' of 2.1 is almost certainly the 120 and not just the twelve. The πάντες most naturally refers to the whole body involved in the preceding verses; that more than twelve languages were heard implies that there were more than twelve speakers; 2.15, and perhaps 2.33, probably refers to other than the eleven, who were standing with Peter; the 'us' of 11.15 includes 'the brethren who were in Judea' (11.1). There is certainly no room for the Catholic view which singles out the apostles for special or exclusive endowments of the Spirit (contra Adler 137f.), and which makes it possible to regard the apostles as the sole 'channel' of the Spirit to others. The one gift and the same gift was common to all.

To see this most clearly we must retrace our steps a little, and, bearing in mind that Luke–Acts is the work of a single author, take a comprehensive look at the total scheme of the two books. Luke sees history as falling into three phases – the period of Israel, the period of Jesus, and the period between the coming of Jesus and his parousia.[7] Jesus is the one who effects these transitions, and in his own life each phase is inaugurated by his entering

[5] Cf. F. J. Foakes-Jackson, *The Acts of the Apostles* (Moffatt 1931) 9f.; Kraft 410; G. Stählin, *Die Apostelgeschichte*[10] (NTD 1962) 39. See also p. 99 below.
[6] von Baer 167; see also O. Procksch, *TDNT* I 103f.
[7] Conzelmann, *Theology* 150, and earlier von Baer 77–84.

into a new relationship with the Spirit:[8] first, when his human life was the creation of the Spirit (Luke 1.35); second, when he was anointed with the Spirit and thus became the Anointed One, the unique Man of the Spirit (Luke 3.22; 4.18);[9] third, when he received the promise of the Spirit at his exaltation and poured the Spirit forth on his disciples, thus becoming Lord of the Spirit. The transition from first to second was made possible and 'triggered off' by his submission to John's baptism; the transition from second to third by his submission to the baptism of the cross.

It is important to realize that this threefold scheme of salvation-history is a development on the older Jewish view of two ages in which the new age and covenant simply succeeded the old. The epoch of Jesus as something distinct and unique was unforeseen. John the Baptist expected the Coming One to bring in and into the new age by baptizing in Spirit-and-fire straight off. When this confident prediction was not fulfilled he lost his assurance and began to question whether Jesus was the one whose coming he had foretold and whether his own message was true after all (Luke 7.18–19). Jesus reassured him by pointing to other messianic Scriptures (Isa. 29.18f.; 35.5f.; 61.1), thereby reminding John that his ministry was broader than John's conception of it (cf. Luke 9.54f.). But, none the less, John's hope had not been fulfilled with the immediacy that John expected. What had happened?

The answer, I suggest, lies in Luke's twofold understanding of the events at Jordan. As we have already seen, the descent of the Spirit upon Jesus was Jesus' *own* entry into the new age and covenant. Before he could baptize others in the Spirit he himself had to be baptized in the Spirit.[10] In the wilderness Jesus was tempted for himself, not vicariously. The new age and covenant had come, *but only in him*; only he had begun to experience them. He alone was the Man of the Spirit, the first-fruits of the future harvest. Why was this?

This leads to the second aspect of Jesus' experience at Jordan.

---

[8] Cf. G. Smeaton, *The Doctrine of the Holy Spirit* (1882, reprinted 1958) 121–36; J. Schniewind, *Das Evangelium nach Matthäus* (NTD 1956) 27.

[9] He is not yet Lord of the Spirit (contra Schweizer, *TWNT* VI 402, and Conzelmann's odd comment in *Theology* 28). Luke does soften the strong words of Mark (τὸ πνεῦμα αὐτὸν ἐκβάλλει εἰς τὴν ἔρημον), but he still says Jesus 'was led by the Spirit' (Luke 4.1 – ἤγετο ἐν τῷ πνεύματι), a phrase which distinctly recalls Christian experience of the Spirit (Rom. 8.14; Gal. 5.18).

[10] Cf. Berkhof 18.

Not only was it his own entry into the age of the Spirit, but it was
also his anointing with the Spirit as Messiah and Servant (Luke
3.22; 4.18; Acts 4.27), and his installation into the messianic office
of Servant and Representative of his people.[11] For Luke this work
culminated in the cross where Jesus accepted and endured the
messianic baptism in Spirit-and-fire on behalf of his people. The
key passage here is Luke 12.49f., where occur the concepts both of
fire and of baptism. Here we have confirmation that John's prediction regarding the Coming One's ministry is accepted by Jesus: he
came to cast fire on the earth. Here too he is looking for a baptism,
one which is to be accomplished on himself. These two verses are
undoubtedly to be taken as parallel members of the one idea:

πῦρ ἦλθον βαλεῖν ἐπὶ τὴνγῆν, καὶ τί θέλω εἰ ἤδη ἀνήφθη.
βάπτισμα δὲ ἔχω βαπτισθῆναι, καὶ πῶς συνέχομαι ἕως ὅτου τελεσθῇ.

It follows that we must understand the thought of the verses thus:
Jesus came to cast fire on the earth, and how he wishes it were
already kindled *on himself*. How he longs for the baptism, *which he
came to administer*, to be accomplished on himself. This baptism is
undoubtedly to be linked with the cup (of wrath) of Luke 22.42.[12]
Thus we may say that for Luke Jesus' ministry as Servant and
Representative is consummated by his suffering the messianic
baptism of fire on behalf of his people.[13]

I suggest, therefore, that in Luke's presentation Jesus' fulfilment
of the role predicted for him by John – as the one who would
bring in the New Age and initiate into it by baptizing in Spirit-
and-fire – was delayed for two reasons. First, Jesus must enter that
New Age himself by being himself baptized in the Spirit; and must
be tested and proved as the new Israel and Son of God. Second,
having been thus initiated and tested himself, he can take up his
role as Servant and Messiah. This role culminates in his vicarious
suffering on the cross, where he received in himself as Representative of his people the messianic baptism in fire. It is only after
fulfilling this role that he can begin to fulfil the role predicted for
him by the Baptist – only after his death, resurrection and ascension that he begins to baptize in the Spirit.

[11] See ch. III, and cf. Berkhof's suggestive treatment (17ff.).
[12] Cf. Mark 10.38; 14.36, and see Taylor 554; Cranfield, *Mark* 433; Grundmann, *Markus* 292f.
[13] So Lang, *TWNT* VI 943; cf. Delling, *NovTest* 2 (1957) 103–12.

The reason for this is, presumably, that whereas Jesus can receive the messianic baptism on his own behalf because he is without sin – so that there is nothing to be refined away and his baptism is only in Spirit – his people are so sinful (cf. Luke 5.8; 18.13) that the messianic baptism would be for them one of destructive πνεῦμα and fire – a cup of wrath so terrible that even Jesus quails before it (Luke 12.49f.; 22.42). Since this would destroy them, Jesus, as Servant, suffers on their behalf; the fire is kindled on him; he is baptized with the messianic baptism of others; he drains the cup of wrath which was the portion of others. This means that when Jesus comes to baptize others it is a baptism no longer of Spirit and fire, but now only of Spirit: Acts 1.5 – 'John baptized with water, but you will be baptized with the Holy Spirit' – not with Spirit-and-fire, as John had said. Perhaps we may say that in some sense Jesus has exhausted the fire that was kindled on him, just as he drained the cup of wrath, so that the means of entry into the New Age is now only a baptism in Spirit, not Spirit-and-fire, but a baptism in the Spirit of Jesus, he who endured the messianic tribulation which was necessary before the messianic Kingdom could be established, and which all must undergo before and if they would see the Kingdom.

In terms of Luke's scheme of salvation-history all this simply means that the new age and covenant does not begin for the disciples until Pentecost. In the *second* epoch only Jesus, the pioneer of our salvation, has entered into that age; he alone has been baptized in Spirit. It is only with the *third* epoch that the disciples enter into the new age; only when Jesus has been exalted that they are initiated into the new covenant by receiving the Spirit; only when Jesus has completed his ministry as Servant and Lamb of God that they experience his ministry as Baptizer in the Spirit. Where up till then only Jesus had experienced life in the new age, now they too can experience that life – for they share in his life. Where only he had participated in the Spirit, now the Spirit comes to all his disciples as his Spirit.[14]

Still with John 20.22 in mind Pentecostals might well ask whether it was not immediately after the resurrection that the disciples were initiated into the new age. If it was then that they

---

[14] Cf. Conzelmann, *Theology* 103 nn. 1, 2, 179. To say that 'no real function of the Exalted Lord is expressed in Luke' (176) is to ignore the exalted Lord's ministry as baptizer in the Spirit.

received the new life which he had won in his death and resurrection, this would mean that Pentecost was still a second,
post-regeneration experience. But this is certainly not Luke's
view.

(*a*) For Luke Pentecost is the climax of all that has gone before.
From the start of the ministry of Jesus we are pointed forward,
not to the death of Jesus, but beyond that to the baptism which he
will give (Luke 3.15–17). And even at the Ascension we are still
looking forward to that baptism, still unfulfilled, and still awaited
as the culmination of Jesus' ministry (Acts 1.5). The same point
becomes evident in Peter's speech (2.29–33). The climax and
purposed end of Jesus' ministry is not the cross and resurrection,
but the ascension and Pentecost. More precisely, as the exaltation
was the climax of Jesus' ministry for Jesus himself,[15] so Pentecost
was the climax of Jesus' ministry for the disciples. It was only at
Pentecost by the gift of the Spirit that the benefits and blessings
won by Jesus in his death, resurrection and ascension were applied
to the disciples. As Moberly put it: 'Calvary without Pentecost
would not be an atonement *to us*.'[16] Jesus' death and resurrection
go for nothing and are wholly ineffective without the gift of the
Spirit.

(*b*) The fact that Pentecost is the climax of Jesus' ministry for
the disciples should not blind us into thinking that Pentecost is
merely a continuation of what went before. Pentecost is a new
beginning – the inauguration of the new age, the age of the Spirit –
that which had not been before.[17] Luke makes this very clear in
several ways.

First, there is the simple fact that Luke wrote two books – an
observation of no little significance.[18] The first book is rounded
off by the ascension, and Luke, for one reason or another, is at no
pains to separate it from the resurrection. In the Gospel the single
complex of events, resurrection and ascension, ends the story of
Jesus. Then comes a new beginning. Acts marks a new phase, and
begins with a new account of the ascension. But this time it is

[15] Von Baer 95; cf. Flender 106, also 98–106. Cf. Phil. 2.6–11; Heb. 12.2.
[16] Moberly 152. See also Michaelis 133; Wotherspoon, *Pentecost* 26–30;
Church of Scotland, *Biblical Doctrine* 37f.; J. A. T. Robinson, *Studies* 167.
[17] Cf. C. H. Dodd, *The Apostolic Preaching and its Developments* (1936,
reprinted 1963) 26; Schweizer in *BNTE* 503f.
[18] As C. K. Barrett shows in *Luke the Historian in Recent Study* (1961) 53ff.;
cf. P. van Stempvoort, *NTS* 5 (1958) 30–42.

linked with Pentecost and what comes after, rather than with the resurrection and what went before.[19] In other words, the ascension from one standpoint brings to an end the story of Jesus, and from another begins the age of the Spirit (Acts 2.33).

But, second, that which ushers in the age of the spirit is Pentecost, rather than the ascension. The account of the ascension at the beginning of Acts is only introductory to the account of Pentecost. Even in the former the prospect of the Spirit soon to come is the dominant theme (Acts 1.5, 8). One of the many parallels between his first and second book that Luke intends us to see[20] is, no doubt, that as Luke 1 is essentially a preparation for Luke 2, so Acts 1 is essentially a preparation for Acts 2.[21]

Moreover, third, it is evident that Luke wants to press home upon us this fact, that the ascension is properly the end of the old (or second) epoch of salvation, and Pentecost is the beginning of the new, for he highlights the significance of the ten-day break between the two events.[22] 1.15–26 is an interregnum – a between-time. In it there is no activity of the Spirit. He has been active in the old epoch (1.2, 16), and he will initiate the new (1.5, 8), but in the between-time he is not in evidence. To emphasize this Luke relates the election of Matthias, and in the method of election the absence of any mention of or dependence on the Spirit is most noticeable. Whatever the rights and wrongs of the election[23] (Luke maintains an impartial silence, as in 15.36–40; cf. 6.1; 8.1), Luke has obviously included his account of it to point the contrast of 'before and after' Pentecost. Before Pentecost choice to office depends on temporal relation to Jesus of Nazareth; after Pentecost it depends on Spirit-possession (6.3). Before Pentecost (the beginning of the 'Peter section') choice depends on the lot; after

---

[19] Barrett, *Luke* 56; cf. D. P. Fuller, *Easter Faith and History* (1965) 197f.

[20] For parallels between Luke and Acts see Stählin 13f.; J. C. O'Neill, *The Theology of the Acts* (1954) 65–67; M. D. Goulder, *Type and History in Acts* (1964) 61, 74.

[21] R. B. Rackham, *The Acts of the Apostles* [14](1951) 14; F. F. Bruce, *The Book of the Acts* (1954) 54–56.

[22] In what follows I draw on von Baer, especially 78–84.

[23] Cf. Stählin 28; E. M. Blaiklock, *The Acts of the Apostles* (1959) 50. One might ask, for example, why a new apostle was elected in the interval between the ascension and Pentecost, and not appointed by the risen Christ himself, which one would have thought to be the only qualification of an apostle which finally differentiated him from the other early disciples (Luke 6.13; Acts 26.15–18; cf. I Cor. 15.7f.). See also K. H. Rengstorf, *Studia Theologica* 15 (1961) 35–67.

Pentecost (13.2 – the beginning of the 'Paul section') choice depends on the Spirit.[24]

It could be argued that for Luke the use of lots has a very high pedigree: an apostle has to be accredited by the Lord himself (1.24f.) and the 'superhuman' method of lots is the only method adequate to this unique occasion (cf. E. Haenchen, *Die Apostelgeschichte* [1956] 131). Yet even if this is so, the contrast between the dispensations remains – not a contrast which disparages the earlier as 'inferior', but one which merely highlights the great difference between the two dispensations – viz. only in the age of the Spirit can guidance be direct and through the Spirit. W. A. Beardslee, however, has suggested that Luke has here taken over an earlier tradition in which Matthias was chosen by the *community* (as representatives of Christ) and has objectified the metaphorical language which used 'lot' to mean 'decision' (a usage evidenced in Qumran) (*NovTest* 4 [1960] 245–52; so also Leaney, cited by Hull 43, and J. Munck, *The Acts of the Apostles* [Anchor Bible 1967] 10; cf. Jackson and Lake, *The Beginnings of Christianity Part I, The Acts of the Apostles* IV [1933] 15).

Fourth, the third stage of history does not begin until Jesus has been given and has received the Spirit, that is, when he becomes Lord of the Spirit and begins to initiate others into the new age through his ministry as Baptizer in the Spirit (Acts 1.5; 2.33). Until that time he is still only the Man of the Spirit. Acts 1.2 makes this clear: he is still dependent on the Spirit for the inspiration of his teaching (ἐντειλάμενος τοῖς ἀποστόλοις διὰ πνεύματος ἁγίου) in a way very similar to that of the NT prophets (11.28; 21.4; cf. 4.25). And this dependency continues right up to his ascension – hence the order of the Greek in 1.2 which stresses that this ministry διὰ πνεύματος ἁγίου continued *right up until* the day (ἄχρι ἧς ἡμέρας) on which he was taken up.

Fifth, and perhaps clearest of all, it was only at Pentecost that the Joel prophecy was fulfilled. In the old two-age view of Jewish eschatology the gift of the Spirit was one of the decisive marks of the new age.[25] Certainly for the first Christians the gift of the Spirit was *the* decisive differentia which marked off the old dispensation from the new (Mark 1.8; John 7.39; Acts 2.17, 33; 19.2;

---

[24] Cf. Flender 119; R. Allen, 'Pentecost and the World', reprinted in *The Ministry of the Spirit* (1960) 45.

[25] E.g. Isa. 32.15; 34.16; Ezek. 11.19; 36.26f.; 37.4–14; and perhaps Zech. 12.10, as well as Joel. 2.28ff. 'The bestowal of the Spirit is the primary characteristic of the age of final redemption' (Lampe in *Studies* 162).

Rom. 8.9; II Cor. 3.3, 6–8; Heb. 6.4f.). The 'last days' did not begin for the disciples till Pentecost (Acts 2.17). Only then did they enter into the distinctively Christian dispensation and into the distinctively Christian experience of the Spirit.

Dispensationalists often argue that Peter did not consider Pentecost a fulfilment of the Joel prophecy; e.g. M. F. Unger: ' "This is that" means nothing more than that "this is (an illustration of) that which was spoken by the prophet Joel" ' (*Bib.Sac.* 122 [1965] 177). This is special pleading. Luke (and Peter) clearly regard the outpouring on the 120 as at least the beginning of the outpouring on all flesh, and the 'last days' in which 'whoever calls upon the name of the Lord shall be saved' (2.21) have certainly arrived. It is quite probable that they understood the cosmic signs (2.19f.) as apocalyptic stage-effects which did not belong to the substance of the prophecy or require literal fulfilment (cf. J. M. Kik, *Matthew* 24 – An *Exposition* [1948] 71–75; J. A. T. Robinson, *Jesus and his Coming* [1957] 151).

(*c*) For Luke Pentecost is also the beginning of the new covenant for the disciples. Four times he refers to the Spirit given then as ἡ ἐπαγγελία (Luke 24.49; Acts 1.4; 2.33, 38f.), a word often used both by Paul and by Luke to characterize the covenant promise of God to his people (Acts 2.39; 7.17; 13.23, 32; 26.6; Rom. 4.13, 16, 20; 9.8; Gal. 3.14; etc). Luke seems to share Paul's equation of the 'blessing of Abraham' with the gift of the Spirit (Gal. 3.14), for the words of Acts 2.39 ('the promise is to you and to your children') clearly recall the terms of the Abrahamic covenant (Gen. 17.7–10) – *the* covenant of promise[26] – and v. 38 identifies the covenant promise with the gift of the Spirit. Implicit here, therefore, is the thought of the Spirit as the new covenant fulfilment of the ancient covenant promise. The gift of the Spirit is now the means whereby men enter into the blessing of Abraham; it is through receiving the Spirit that 'all nations of the earth (= all that are afar off?)[27] shall be blessed' (Gen. 12.3; 22.18; Acts 3.25).

Among the specific promises of the Father for the messianic time and the new covenant the parallel between Ezek. 36.27 and

[26] Note the specific reference to it in the conclusion to the next Petrine sermon – Acts 3.25.
[27] The similar phrase in Acts 22.21 refers to the Gentiles. But Rackham 31, B. Reicke, *Glaube und Leben der Urgemeinde* (1957) 51, Stählin 54, Munck 21, take it as a reference primarily to the Jews of the dispersion. Alternatively, 'those who are far away' are the new covenant equivalent to the foreigners who were to be included within the Abrahamic covenant (Gen. 17.12f.).

Jer. 31.33 is particularly noticeable: both promise ability to keep
the law, the law written in the heart (the enabling factor in
Jeremiah) being precisely equivalent to the gift of the Spirit
(the enabling factor in Ezekiel). In any new covenant theology,
therefore, the Spirit is to be seen as the agent of the new covenant
and its supreme blessing – the one who will write the law in their
hearts, the one we may say who is the law written in their hearts.
Moreover, in any antithesis between the old and new covenants
the external written law will be set against the inward gift of the
Spirit. Each stands as the embodiment and motivating principle of
its respective covenant. With the law the old covenant stood or
fell; so it is with the Spirit in the new. This is certainly Paul's
understanding of the situation (II Cor. 3.3, 6–8), but Paul is
simply drawing out the logical corollary to Pentecost – the fulfilment of the promise of the Father. It is very probable therefore
that Luke also saw the Spirit as the essence and embodiment of the
new covenant, as that which most distinguished it from the old.

This would appear to be confirmed by the fact that Luke
presents the outpouring of the Spirit as taking place on the Feast
of Pentecost. For Pentecost was more and more coming to be
regarded as the feast which commemorated the lawgiving at Sinai.

E. Lohse claims that the old form of the feast (the bringing of the
first fruits to the Temple) would persist till the destruction of the
Temple, and only after AD 70 would the Rabbis give the feast new content (*EvTh.* 13 (1953) 429f.; cf. Stählin 37f.). S. Maclean Gilmour states
bluntly that 'No association of Pentecost with the Sinai event can be
documented from Jewish sources before the second century' (*JBL* 81
[1962] 65). However, from the middle of the second century BC Pentecost was undoubtedly regarded as the feast of covenant renewal, for the
Book of Jubilees celebrated the giving of the Sinaitic covenant (as well
as the Noahic and Abrahamic covenants) on the Feast of Weeks (Jub.
6.17–21; 15.1–24), and the annual renewal of the covenant at Qumran,
where they seem to have followed the same calendar as we find in
Jubilees, most probably fell at the same feast (1QS 2); nor should we
neglect the fact that the renewal of the covenant in II Chron. 15.10–12
took place in the same month as the law-giving at Sinai (Ex. 19.1), and
the other evidence which strongly suggests that Ex. 19 was an established reading for the Feast of Weeks in the century before Christ
(see G. Kretschmar, *Zeitschrift für Kirchengeschichte* 66 [1954–55] 222–9;
R. de Vaux, *Ancient Israel* [ET ²1965] 494; N. Adler, *Lexikon für
Theologie und Kirche* 8 [1963] 421; Leaney, *Rule* 95–107; C. S. Mann in

Munck's *Acts* 272; Hull 53–55; J. C. Kirby, *Ephesians: Baptism and Pentecost* [1968]; and on the parallels between Acts 2 and Qumran see W. Grundmann *Studia Evangelica* II Part I [1964] 592f.). Besides, it is unlikely that the Rabbis after AD 70 created a new significance for Pentecost *de novo*; they doubtless took over a tradition of some antiquity and respectability.

This does not mean that the concept of the new covenant and of the renewal of the law for Judaism all over the world has 'powerfully moulded the story of the Spirit's first appearance',[28] for the indications of such a moulding are lacking. But it is fairly safe to conclude that the thought of Sinai is present,[29] and it may even be as Knox suggests, that 'the devout proselytes no doubt regarded the sending of the Holy Spirit as the giving of the new Torah written on the tables of their hearts'.[30] At all events the thought of Pentecost as the giving of the new Torah (or rather as the writing of the law upon the heart by the Spirit) indicates that for Luke Pentecost was the beginning of the new covenant in the experience of the disciples, and that the Spirit is the essence of the new covenant without whom there is no new covenant and no entry into or participation in it.

(*d*) Pentecost inaugurates the age of the Church. For Luke Pentecost constitutes the disciples as the new covenant people of God, and is 'the beginning of the period of the Church'.[31] In Luke's eyes the Church is basically a missionary body or, more accurately, the Church is composed of witnesses to Jesus Christ. That 1.8 is the 'contents page' for the book of Acts need hardly be reiterated, but it is the Spirit on whom the outworking of this theme depends (the Acts of the Holy Spirit), and it is not till Pentecost that the mission begins. No attempt is made to start work even on the first stage of the 1.8 plan of campaign until the Spirit is given at Pentecost. But when the Spirit comes, then, and only then, the world-wide mission starts at full gallop, and the gospel is preached to representatives 'from every nation under heaven' (2.5) no less! The Christian Church is a confessional Church, and its basic (or one of its basic) confessions is 'Jesus is Lord' (Acts 10.36; Rom.

[28] Schweizer, *TWNT* VI 408f., following W. L. Knox, *The Acts of the Apostles* (1948) 81–84; also Hull 53f.

[29] Kirby 118.

[30] Knox, *Acts* 86; cf. Rackham 18.

[31] Schweizer, *TWNT* VI 409; so many; 'The Spirit is the reality on which the Church is founded' (E. Stauffer, *New Testament Theology* [ET 1955] 165).

10.9; I Cor. 12.3).[32] But this confession only becomes possible
with the ascension, when Jesus is made 'both Lord and Christ'
(Acts 2.36). And it is no doubt the outpouring of the Spirit which
brings the full and final certainty about Jesus' exaltation and lordship home to the disciples (Acts 2.33).[33] At all events it is not until
Pentecost that this foundational belief of the Church is realized and
promulgated, and it is only as a result of Pentecost that the invitation of Acts 2.21 ('whosoever calls on the name of the Lord shall
be saved') can be issued in the name of Jesus and the promise of
the Spirit be made on condition of repentance and baptism in the
name of Jesus Christ (Acts 2.38).

Nor can we say that the other essential notes of the Church are
present until after Pentecost. The apostolic teaching cannot
properly be said to have begun till 2.42;[34] nor the κοινωνία (2.42),
which for Paul particularly denotes the Christian community's
common participation in or mutual sharing of the one Spirit
(II Cor. 13.14; Phil. 2.1). Christian water-baptism – that is, baptism
in the name of the Lord Jesus Christ – was certainly not administered till after Pentecost (2.41); nor was the common meal, which
may have included the Lord's Supper,[35] shared in till 2.42. Yet, no
sooner has Pentecost come than we find these four features
suddenly becoming the mark of the primitive community.

It would be premature to say that for Luke Acts 2.42–47 represents the ideal state within the young Church,[36] or that in 2.42 we
have necessarily 'the sequence of an early Christian service'.[37] Even
less can we say that for Luke 'the real, primary and enduring
result of the Spirit's coming' at Pentecost was 'the "Fellowship"
(ἡ κοινωνία)',[38] or that Luke has a developed theology of the

---

[32] O. Cullmann, *The Earliest Christian Confessions* (ET 1949) 54–64; but see
also V. H. Neufeld, *The Earliest Christian Confessions* (1963).

[33] Von Baer 84, 93–95. Cf. Jesus' own reception of the Spirit at Jordan
which may properly be said to have brought final certainty to Jesus as to his
divine sonship.

[34] If 1.15ff. is upheld as an example of apostolic teaching, it can equally
well be argued that it is an example of mistaken teaching (see p. 45 n. 23).
Besides, it is clear that the apostles' understanding of even basic matters was
deficient before Pentecost, in Luke's eyes at least (1.6; and see Wotherspoon,
*Pentecost* 19–26; C. S. C. Williams, *The Acts of the Apostles* [1957] 56; Blaiklock
50).

[35] J. Jeremias, *The Eucharistic Words of Jesus* [3](ET 1966) 120.

[36] Adler, *Pfingstfest* 138.

[37] Jeremias, *Eucharistic Words* 119.

[38] C. A. A. Scott in *The Spirit* (ed. B. H. Streeter 1919) 136ff., followed by

Church as the Body of Christ (though cf. 9.5). What we can say is that Luke shows us in 2.41ff. the Church operating in a manner which exemplifies Paul's concept of the Church as the Body of Christ. Luke's history at this point demonstrates Paul's doctrine. We can therefore say that Pentecost is the beginning of the Church and the coming into existence of the Church as the Body of Christ. And this is the work of the Spirit; for Luke evidently intends us to understand 2.41–47 as the direct and immediate result of the Spirit's coming, just as 4.32–37 is the immediate and direct consequence of 4.31.[39]

It could be argued that Acts 4.32–37 is simply one of Luke's generalizing summaries. But this need not exclude my point. Certainly the story of Ananias and Sapphira which follows shows that in Luke's view the life of the community as depicted in 4.32–37 was the work of the Spirit, for it is precisely the abuse of this community life which Peter calls a lie to the Holy Spirit and a testing of the Spirit of the Lord (5.3, 9).

In brief, then, the Church properly conceived did not come into existence until Pentecost.[40] Apart from everything else the vital experience and possession of the Spirit, the constitutive life principle and hallmark of the early Church, was lacking. And as one cannot say 'Christian' without also saying 'Church', since a Christian is by definition a member of the Church (see chapter VIII), non-existence of the Church prior to Pentecost means that there were no Christians (properly speaking) prior to Pentecost.

(*e*) One further piece of evidence must be called in – the testimony of Peter in Acts 10–11. There Peter tells us not only that Cornelius's experience of salvation and forgiveness was precisely that of the 120 at Pentecost, but also that the spiritual state of the 120 prior to Pentecost was precisely that of Cornelius prior to his reception of the Spirit. As we shall see in chapter VII, no less than

---

L. Dewar, *The Holy Spirit and Modern Thought* (1959) 46; cf. Hull 73, 75. But see especially J. Y. Campbell, *JBL* 51 (1932) 352–80; also H. Seesemann, *Der Begriff KOINΩNIA in Neuen Testament* (1933).

[39] Adler, *Pfingstfest* 138.

[40] This is not to deny that the Church is foreshadowed and prepared for by Jesus (see e.g. R. N. Flew, *Jesus and his Church* [1938] 35–88), but even passages like Matt. 16.18; 18.17 look forward beyond Jesus' departure to Pentecost.

four times (10.47; 11.15, 17; 15.8) is the direct equation between the two experiences of the Spirit clearly and firmly drawn. In particular we should note 11.15, 17:

> 11.15: 'The Holy Spirit fell on them as on us *at the beginning*.'
> 11.17: 'God gave the same gift to them as he gave to us *when we believed* in the Lord Jesus Christ.'

The *beginning* for the apostolic circle was the beginning of the Church at Pentecost. The reception of the Holy Spirit was the beginning of their *Christian* experience as it was for Cornelius, their baptism in the Spirit into the new covenant and the Church as it was for him.

Not only so, but Pentecost came in the experience of the 120 'when they believed in (πιστεύσασιν ἐπί) the Lord Jesus Christ'. Now πίστευσαι (aorist) ἐπί in Luke always signifies the act of faith, the decisive commitment by which one becomes a Christian (Acts 2.44; 9.42; 16.31). 11.17 is no different. The act of faith which resulted in the gift of the Spirit to the 120 did not take place till Pentecost. However highly they esteemed their Master while with him on earth, however deep their insights into his character and person (Luke 5.5; 9.20), and however greatly they reverenced him when gone from them (Acts 1.21),[41] so far as Peter was concerned their belief in him and commitment to him as Lord and Christ did not begin until Pentecost. It was only at that moment of believing committal that they received the Spirit, only at Pentecost that their faith reached the level of Christian committal, only then that they became Christians in the NT sense of that word.

The conclusions for the Pentecostal theology of Pentecost are plain. Their appeal to the experience of the 120 is a broken reed, at least so far as it is based on the record of Luke–Acts. In Luke's understanding of salvation-history the 120 before Pentecost were in a position analogous to that of Jesus before Jordan. They were in the old epoch of salvation, and while they may well have experienced many of the blessings of the old age and covenant, they were still outside the new – for until Pentecost the new age and covenant had not come into operation for any but Jesus. Only at Pentecost did they enter into that relationship with the Father

---

[41] The prayer of 1.24 is addressed to God, not Jesus. It is God who is described as καρδιογνώστης (15.8).

which was made possible through the death, resurrection and exaltation of the Son, and which was effected through the ascension gift of the Spirit. Whatever their old covenant experience of the Spirit, it was only at Pentecost that they entered into what Paul might have called the ἀββά-relationship with the Father, in which the filial relation of Jesus to God is repeated in the experience of the Christian through his reception of the Spirit of the Son. And since it is this relationship which alone may be called 'Christian', it was only at Pentecost that the 120 became Christians.

Luke 10.20 has to be understood in terms of the blessings of the old covenant. To have one's name written in the book of life or in heaven was as possible in the old dispensation as in the new (Ex. 32.32f.; Dan. 12.1; I Enoch 104.1; 108.3). Luke 11.13 is to be referred either to the once-for-all occasion of Acts 1.14, 2.1, or to the frequent request of the Christians for a renewed 'filling' with the Spirit, as in Acts 4.29–31.

The epochal significance of Pentecost raises the whole course of salvation-history to a new plane. As the beginning of the new age of the Spirit, the new covenant, the Church, it is what happened at Pentecost and not before which is normative for those who would enter that age, covenant and Church. The (pre-Christian) experience of the 120 prior to Pentecost can *never* provide a pattern for the experience of new Christians now. As well we might make the civilization of the Roman Empire the standard for civilization today as make the experience of the earthly contemporaries of Jesus the standard for spiritual experience today. The new age has come, and in comparison the old age reeks of condemnation and death (II Cor. 3.6–8). It is Pentecost which opens the door to that realm of faith and experience which the NT calls Christian. For those who live in the Pentecostal age there is no going back through that door. 'There is no genuine Christianity "on the wrong side of Pentecost".'[42]

In one sense, therefore, Pentecost can never be repeated – for the new age is here and cannot be ushered in again. But in another sense Pentecost, or rather the experience of Pentecost, can and must be repeated in the experience of all who would become Christians. As the day of Pentecost was once the doorway into the new age, so entry into the new age can only be made through that doorway, that is, through receiving the same Spirit and the same

[42] G. Johnston, *TWBB* 239, citing W. R. Forrester, *Conversion* 5.

baptism in the Spirit as did the 120.[43] This, of course, is why the great thing which Peter offers above all at the conclusion of his sermon is the gift of the Spirit (Acts 2.38). As the 120 received the benefits of the death and resurrection of Christ at Pentecost through receiving the outpoured Spirit, so do all now become Christians by receiving the same Spirit.

As in the case of Jesus' experience at Jordan the Pentecostals are quite right to emphasize that Pentecost was an experience of empowering (Luke 24.49; Acts 1.8).[44] However, they, and by no means only they, are again wrong in making Pentecost only and primarily an experience of empowering. On the contrary, the Baptism in the Spirit, as always, is primarily initiatory, and only secondarily an empowering. The fact is that the phrase 'baptism in Spirit' is never directly associated with the promise of power, but is always associated with entry into the messianic age or the Body of Christ.

The positive value of the Pentecostal's emphasis is his highlighting of the dramatic nature of the initiating Spirit-baptism: the Spirit not only renews, he also equips for service and witness. Yet, however correct Pentecostals are to point to a fresh empowering of the Spirit as the answer to the Church's sickness, they are quite wrong to call it 'the baptism in the Spirit'. One does not enter the new age or the Christian life more than once, but one may be empowered by or filled with the Spirit many times (Acts 2.4; 4.8, 31; 9.17; 13.9; Eph. 5.18).

[43] To talk of becoming members of the Spirit-baptized Church as a means of maintaining that there was only one Baptism in the Spirit is a hopeless device. It was not a structure or institution which was baptized in the Spirit at Pentecost, but people, and others became (spiritually) one with that group only by themselves being baptized in Spirit (Acts 11.16; I Cor. 12.13).

[44] Cf. N. H. Snaith, *ExpT* 43 (1931–32) 379f.

# V

# THE RIDDLE OF SAMARIA

THE problem of Acts 8, long the chief stronghold of Pentecostal (baptism in the Spirit) and Catholic (Confirmation) alike, centres on two facts: the Samaritans believed and were baptized; they did not receive the Spirit until some time later. The problem is that in the context of the rest of the NT these facts appear to be mutually exclusive and wholly irreconcilable. If they believed and were baptized (v. 12) in the name of the Lord Jesus (v. 16) they must be called Christians. But if they did not receive the Holy Spirit till later they cannot be called Christians until that time (most explicitly Rom. 8.9). The usual course has been to build on the foundations of vv. 4–13 and to call in question the statements of vv. 14–24: in Lukan theology the language of vv. 12f. means that the Samaritans became Christians at that point; therefore, it is said, the statements of vv. 14–17 cannot mean what they seem to mean. Either (1) the Samaritans had already received the Spirit and vv. 14–17 record only a charismatic manifestation,[1] or (2) they record a second reception of the Spirit;[2]

[1] Most recently, Beasley-Murray 119; earlier, Bruce, *Book* 182f., and J. E. L. Oulton, *ExpT* 66 (1954–55) 238f., who refers back to F. J. A. Hort, *The Christian Ecclesia* (1897) 54. This interpretation has been most popular among commentators of the Reformed school: e.g., Calvin, *The Acts of the Apostles* (Torrance edition 1965) 235f; J. C. Lambert, *The Sacraments in the New Testament* (1903) 95f; N. B. Stonehouse, *Paul Before the Areopagus* (1957) 78–80; R. A. Finlayson in *The Encyclopedia of Christianity* (ed. E. H. Palmer, I 1964) 539; A. M. Stibbs and J. I. Packer, *The Spirit Within You* (1967) 35. Similarly the Lutheran, R. C. H. Lenski, *The Interpretation of the Acts of the Apostles* (1934) 324f. Hull argues that the Samaritans in fact had the Spirit prior to the visit of Peter and John, but that in Luke's eyes the Spirit had not come unless he manifested himself visibly (106–9).

[2] The view of most Pentecostals and many Catholics: e.g., Riggs 52; Ervin 92–94; B. Neunheuser, *Baptism and Confirmation* (ET 1964) 19; P. T. Camelot in *New Catholic Encyclopedia* (1967) IV 145, 148.

or (3) the gift of the Spirit belongs only to the laying on of hands;

or (4) Luke has separated what was in fact joined;

or (5) God in his sovereignty withheld the Spirit from Christians.

1. This hypothesis founders on the explicit statements of Luke, that before Peter's and John's appearance the Spirit had 'not yet fallen on any of them' (v.16), and that only when Peter and John laid hands on them was the Holy Spirit given (v. 18) and received (vv. 15, 17, 19). Charismatic manifestations are implied, of course, but only implied, and, as elsewhere in Acts, they come *with* the Spirit and are the immediate result and indication of *his coming* (2.4; 10.45f.; 11.15; 19.6). The force of this argument cannot be blunted by taking πνεῦμα ἅγιον to mean only 'the charismata of the Spirit'.[3] As I show on pp. 68ff. below, one cannot so easily drive a wedge between τὸ πνεῦμα τὸ ἅγιον and πνεῦμα ἅγιον.[4] The clearest indication of all that for Luke these are equivalent titles of the Holy Spirit is the fact that he identifies the πνεῦμα ἅγιον of vv. 15, 17, 19 and τὸ πνεῦμα of v. 18 with ἡ δωρεὰ τοῦ θεοῦ, which in Luke always refers to the Holy Spirit (Acts 2.38; 10.45; 11.17). The true formula is not πνεῦμα ἅγιον = charismata (alone), but πνεῦμα ἅγιον = Holy Spirit + charismata, or more precisely, the Holy Spirit bringing and manifesting his coming and presence by charismata. It was not merely charismata which the exalted Lord poured out on the disciples at Pentecost (2.33), but the Spirit of the Lord (2.17f.), who manifested himself and his coming by these gifts. As Mason once put it: 'It is the Holy Ghost Himself who falls upon men, and not His gifts.'[5] Certainly Peter and John missed the manifestations, but they concluded that the Samaritans lacked the Spirit, not spiritual gifts. No gifts meant no Spirit.[6] And in the event what they actually prayed for and what the Samaritans actually received was the Holy Spirit. To claim that Peter and John were interested only in gifts is to exalt charismata far above their NT status, to 'out-Pentecostalize' the Pentecostals. Peter and

[3] Contra Beasley-Murray 119, who points to Luke 11.13 as a parallel case; see also the authors cited in Adler, *Taufe und Handauflegung* (1951).

[4] Originally suggested by F. J. A. Hort, *The First Epistle of St Peter* (1898) 61, and now revived by N. Turner, *A Grammar of New Testament Greek* III (1963) 175. At a more popular level see E. W. Bullinger, *The Giver and his Gifts* (1905) 24–41.

[5] Mason 23 n. 3. Cf. II Cor. 6.6; I Thess. 5.19.

[6] 'No one seems to have said, "Perhaps these believers have received the Spirit quietly and unconsciously"' (Harper, *Power* 26).

John acted because the Holy Spirit had not yet fallen on them, and only when they acted did the Samaritans receive the Spirit.

2. Like the first, this suggestion cannot stand before Luke's unequivocal statements: the Spirit had not yet fallen on them = not one had received the gift of the Holy Spirit. The parallels between 8.5–13 and 2.41–47, and the miracles and joy present among the Samaritans (8.6–8) do not indicate that they already possessed the Spirit or were already converted.[7] H. Schlier tries to cut the knot by distinguishing between the 'grundlegende Pneuma', which Luke does not mention, and the 'Charismengeist',[8] and it has sometimes been argued that ἐπιπίπτειν ἐπί and perhaps λαμβάνειν here carry in themselves the thought of a special second coming of the Spirit.[9] But when we compare Luke's language here with his description of the Spirit's coming elsewhere (see pp. 70ff. below), it becomes evident, first, that Luke knows of *no earlier* coming of the Spirit than the one he describes by using λαμβάνειν, ἐπιπίπτειν and δίδοσθαι, and second, that Luke knows of *no other coming* of the Spirit than the one thus described (apart from the 'filling' with the Spirit, which is not relevant here).[10] This coming of the Spirit is described in various ways and may manifest itself in various ways, but it is essentially one and the same coming. As there is no ground for distinguishing between πνεῦμα ἅγιον and τὸ πνεῦμα τὸ ἅγιον, so there is no ground for distinguishing between the 'grundlegende Pneuma' and the 'Charismengeist'. For Luke it is the one Spirit and the one coming.

Perhaps some are prepared to say that Luke's reporting was so superficial that only the external and visible workings of the Spirit interested him (see n. 1); that the first coming, even though that was what made a man a Christian, had such little significance for him that he never mentioned it;[11] that the really important even

[7] S. I. Buse in *Christian Baptism* (ed. A. Gilmore 1959) 118f; Adler *Taufe* 83; contra Oulton 238f; Beasley-Murray 118f; Horton 4.

[8] *Die Zeit der Kirche* (1956) 116; cf. Haenchen 261; A. Wikenhauser, *Die Apostelgeschichte* (1961) 98; O. Kuss, *Auslegung und Verkündigung* (1963) 100–2; also Lampe in *Peake* 782 gh. The equivalent Pentecostal distinction is between the regenerating Spirit and the empowering Spirit.

[9] So Wirgman 63; G. C. Richards, *Baptism and Confirmation* (1942) cited in Lampe, *Seal* 66; Oulton 238 (ἐπιπίπτειν); and Th. Zahn, cited in Adler, *Taufe* 83; Dewar 53 (λαμβάνειν). 'To receive the Holy Spirit' has become the Pentecostals' technical phrase for Spirit-baptism.

[10] Contra Ervin; see pp. 70ff. below.   [11] Cf. Wikenhauser 98.

essential coming of the Spirit was the one which resulted in a display of spiritual gifts.[12] But this will hardly do. For Luke the one reception of, falling upon, gift of the Spirit is the *beginning* of a man's Christian experience and life. The Spirit is *received* as God's gift when a man repents and commits himself to Jesus Christ (Acts 2.38), is *given* when a man puts his trust in the Lord Jesus Christ (11.17), and *falls upon* him to bring him forgiveness and salvation (10.43f.; 11.14f.).[13] It is precisely because the Spirit, who usually came thus at initiation, had *not yet* (οὐδέπω) come upon any of them, and the only (μόνον) thing they had experienced was their water-baptism ('that and nothing more' – v. 16 NEB), that the two senior apostles came down hot-foot from Jerusalem to remedy a situation which had gone seriously wrong somewhere.

3. Why was the Spirit not yet received through Philip's ministry? Why was the promise of Acts 2.38 not fulfilled when its conditions seem to have been met? Some take the bull by the horns and reply: Because for Luke the Spirit could be conferred only through the laying on of apostolic hands.[14] But this view cannot stand in the face of Luke's other reports, let alone the rest of the NT. How absurd that Luke should go to such lengths to demonstrate that the Spirit is given only through apostles, and then immediately go on to relate the conversion and water-baptism of the eunuch by the same unqualified Philip! Or does he mean us to believe that the Ethiopian never received the Spirit?[15] Paul certainly was not 'confirmed' by an apostle.

Lampe does ascribe to Ananias apostolic status 'for this particular task', that is, of ministering to Paul (*Seal* 68; cf. Swete 95f.). But this is surely to destroy the very thing which the ideas of 'Apostle' and

[12] This is a necessary corollary, otherwise Peter and John would not have been so anxious here (like Paul in Acts 19) for the disciples they met to receive the Spirit; and obviously no one was satisfied with the Samaritans' Christian standing till they burst forth in tongues and prophecy, or whatever it was.

[13] Cf. R. Schnackenburg, *Baptism in the Thought of St Paul* (ET 1964) 109.

[14] K. Lake, *Beginnings* IV 92, V 53; Foakes-Jackson 72f; G. H. C. Macgregor, *IB* 9 (1954) 110; Williams 116; Flemington 41; von Allmen, *Voc.B.* 32f; Munck, *Acts* 75; C. E. Pocknee, *Water and the Spirit* (1967) 28. It is an explanation long popular in some Catholic circles – e.g. Chase 26; Lowther Clarke 8; Adler, *Taufe* 97, 110f; Rackham 116; Leeming 216–218; Dewar 51–57.

[15] But cf. the Western text: 'The Holy Spirit fell on the eunuch, and an angel of the Lord seized Philip'; and see p. 93 below.

'apostolic confirmation' are designed to safeguard. For it means that *any* Christian may be commissioned by God as an apostle for some particular task; and since this joins the distinctive essence of apostolicity to apostolic *work* rather than *persons*, it means that all who are sent by God to do apostolic work are apostles – a definition which I prefer.

Again in Acts 11.19–24, the situation most parallel to Acts 8, there is complete silence about any confirmatory coming of the Spirit: Barnabas does not act to remedy a defective situation, but rather acknowledges and rejoices over the already manifest grace of God.[16] The picture of apostles scurrying hither and thither up and down the eastern end of the Mediterranean in an attempt to keep up with the rapid expansion of the Christian gospel, with little time for anything but 'confirmation services', is amusing but incredible.[17]

Nor can the day be saved by deleting 'apostolic' and attributing the gift of the Spirit merely to the laying on of hands. For baptism is the only ritual action required for the Spirit to be received in 2.38,[18] and is usually the only rite performed (2.41; 8.38; 10.48; 16.15, 33; 18.8). Luke's treatment of the eunuch would then be almost as inconsistent as before,[19] and the case of Cornelius (and Paul?) is hardly possible.[20] Besides, why did Philip not lay his own hands on the Samaritans? Far from answering our question this theory makes the delay of the Spirit even more incomprehensible.

The Pentecostal often ignores the question of ritual act and argues simply that the Samaritans show reception of salvation to be distinct from reception of the Spirit.[21] But if Mark 16.15f. is cited as proof that they were saved,[22] we must call attention to the much more relevant Acts 2.38. The Spirit is promised on the same conditions as salvation (cf. 16.31 – faith-repentance being two sides

16 See Beasley-Murray 93.
17 See further G. B. Caird, *The Apostolic Age* (1955) 69–71; Beasley-Murray 113–15; Lampe, *Seal* 67.
18 Contra Lowther Clarke 17, 21.
19 See Oulton 239.
20 Dewar 53 and A. Richardson, *Introduction to the Theology of the New Testament* (1958) 356, both speak of Cornelius being confirmed before his baptism. God apparently does not observe correct ecclesiastical procedure!
21 Prince, *Jordan* 68; also *Baptism in the Holy Spirit* (1965) 13; J. D. Stiles, *The Gift of the Holy Spirit* (n.d.) 67; Horton 4; Harper, *Power* 26f; Allen, *Life* 9f; D. Basham, *A Handbook on Holy Spirit Baptism* (1969) 15f., 17. They thus have the unhappy precedent of Christians who have done all that God requires of them and yet have still not received the Spirit – a situation they are all too familiar with in their own assemblies ('chronic' seekers – Lindsay 57).
22 Prince, *Jordan* 67f; Lindsay 34.

of the same coin), and Luke knows no other condition required of the individual for his reception of the Spirit (11.17; 19.2; cf. John 7.39; Gal. 3.2).[23] If the argument is posed in these terms, then either the Samaritans were not 'saved' prior to v. 17, or else they received the Spirit when they believed and were baptized.

4. Has Luke himself created the difficulty by expanding a straightforward story about Philip and Simon, in which the Samaritans received the Spirit through Philip's ministry, and in which Peter and John did not originally feature at all?[24] The disappearance of Philip from the story after v. 13 is certainly striking, as is the very problem we are dealing with – the long delay between baptism and the reception of the Spirit.[25] Has Luke simply adapted the authentic(?) Philip tradition in order to present a picture of a unified Church with Jerusalem as the fountain head of authority and mission?[26] The arguments in favour of an affirmative answer fail to reckon with Luke's treatment elsewhere. It is characteristic of Luke's style that in recording an incident which involved a number of people he concentrates only on the central figure(s).

In the Peter and John narratives (3.1–4.22; 8.14–24) John almost fades entirely from view, although as active as Peter (4.13; 8.18); all attention is on Peter. So with Paul. We know, e.g., that Silas became his companion after the breach with Barnabas (15.39f.), but in 15.41; 16.1 Luke speaks of their travels solely in terms of Paul – '*he* went . . . *he* came' (see also 16.3; 18.7, 11). After Timothy joins them (16.3) his name is mentioned again only on occasions when they parted or reunited (17.15; 18.5; 19.22). 19.22 shows that Paul must have been accompanied by helpers on most of his journeys, but we hear nothing of his companions, except when the narrative uses the all but anonymous 'they' or the self-effacing 'we' – and these occur usually in the travel notes linking the incidents in which Paul alone figures. It is often only these travel notes which show that Paul was not alone.

[23] Acts 5.32 is no exception. Either the obedience is the obedience (ὑπακούω) to the faith = conversion of 6.7 (cf. Rom. 1.5; 10.16; 16.26; II Thess. 1.8); or else the obedience is the sort described in 5.29 (πειθαρχέω) and the gift of the Spirit spoken of is the filling of the Spirit for bold witness (4.8, 31).

[24] M. Dibelius, *Studies in the Acts of the Apostles* (ET 1956) 17; Haenchen 263–65; H. Conzelmann, *Die Apostelgeschichte* (1963) 54f.

[25] E. Preuschen, *Die Apostelgeschichte* (1912) 50.

[26] E. Käsemann, *Essays on New Testament Themes* (ET 1964) 145f; also *RGG*³ II (1958) 1277; Haenchen 265f; Stählin 122–4; Conzelmann, *Apg.* 55; E. Dinkler *RGG*³ VI (1962) 634; A. Ehrhardt, *The Framework of the New Testament Stories* (1964) 79, 92.

The fact that a person is not mentioned by Luke in a narrative therefore does not necessarily imply that person's absence. So here, Peter holds the centre of the stage; John is barely noticed in the background; and Philip is ignored in the wings. Moreover, it is very probable that the 'they' of the travel note in v. 25 includes Philip, in accordance with Luke's habit. For the command of v. 26 is that Philip should 'go southwards *on* (ἐπί) the road that goes down from Jerusalem to Gaza',[27] and is best understood as a command to leave *Jerusalem*. Philip's journey from Samaria to Jerusalem is almost certainly covered by v. 25.

As to the supporting arguments: Käsemann has no grounds for his two assertions, that Luke stigmatizes Philip's baptism as defective,[28] and that for Luke the Spirit 'is accessible solely within the boundaries of the apostolic fellowship'.[29]

I do not deny that Jerusalem exercised, at least initially, a general supervision over the expanding work of evangelization (8.14; 11.1ff., 22). But for Luke the authorization of the Spirit is always more important than any authorization by Jerusalem (10.1–11.18; 13.1–3; cf. 26.16–18). And the signs and wonders performed by Philip imply that the Spirit was using him and had therefore authorized him (cf. 10.38; Rom. 15.18f.; Heb. 2.4). Moreover, it is Luke himself who shows us that the Hellenists spear-headed the wider mission while the apostles remained in Jerusalem (8.14; 11.19–21), and he can hardly have considered the great majority of the churches in Judea, Samaria, Phoenicia and Syria to be unauthorized (cf. Beasley-Murray 115f.).

Luke casts no slur on Philip's baptism: it was administered on confession of faith and in the name of the Lord, as were all the other Christian baptisms in Acts; it was not repeated, and the rest of Acts offers no proof for the contention that the Spirit *must* have come with or been 'conferred' by Philip's baptism in the original tradition (2.4; 10.44–48).[30] And as for Luke's alleged desire to preserve an unblemished picture of the *Una sancta*, we need only point to 8.26–40; 9.1–19; 11.19–24; 18.24–28 to show how ill it accords with Luke's over-all presentation.

[27] Lake and Cadbury, *Beginnings* IV 95; Munck, *Acts* 37; JB.
[28] *Essays* 146. Schlier calls it a 'half-baptism' (*Zeit* 116).
[29] *Essays* 145.
[30] Cf. Kittel 35; Bieder 127. Even in 2.38 baptism is only a *condition* for receiving the gift of the Spirit. For Bultmann, *History* 247 n. 1, and Conzelmann, *Apg.* 55, to maintain that this passage really 'presupposes' and 'teaches the inseparability and solidarity of baptism and Spirit' is really too extraordinary for words. See further in ch. IX.

Haenchen's argument that Simon must have dealt with Philip since he would desire the power of miracles more than the authority to give the Spirit (264f.) ignores the clear implication that the descent of the Spirit on the Samaritans was rather spectacular.

5. One of the most influential English interpretations in recent years has been that of Lampe, who stresses that Samaria was a unique situation and one of the chief turning points in the missionary enterprise. Before Samaria, a region long at odds with the Jews, could be established as a nucleus for further expansion, the continuity with Jerusalem had to be maintained, otherwise the unity of the Spirit-possessed community would be impaired.[31] Undoubtedly the most satisfactory of the explanations so far proposed, yet I must confess that it leaves me unconvinced. The conversion of the Ethiopian eunuch was an advance of no little significance, yet absolutely nothing is made of it in terms of continuity with Jerusalem. And why did the Spirit await apostolic 'confirmation' in the case of the Samaritans when he did not do so with Cornelius? Again, Antioch was at least as significant a centre of expansion as Samaria, and, as the springboard for the most important expansion of all (Paul's missions), even more important than Ephesus, yet Luke does not so much as mention the Spirit in connection with Antioch (except in his description of Barnabas). Nor is there any cementing of the apostolic unity by the Spirit in the case of Apollos, surely too strategic a figure to be left unattached to Jerusalem.[32] Above all, this view shows us a considerable number of *baptized believers* who do *not* have the Spirit and who are *not* yet incorporated into the Church.[33] This means that belief and baptism 'in the

[31] Lampe, *Seal* 70–72, and xxf.,; also in *Peake* 782h. Those who follow Lampe's line more or less include Bruce, *Book* 182f.; Oulton 239; Caird, *Age* 71f.; Williams 116; Richardson 356; White 198; Hill 264. It is very close to the *Heilsgeschichte* interpretation of Schweizer, *TWNT* VI 412 and Wilkens, *TZ* 23 (1967) 27, which sees the coming of Peter and John from Jerusalem as proof of Luke's desire to link the revelation of God to Jerusalem as the centre of salvation-history (cf. n. 26, and Bieder 129, 137f.).

[32] The weak link in Wilken's exposition is his treatment of Apollos, who is Pneumatiker before his meeting with Priscilla and Aquila (37–39). Any *Heilsgeschichte* thesis which postulates a necessary dependence on Jerusalem comes to grief on the contrasts central to the twin stories of Apollos and the twelve 'disciples' (see ch. VII').

[33] There seems to be some confusion at this point. Were the Samaritans not incorporated into the Church until the laying on of apostolic hands (Lampe, *Seal* 72), or were they merely being assured 'that they *had* really become members of the Church' (69f.)? Similarly Beasley-Murray 118.

name of the Lord Jesus' do *not* result in the gift of the Spirit (contrary to 2.38) and do *not* incorporate into the Church (contrary to 2.41 and the descriptions of the Christian community as οἱ πιστεύσαντες – 2.44).[34] In short, we are back at the same dilemma as faced the Catholic and Pentecostal above: Can we regard as Christians those who have *not* received the Spirit and have *not* been incorporated into the Church?

The usual method of treating Acts 8 – of accepting what vv. 12f. seem to say and calling in question what follows – has thus led to a serious impasse. It may be that Acts 8 stands in complete contradiction to Paul, and indeed to the rest of the NT so far as it sheds light on these matters. Luke may be much more dependent on and faithful to his sources than is often believed, and may be content simply to show that the Samaritans were in the end fully accepted, without speculating on their spiritual status and state between their baptism by Philip and the mission of Peter and John.[35] But before resigning ourselves to this conclusion we should try reversing the strategy. Verses 14–17 have proved unyielding in their implications. Perhaps the preceding section will yield a few clues.

Were the Samaritans Christians before Peter and John arrived? Philip's preaching seems to have been no different from that recorded elsewhere in Acts. The Samaritans' response seems to have been entirely satisfactory. And their baptism was fully Christian. However, there are a number of reasons for believing not only that their response and commitment *was* defective, but also that Luke intended his readers to know this.

(*a*) For the Samaritans 'kingship was . . . something special', and they looked for the coming of a 'Messiah', or Taheb, who would introduce 'a period of divine favour, a second Kingdom', by uniting all Israel, crushing her enemies and exalting the Samaritan people.[36] Judging by their response to Simon's magic and the

---

[34] Beasley-Murray calls this view 'a theologically impossible abstraction' (118).

[35] Cf. White 194f.

[36] See J. Macdonald, *The Theology of the Samaritans* (1964) 74f., 79f., 359–71. While Macdonald's survey is drawn chiefly from documents deriving from a period later than that covered in Acts, there is no reason to doubt that the traditions they embody are in essentials much older and have their roots in the centuries before Christ. Comparison with John 4. 19–26 and the adulation accorded by the Samaritans to Simon (8.10) give strong support to the view that the beliefs we have cited were prevalent in Samaria at the time of Christ

high-sounding title they gave him (v. 10),[37] the Samaritans' excitement and eschatological expectation must have been roused to near fever-pitch. Into this situation came Philip proclaiming the Christ and preaching about the Kingdom of God. Now ὁ χριστός *simpliciter* is always used in Acts of the Messiah of pre-Christian expectation (2.31, 36; 3.18; 4.26; 9.22; 17.3; 26.23), and when the Kingdom is preached elsewhere to non-Christians it is always with reference to the Kingdom of Jewish expectations (19.8; 28.23, 31; cf. 1.3, 6; 20.25).

To the Samaritans Philip's message could only be about the Taheb, and must mean that the long-awaited second Kingdom was about to be ushered in. Coming as Philip did in succession to Simon, working even greater signs, they would welcome his preaching enthusiastically (v. 8) and accept it unreservedly; baptism would probably be seen as the rite of entry into the Kingdom (v. 12) and the token of allegiance to Jesus the Taheb, and as such would be submitted to gladly. This does not mean that Philip's preaching was defective, only that his particular emphasis (perhaps due to a desire to speak in terms familiar to his audience) could well have given the Samaritans a false impression and resulted in a response which was sincere and enthusiastic, but wrongly directed.

(*b*) The Samaritans seem to have been a rather superstitious people. Their response to Simon was certainly of this nature, indicating very little discernment and depth (vv. 9–11). The whole area – even τὸ ἔθνος τῆς Σαμαρίας . . . ἀπὸ μικροῦ ἕως μεγάλου (vv. 9f.) – seems to have been caught up in a wave of mass emotion. It is significant then that Luke describes their response to Simon with precisely the same word as he uses for their response to Philip (προσέχω – vv. 6, 10f.). This suggests that their reaction to Philip was for the same reasons and of the same quality and depth as their reaction to Simon (cf. vv. 6–8 with 10f.). It is hardly to be compared with Lydia's response to Paul's message (16.14), and the implication is that the Samaritans' acceptance of baptism was

---

and after. Samaria cannot have escaped influence from the current apocalyptic expectations in Judaism. Josephus also tells us that 'Pontius Pilate lost his office in Palestine because of the savage way in which he quelled a riot in Samaria, which arose as the result of one claiming to be the expected "Messiah"' (Macdonald 361, citing *Ant* 18.85–89).

[37] See Bruce, *Book* 179; Conzelmann, *Apg.* 53.

prompted more by the herd-instinct of a popular mass-movement (ὁμοθυμαδόν – v. 6) than by the self- and world-denying commitment which usually characterized Christian baptism in the early years.

(*c*) πιστεύειν also cannot bear the weight usually put on it. It is not here πιστεύειν εἰς or ἐπὶ τὸν κύριον, but ἐπίστευσαν τῷ Φιλίππῳ; and when πιστεύειν governs a dative object (except perhaps κύριος or θεός) it signifies intellectual assent to a statement or proposition, rather than commitment to God (24.14; 26.27).[38] This use of πιστεύειν, unique in Acts, can surely be no accident on Luke's part. He indicates thereby that the Samaritans' response was simply an assent of the mind to the acceptability of what Philip was saying and an acquiescence to the course of action he advocated, rather than that commitment distinctively described elsewhere which alone deserves the name 'Christian' (cf. John 2.23–25).

(*d*) As if this was not enough, Luke immediately adds ὁ δὲ Σίμων καὶ αὐτὸς ἐπίστευσεν, καὶ βαπτισθείς . . ., and then in the sequel reveals just how little his profession and action meant. Despite his belief and baptism Simon had neither part (μερίς) nor lot (κλῆρος) in the matter of salvation (v. 21); that is, he never had become a member of the people of God.[39] His heart was not right before God (v. 21) but was crooked and unbelieving like that of the Israelites who were cast off in the wilderness (Ps. 78.37).[40] He was 'doomed to taste the bitter fruit (χολὴν πικρίας) and wear the fetters of sin' (v. 23 NEB), for, like Esau (Heb. 12.15–17), he had 'a root bearing poisonous and bitter fruit' (ἐν χολῇ καὶ ἐν πικρίᾳ) and therefore would know not the pardon but the anger of the Lord (Deut. 29.18–20). In other words, Simon had not really fulfilled the conditions for the gift of the Spirit (Acts 2.38), and had so little spiritual understanding of these matters that he thought it (or at least the power to bestow it) could be bought (8.20). He was a Christian in outward form only, not in the NT sense of the word. His profession and baptism mean nothing in face of the devastating exposure

---

[38] See Arndt and Gingrich. Acts 5.14(?); 13.12(D); 16.34; 18.8 should also probably be given the sense of accepting the disclosures about rather than commitment to. Cf. the distinction between παραλαμβάνειν and λαμβάνειν especially as it bears on Col. 2.6 (see p. 95).

[39] Cf. Col. 1.12; Acts 26.18. The verse recalls Deut. 12.12, and indicates not excommunication from the Church (contra Haenchen 262; Lampe in *Peake* 782i), but that Simon had never possessed a 'share (μερίς) in the inheritance (κλῆρος) of the saints'.

[40] 8.21 is almost a direct quotation of Ps. 78.37. Cf. Acts 13.10; II Peter 2.15.

by Peter. His only hope – and a forlorn one – was the repentance which he had not so far experienced (v. 22).[41] What belief he had was from start to finish centred on man – first Philip (v. 13) then Peter (v. 24); he had no idea of what it was to repent before God and to put his trust in the Lord.[42] And Luke makes it clear (vv. 12f.) that Simon's faith and baptism were precisely like those of the other Samaritans, as if to say, Note carefully what I say, and do not miss the point: they all went through the form but did not experience the reality.

(e) It is not sufficiently realized that in NT times the possession of the Spirit was *the* hallmark of the Christian. Cornelius's reception of the Spirit was unquestionable proof of his acceptance by God; just as the Ephesians' lack of the Spirit in Acts 19 was unquestionable proof that they had yet to come to full *Christian* faith. Thus we are not surprised that Philip did not conclude, as many would today, 'They have been baptized, and therefore they have received the Spirit, even though neither we nor they know it.' For possession of the Spirit was not inferred from baptism, but the genuineness (or otherwise) of the faith expressed in baptism was proved by the reception (or otherwise) of the Spirit: if God responded to the baptizand's commitment by giving the Spirit, his acceptance of the commitment showed it to be genuine (the lesson Peter learned with Cornelius [11.17] and Paul practised with the Ephesians).[43] In other words, the Spirit's absence from and coming to the Samaritans is the critical factor in this narrative. Luke's aim is to highlight the difference between true and false Christianity, and he does so by devoting most attention to Simon (not Philip and not Peter) in order to draw out the ultimate contrast between him and the Samaritans. The narrative alternates between the Samaritans (vv. 5–8, 12, 14–17) and Simon (vv. 9–11, 13, 18–24). At first each step taken by the Samaritans is paralleled by a similar

[41] It is unlikely that Simon thereupon repented and was converted (contra Foakes-Jackson 73). Such a notable success for the gospel would surely have been recorded. And all other available traditions about Simon are unanimous against this suggestion.

[42] Stählin notes that Simon still thinks as a magician: he believes that Peter's prayer will have greater magical power than his own; and his prayer is not for forgiveness but for escape (125). See also Wikenhauser 98; and cf. Blaiklock 80.

[43] This was why Philip was not wrong to baptize those who came to him with enthusiastic and sincere desire for baptism. Only God is καρδιογνώστης (15.8).

step taken by Simon: they turn from magic to Philip, so does he; they believe Philip, so does he; they are baptized by Philip, so is he. But then their paths diverge – *they* receive the Spirit, whereas Simon receives only a curse.[44] This contrast is the climax of the whole incident – the Samaritans receive the Spirit, which indicates that they have come to genuine faith, but Simon continues to see and be interested in only the external. For Luke, as for Paul, the great difference between the Christian and non-Christian is that only the former has received the Spirit; to illustrate this fundamental belief is one of Luke's principal reasons for including this narrative.

(*f*) Perhaps the full flowering of the Samaritans' faith was also delayed by the cold wind of religious and racial animosity which blew from Jerusalem to Samaria:[45] they lacked the assurance that they were really accepted into a Christian community so far composed of Jews and proselytes,[46] and the fact that their evangelist was a Hellenist independent of Jerusalem (8.1–3)[47] could not dispel their fears. This would be a further reason why the two most senior apostles were sent to Samaria.[48] And it would only be when Peter and John, as chief representatives of the Jerusalem Church, proffered the right hand of fellowship that this particular stumbling block was removed and they came to fullness of faith in the One who had died and risen again at Jerusalem.

It is unfortunate that Luke has compressed the account of Peter and John's mission so much. Evidently he wants to make only two points: the Samaritans received the Spirit only through the apostles' ministry (reiterated six times in six verses), and the exposure of

[44] It is improbable that Peter and John laid hands on Simon (Haenchen 262). The tenses of vv. 17f., imply that Simon followed Peter and John about, carefully observing their actions and 'technique', until his amazement and greed got the better of him and led him to make his fateful request.

[45] The Samaritans were the ancient enemies of the Jews, detested by them as racial and religious half-breeds (Lampe in *Peake* 872c).

[46] Cf. Lampe, *Seal* 69f.; Bruce, *Book* 182f.

[47] The persecution arose largely as a result of the Hellenists' views on the Temple, expressed by Stephen, and it was principally they who were scattered. 8.1–3 marks something of a cleavage in the ranks of the Christians themselves (cf. O. Cullmann, *The Early Church* [ET 1956] 190f;. L. Goppelt, *Jesus, Paul and Judaism* [ET 1964] 107f.).

[48] When Peter and John discovered that the Spirit had not been given is not clear. But the fact that the senior apostles were sent (contrast 11.22) suggests that the information came with the original news. It is probably most just to assume that the apostles' chief purpose was to do what they in fact did οἵτινες καταβάντες προσηύξαντο περὶ αὐτῶν . . .).

Simon. He stops for nothing else. No explanations are given as to why the Spirit was not received before, no indications as to what reaction greeted the news that the Spirit had not been given, no hint of what Peter and John said on arrival (contrast 11.1ff., 23; 19.1ff.). Certain things are made clear: they had only been baptized; they had not received the Spirit; Simon's conversion was spurious. Certain things are implied: the ideas Philip used, the nature of their response, the dramatic nature of the Spirit's coming. And certain conclusions drawn from Luke's thought overall have to be applied to the passage: the Spirit both as the hallmark of the new age and of the Christian, the man of the new age, and as God's response to the act of faith (see pp. 91f. below). The mistake of many commentators is to assume that because the conditions of 2.38 had apparently been fulfilled, therefore they were Christians and/or the Spirit had been given. The NT way is rather to say: Because the Spirit has not been given, therefore the conditions have not been met. This is why Luke puts so much emphasis on the Samaritans' reception of the Spirit (vv. 15–20), for it is God's giving of the Spirit which makes a man a Christian, and, in the last analysis, nothing else.

## ADDITIONAL NOTES

### *1. πνεῦμα ἅγιον, τὸ πνεῦμα, τὸ πνεῦμα τὸ ἅγιον, τὸ ἅγιον πνεῦμα*

As indicated above (p. 56 n. 4) the opinion has sometimes been offered that Luke makes a distinction between πνεῦμα ἅγιον with the article and the same phrase without. The most recent and fullest presentation of the argument is to be found in N. Turner's *Grammatical Insights into the New Testament* (1965) 17–22, where he takes the fuller phrase to signify 'the third person of the Trinity' and the shorter phrase to signify 'a holy spirit, a divine influence possessing men' (19).

In my opinion such a distinction is unjustified. Consider the following parallels:

(*a*) Jesus' promise to the disciples before his ascension is put in two ways:

Acts 1.5: After not many days you will be baptized ἐν πνεύματι ἁγίῳ.

Acts 1.8: You shall receive power ἐπελθόντος τοῦ ἁγίου πνεύματος. In the event their experience is described thus:

Acts 2.4: They were all filled πνεύματος ἁγίου, and Joel 2.28ff. is said to be thereby fulfilled: God says ἐκχεῶ ἀπὸ τοῦ πνεύματός μου.

(b) With Acts 2.4 and the other examples of πνεῦμα ἅγιον with πίμπλημι (4.8; 9.17; 13.9, 52)
cf. Acts 4.31: ἐπλήσθησαν ἅπαντες τοῦ ἁγίου πνεύματος (hardly · an anaphoric reference to 4.25).

(c) The experience of the Samaritans is described not just in terms of πνεῦμα ἅγιον.
Cf. Acts 8.17: they laid their hands on them and ἐλάμβανον πνεῦμα ἅγιον, and Acts 8.19: Give me also this power, that anyone on whom I lay my hands λαμβάνῃ πνεῦμα ἅγιον, with Acts 8.20: You thought you could obtain τὴν δωρεὰν τοῦ θεοῦ with money! In other occurrences of the phrase ἡ δωρεὰ τοῦ θεοῦ (2.38; 10.45; 11.17) it is clearly the Holy Spirit who is referred to.

(d) The experience of Cornelius is described in a variety of ways:
Acts 10.44; 11.15: τὸ πνεῦμα τὸ ἅγιον fell on them just as on us at the beginning;
Acts 10.45: ἡ δωρεὰ τοῦ πνεύματος ἁγίου had been poured out;
Acts 10.47: who had received τὸ πνεῦμα τὸ ἅγιον just as we have;
Acts 15.8: giving them τὸ πνεῦμα τὸ ἅγιον just as he did to us.
But in Acts 11.16 Peter connects the incident with Acts 1.5: You shall be baptized ἐν πνεύματι ἁγίῳ.

(e) Luke's descriptions of Jesus' own experience are also interesting:
Luke 3.22: τὸ πνεῦμα τὸ ἅγιον descended on him;
Acts 10.38: God anointed him πνεύματι ἁγίῳ καὶ δυνάμει.

(f) He then goes on to tell how:
Luke 4.1: Jesus was full πνεύματος ἁγίου,
and Luke 4.14: he returned in the power τοῦ πνεύματος;
surely the same πνεῦμα as in Luke 4.18: πνεῦμα κυρίου is upon me.

(g) Luke uses λαμβάνειν four times out of five with πνεῦμα ἅγιον (8.15, 17, 19; 19.2), but in 10.47 he describes the Gentiles as those who have received τὸ πνεῦμα τὸ ἅγιον.

(h) Interesting too is the comparison of
Luke 1.35: πνεῦμα ἅγιον ἐπελεύσεται ἐπὶ σέ, with Acts 1.8: ἐπελθόντος τοῦ ἁγίου πνεύματος ἐφ᾽ ὑμᾶς.

(i) Finally we might compare
Acts 1.16: προεῖπεν τὸ πνεῦμα τὸ ἅγιον διὰ στόματος Δαυείδ, with Acts 4.25: ὁ . . . διὰ πνεύματος ἁγίου στόματος Δαυείδ . . . εἰπών.

This evidence indicates that for Luke at least there is no significant difference between πνεῦμα ἅγιον and τὸ πνεῦμα τὸ ἅγιον – for the same experience and same kind of experience can be described variously by πνεῦμα ἅγιον with or without the article. At most the difference could mean the Holy Spirit in personal capacity and the Holy Spirit manifesting himself in an impersonal way – in power, or charismata, or inspired utterance. πνεῦμα ἅγιον certainly cannot mean a power or influence or spirit distinct and separate from the Holy Spirit. It is incredible, for example, that Luke should suggest that the experience of the 120 on the Day of Pentecost (1.5; 2.4) was different from and less significant than their experience with others in 4.31 (see (b) above). And, indeed, it is incredible that for Luke *holy* spirit should be something different from the Holy Spirit (cf. C. F. D. Moule, *An Idiom Book of the New Testament* [1959] 112f.).

The true explanation seems to be that the variation is due to stylistic reasons and lacks any real theological significance. I therefore accept Adler's conclusion: 'Where πνεῦμα ἅγιον confronts us in the NT it never designates a charismatic endowment without the Holy Spirit, but the Spirit himself' (*Taufe* 86).

### 2. The Phrases used by Luke to Describe the Coming of the Spirit in Acts

(a) βαπτίζεσθαι ἐν πνεύματι ἁγίῳ 1.5; 11.16

(b) (ἐπ)έρχεσθαι τὸ πνεῦμα ἅγιον 1.8; 19.6

(c) πλησθῆναι πνεύματος ἁγίου 2.4; 4.8, 31; 9.17; 13.9, 52 (ἐπληροῦντο)

(d) ἐκχέειν ἀπὸ τοῦ πνεύματος 2.17, 18, 33; 10.45 (ἐκκέχυται)

(e) λαμβάνειν πνεῦμα ἅγιον 2.38; 8.15, 17, 19; 10.47; 19.2

(f) διδόναι πνεῦμα ἅγιον 5.32; 8.18 (δίδοσθαι); 11.17; 15.8

(g) ἐπιπίπτειν τὸ πνεῦμα τὸ ἅγιον 8.16; 10.44; 11.15

I do not include 10.38 – χρίειν πνεύματι ἁγίῳ – since it refers to Jesus' anointing with the Spirit and not to a post-Pentecostal reception of the Spirit.

The seven different verb-phrases are used in Acts 27 times; most Pentecostals would probably say 23 times in reference to the baptism in the Spirit, since the third phrase is used of the same person more than once (e.g. Riggs 63; Prince, *Jordan* 68f.). Ervin is the principal exception: he focuses attention on πίμπλημι as the key description of Spirit-baptism and argues that to be filled with the Spirit was a once-for-all experience. 4.31 he refers solely to the 3,000 converts of the day of Pentecost, who did not receive the Spirit till then! 4.8 and 13.9 he refers back to Peter's and Paul's earlier Spirit-baptism (πλησθείς – who *had* been filled). 13.52 he takes to signify that the disciples were filled one after another with joy and with the Holy Spirit (59–67, 71–73). But while his interpretation of 13.52 is quite possible (cf. 8.18) his treatment of 4.31 involves some rather unnatural and tortuous exegesis which cannot be accepted. The 'all' of 4.31 obviously includes the Christian comminity as a whole and Peter and John in particular – all in fact who took part in the prayer of 4.24–30. As for the formula πλησθεὶς πνεύματος ἁγίου εἶπεν, when an aorist participle is used with εἶπεν, it always describes an action or event which takes place immediately prior to or which leads into the act of speaking (e.g. Acts 1.15; 3.4; 5.19; 6.2; 9.17, 40; 10.34; 16.18; 18.6; 21.11). So with 4.8 it describes the sudden inspiration and empowering of the Spirit which Jesus had promised for the special occasion (Luke 12.11f.: ἐν αὐτῇ τῇ ὥρᾳ) and which would not last beyond the hour of need. The same is probably true of 13.9. When Luke wants to indicate a lasting state of 'fullness' resulting from a past 'filling' the word he uses is πλήρης (Luke 4.1; Acts 6.3, 5, 8; 7.55; 11.24).

When we turn to the more usual Pentecostal view, several comments are called for. First, a number of these different phrases are often used to describe the same incident. All 7 are used for Pentecost (1.5; 1.8; 2.4; 2.17; 10.47; 11.17; 11.15); for Samaria 3, for Caesarea 5, for Ephesus 2. This means that they are all equivalent ways of describing the same coming of the Spirit – a coming which was such a dramatic and over-powering experience that it almost exhausted Luke's vocabulary to find language which would give an adequate description of its richness and fullness.

Second, these 7 phrases are the only ones Luke uses to describe a coming of the Spirit. Luke knows of no other coming of the Spirit than that described in these phrases. In all the key incidents Luke says nothing of an earlier coming of the Spirit. For him there is only the one coming of the Spirit which he describes in various ways. In other words, in every one of the 23 occurrences which the Pentecostal claims for his second distinctive work of the Spirit, Luke is describing what is for him the first coming of the Spirit.

Third, the two incidents which involve all or most of the six key phrases (Pentecost and Caesarea) are the two in which this coming of the Spirit is most obviously bound up with conversion and entry into the Christian life. I think, for example, of the πιστεύσασιν ἐπί of 11.17 and the δοὺς τὸ πνεῦμα τὸ ἅγιον = in the parallel verse τῇ πίστει καθαρίσας τὰς καρδίας αὐτῶν of 15.8f. (see the full treatment of these incidents). The variety of phrases used and the stress on the parallel with Pentecost rules out the expedient of interpreting the coming of the Spirit in Acts 10 merely in terms of a charismatic display. *All* that the outpouring of the Spirit at Pentecost was for the original disciples, the outpouring of the Spirit at Caesarea was for Cornelius and his friends. (The Catholic is in a cleft stick when he comes to interpret the 'falling upon' of the Spirit in Acts 8 and 10. If he takes the former of Confirmation, what of Acts 10? If he takes the latter merely as a charismatic manifestation, does the 'confirmation' of Acts 8 result only in a charismatic display?

Similarly, the equivalence of these phrases means that the Catholic cannot cling on to Acts 2.38 and 9.17f. as proof texts [the only ones possible in Acts] for the belief that the Spirit is given through water-baptism, while at the same time arguing that the reception of the Spirit in 8 is a second [confirming] coming of the Spirit.)

Fourth, it will not help the Pentecostal to abandon his claim to all 6 of the phrases as descriptions of Spirit-baptism in order to pin his hopes on one or two key phrases. βαπτίζεσθαι is used only of the same two incidents (Pentecost and Caesarea) and is clearly initiatory, both as a metaphor and in the event (cf. I Cor. 12.13). λαμβάνειν is used in 2.38 where the gift of the Spirit is equivalent to the promise of salvation in 16.31 (cf. Rom. 8.15; Gal. 3.2f., 14). The ἐπί-verbs – (ἐπ)έρχεσθαι, ἐκχέειν ἐπί, and ἐπιπίπτειν are the ones which most suggest the dramatic empowering impact of the Spirit's coming, particularly in view of 1.8. But they certainly do not imply a second distinct work of the Spirit, simply the dynamic nature of his first coming (cf. Tit. 3.5–7 – the only Pauline [?] use of an ἐπί-verb with the Spirit).

I conclude that in the 23 instances in question these 7 different phrases describe *not* different operations or experiences of the Spirit (contra Unger, *Bib.Sac.* 101 [1944] 233–6, 484f.), but rather different *aspects* of the *same* operation and experience – the first initiating, i.e. baptizing work of the Spirit.

# VI

## THE CONVERSION OF PAUL

ANOTHER favourite passage among Pentecostals is the story of Paul's conversion. Their case is again simple: Paul was converted on the road to Damascus and *three days later* he was baptized in the Spirit.[1] The view that Paul's conversion was instantaneous and that he was only later filled with the Spirit is very common,[2] but it is one which must be sharply questioned.

The arguments in favour of this view are principally that Paul called Jesus 'Lord' (9.5; cf. I Cor. 12.3),[3] and that Ananias greeted him as 'brother' (9.17; 22.13).[4] But in each case (9.5; 22.8, 10; 26.15) it is the vocative κύριε that Paul uses, and κύριε often means simply 'Sir' – a title of respect rather than a confession of faith.[5] And since Paul does not recognize who has thus confronted him ('Who are you, κύριε?') we can hardly say that he calls Jesus 'Lord'.

[1] Riggs 110; Stiles 68; Harper, *Power* 27; Ervin 97–99; Basham 17. For the same arguments by Holiness teachers see A. J. Gordon, *The Ministry of the Spirit* (1894) 90; J. Elder Cumming, *Through the Eternal Spirit* (n.d.) 146; M. James, *I Believe in the Holy Ghost* (1964) 31. However, another stream of Holiness teaching holds that Paul was only arrested and convicted on the Damascus road, and was not converted and renewed until ministered to by Ananias. G. C. Morgan, *The Spirit of God* (1902) 175; C. W. Carter and R. Earle, *The Evangelical Bible Commentary of Acts* (1959).

[2] Many commentators explicitly entitle the section 9.1–8 or 3–9 'Paul's conversion' – e.g. Weiss 190; C. T. Wood, *The Life, Letters and Religion of St Paul* [2](1932) 17–22; J. Knox, *Chapters in a Life of Paul* (1954) 61; Blaiklock 87.

[3] 'Paul acknowledges Jesus as Lord' (Lampe in *Peake* 783b); cf. Bruce, *Book* 441, 492; Wikenhauser 108f.

[4] 'The meaning would really be given better by "my fellow Christian"' (Lake and Cadbury, *Beginnings* IV 104); so Macgregor, *IB* 9 (1954) 124; Haenchen 281 n. 1; Stählin 137; Williams 124; Lampe in *Peake* 784b.

[5] e.g. Matt. 13.27; 21.29; 25.11, 20, 22, 24; Luke 13.8; 14.22; 19.16, 18, 20. In Acts note 10.4 and 16.30. Jesus is often called κύριε in Luke's Gospel, but it is very unlikely that the word ever signifies more than a respectful form of address (see Cadbury, *Beginnings* V 360; C. F. D. Moule, *Studies in Luke-Acts* [1966] 160).

Rather, like Cornelius, confronted by a glorious, majestic being, he addresses him with awe, 'Sir' (10.4). It is hardly likely that the κύριε of 22.10 means more – scarcely credible, indeed, that the full implications of Jesus' reply should have been grasped by a dazed and shocked man and translated into full Christian commitment all in a matter of seconds.[6]

As for Ananias addressing Paul as 'brother', it is possible that he is simply hailing his fellow Jew with the word of racial kinship.

ἀδελφός is used 57 times in Acts – 33 times equivalent to 'my fellow Christian(s)' (leaving aside 9.17 and 22.13), and 19 times in reference to the national/spiritual kinship of Jew to Jew. But the absolute use of οἱ ἀδελφοί = 'the Christians' does not become established until 9.30 (and in 22.5; 28.21 the same formula is applied = 'fellow Jews'), and in the 18 cases where ἀδελφός is used in the vocative (as here), 13 mean 'fellow Jews' and only 5 = 'fellow Christians'.

On the whole, however, it is more probable that Ananias was simply putting Paul at ease – telling him that his past was not held against him, something which may well have worried Paul as he thought things through in the dark (cf. 9.13f., 26).[7] It is unlikely that he would call 'Christian' one who had neither yet received the Spirit nor yet been baptized. His procedure is just that of Peter with Cornelius: as Peter put Cornelius at ease by announcing at once that the latter was acceptable both to God and to himself (10.28, 34f.), so Ananias does likewise by calling Paul 'brother'. In neither case do the words mean that the person addressed was already a Christian; in both cases they indicate that he was *in the process* of becoming a Christian.

Three factors indicate that Paul's three-day experience was a unity, that his conversion, properly speaking, was a crisis experience extending over the three days from the Damascus road to his baptism. First, Acts 22.16: in Ananias's eyes Paul had yet to take that step which would clinch his committal and forgiveness. We have no record whatsoever of Paul taking the decisive step *prior* to his baptism; but we *do* have Ananias exhorting him to take that step – to have his sins washed away by calling on the name of the Lord Jesus (cf. 2.21; 9.14, 21; also Rom. 10.13, 14). In short,

[6] κύριε, used by Paul twice in consecutive sentences which together contain six words, will almost certainly have the same significance each time.

[7] Brother – 'the word of forgiveness' (Rackham 135).

Paul did not become a Christian – one of those οἱ ἐπικαλούμενοι τὸ ὄνομα κυρίου – was not saved (2.21), until he ἐπικαλέσεται τὸ ὄνομα αὐτοῦ. The Pauline baptismal references (Rom. 6.4; Col. 2.12) reflect a very personal and profound experience and imply that for himself Paul's own baptism was the means of his commitment to Christ and the moment of his union with Christ in his death.

Second, Paul's commissioning: Paul seems to make no distinction between what commissioning he received outside Damascus, and the commissioning he received through Ananias.[8] In ch. 9 the commissioning comes solely through Ananias; in ch. 22 Ananias's role is more explicit, though an earlier direct word is presupposed in vv. 14f.; in ch. 26 Ananias is not mentioned and the whole commission is received outside Damascus. Paul, it appears, in looking back to his commissioning, did not distinguish the means and the times of God's dealings with him. This is most likely because it was all the one event and experience, and as such it was impossible to disentangle the various elements in it. And since we can no more separate Paul's experience of conversion from his experience of commissioning,[9] we cannot say that Paul was converted on the Damascus road and commissioned three days later, but must recognize that Paul's conversion-commissioning was one experience which extended over three days; his conversion was completed through Ananias just as much as was his commissioning.

Third, Paul's blindness spans three days and forms the connecting link between what happened on the highway and what happened in the house of Judas. The blindness was obviously due, on the psychological level, to the sudden shock of being confronted with the glory of one whom he thought of as a blasphemer and law-breaker justly done to death.

The brilliance of the light also had its physical affect (22.11); but he alone was blinded, although his companions also saw the light (22.9). His neither eating nor drinking during the next three days (9.9) is best explained as the consequence and symptom of a state of shock (Lake and Cadbury, *Beginnings* IV 102; Bruce, *The Acts of the Apostles* (1951) 198; Williams 123; Lampe in *Peake* 783c). It is well known that serious mental shocks often have physical consequences.

When we realize how this encounter with Jesus cut to the very

[8] J. Munck, *Paul and the Salvation of Mankind* (ET 1959) 19.
[9] G. I. Inglis, *Theology* 36 (1937) 225; cf. J. Knox 98.

roots of Paul's personality and world-view it becomes impossible
to think that he was converted in an instant. Some speak as though
in a matter of seconds Paul threw over everything he had hitherto
held dear, broke down everything on which he had built his life,
transferred his allegiance to a new master, and would have been
off into Damascus to preach his new faith within the hour if the
Lord had permitted him![10] This is hardly the Paul we know. Paul's
loyalties and affections ran deep, and he could not switch their
object in a matter of seconds. His encounter with the risen Jesus
was not a slight transaction of shallow consequences completed in
a few seconds – otherwise the blindness would not have been so
severe – rather it was the entry into his mind and understanding of
a new factor which called in question all that he stood for and
which must be the most important factor in the radical re-thinking
of the next few days. The Damascus road experience was not
simply like rounding a sharp corner, but rather like running into a
solid object while in full flight. Paul did not want at once to be up
and preaching a new faith; he needed time and quiet to collect
himself and his thoughts; he wanted to be alone to think things
through, and to let the pieces of his shattered life reassemble themselves round the new and central fact which had broken in upon
him. It was only when this was done, when the tumult in the
depths of his being had been calmed, and his faith had been re-
ordered from its deepest levels – only then was he ready to take
that step of commitment after which there was no going back.[11]
In short, I do not deny that Paul's whole *Weltanschauung* changed
as *a result of* the single incident on the Damascus road; I do deny
that it changed in *a single moment*.

Luke probably regarded the three days of blindness as symbolic,
for conversion was frequently thought of as bringing sight to the
spiritually blind (John 9.39–41; Acts 26.18; II Cor. 4.4–6; Heb.
6.4; 10.32).

Note the constant harping on sight in Paul's commission: 9.17;
22.14f.; 26.16. In these four verses ὁράω is used six times; and in 26.18
the commission stands thus: 'I send you *to open their eyes* that they may

[10] E.g. W. von Loewenich, *Paul: His Life and Work* (ET 1960) 45;
Wikenhauser 108f.
[11] Cf. C. G. Jung's analysis of Paul's conversion cited in Williams 123 –
especially this sentence: 'Unable to conceive of himself as a Christian, he
became blind and *could only regain his sight through . . . complete submission to
Christianity*' (my italics).

turn from *darkness to light* . . .' Moreover, biblical writers frequently regard sight and light as symbolic spiritual terms (e.g. Isa. 42.6f.; Rom. 11.10; Col. 1.12) and Luke is no exception (e.g. Acts 26.23; 28.27).

If Paul's blindness is symbolic here it symbolized a *simultaneous* spiritual blindness and indicates a time of spiritual turmoil and groping for the truth. Paul, as it were, plunged below the surface of his faith to reconstruct it round the new fact, and only after three days was that basic reconstruction complete enough for him to surface again. As the laying on of Ananias's hands brought to an end his physical blindness, so his reception of the Spirit brought to an end his spiritual blindness (cf. pp. 133f. below). Moreover, the three days probably recalled Jesus' three days in the tomb;[12] and as Jesus' death and resurrection are not properly to be regarded as two separate events but two sides of the one event, so the three days' blindness do not separate two distinct experiences but tie the events at each end of the three days into a single indivisible whole.

Perhaps the simplest way to regard Paul's blindness, so far as symbolism goes, is to see it as indicative of the deep and crushing sorrow and conviction which must have weighed him down like a millstone during these three days. He had sought to devastate the Church of God (Gal. 1.13); he had been resisting the Holy Spirit and had approved the murder of God's Righteous One (Acts 7.51f.); he had all that time gone on persecuting the risen Lord. Do those who think Paul was converted in an instant believe that he could sweep aside the enormity of his manifold crime in an instant? The three days' abstinence and inactivity are difficult to explain on such a hypothesis; but they make excellent sense when seen as the occasion of a deep heart-searching and repentance.[13]

We conclude then that Paul's conversion was one single experience lasting from the Damascus road to the ministry of Ananias. As John Wesley – no stranger to instantaneous conversion – says of the three days, 'So long he seems to have been in the pangs of the new birth.'[14] The experience of being filled with the Spirit was as much an integral part of his conversion as his meeting

---

[12] Cf. Rackham 132f.; Lampe in *Peake* 783c. The comparison is certainly present to Paul himself (Rom. 6.4; Col. 2.12).

[13] See Weiss 194; cf. Wikenhauser 109.

[14] Wesley, *Notes on the New Testament* (1754) on 9.9; cf. Beasley-Murray, *Baptism Today and Tomorrow* (1966) 38.

with Jesus and the three days of solitude and prayer. Paul's conversion was only completed when he called on Jesus as Lord, was filled with the Spirit and had his sins washed away; then, and only then, can he be called a Christian.[15]

[15] Luke's failure to relate Paul's actual reception of the Spirit makes it impossible to decide finally whether it happened at the laying on of Ananias's hands (9.17; cf. 8.17; 19.6) or at his baptism (9.18; cf. 22.16). 9.17f. cannot therefore be used as positive evidence for the relationship either between Spirit-baptism and water-baptism, or between the gift of the Spirit and the laying on of hands.

# VII

## THE CONVERSION OF CORNELIUS

THREE of the key passages which, on the face of it, give strong support to the Pentecostal case have, on closer examination, told a rather different story. With Acts 10 the Pentecostal is in difficulty from the start: there appears to be no grasp between the conversion of Cornelius and his Spirit-baptism. Pentecostals usually argue along one of three lines:

(a) Cornelius 'was born again before Peter preached to him'.[1]

(b) Cornelius came to faith and was cleansed in heart (15.9) during Peter's sermon. The gift of the Spirit followed in close succession, but as a distinct act of grace.[2]

(c) The two things happened simultaneously, and though indistinguishable in this case, they were even here distinct acts of God.[3]

(a) This is obviously not Luke's view. It was only through Peter that the message which led to Cornelius's belief and salvation came (11.14; 15.7); only then that God 'visited the Gentiles, to take out of them a people for his name' (15.14); only then that God 'granted life-giving repentance to the Gentiles' (11.18 NEB) and 'cleansed their hearts by faith' (15.9). Luke would by no means wish to question the spiritual standing of an OT saint or of a pious Jew before God (e.g. Luke 18.14). Cornelius came up to the highest standards of Jewish piety,[4] and even before his meeting with Peter was 'acceptable to God' (10.35; see 10.2, 4; cf. 10.15; 11.9). But

---

[1] K. Southworth, *The Pentecostal* I No. 4 (1965) 7.

[2] Pearlman 317f.; Riggs 111; D. Gee, *Pentecost* (1932) 20; Lindsay 32; Ervin 100f.; Basham 16, though see also 41. For equivalent interpretations in Holiness teaching see J. McNeil, *The Spirit-Filled Life* (1894) 55; A. T. Robertson, *Epochs in the Life of Simon Peter* (1933) 233; James 37. Similarly Lenski 431.

[3] Stiles 69; Prince, *Jordan* 71; Harper, *Power* 28; and in Holiness teaching, A. T. Pierson, *The Acts of the Holy Spirit* (n.d.) 86.

[4] Cf. Bruce, *Acts* 215; Williams 133.

for Luke what made a man a Christian and brought him into the salvation of the new age (the before-and-after watershed for the NT generally), was belief in Jesus Christ and the gift of the Holy Spirit (see ch. IX). Peter was ready to accept Cornelius into his company and friendship from the first,[5] but only when the Spirit fell upon him did Peter realize that he must now accept Cornelius into the community as a *Christian* as well.

Wilckens (66) has argued that the speech of 10.34–43 is really addressed to Christians since the Spirit fell on them at the *beginning* of Peter's speech (11.15). But why then did Luke relate the outpouring of the Spirit in 10.44 as though it interrupted Peter when he was well set in his speech? He hardly intended his readers to understand that there were *two* outpourings of the Spirit. To read such an inference from 11.15 is surely too pedantic. Is 11.15 any more than a vigorous way of speaking intended to highlight the suddenness and unexpectedness of the Spirit's coming (cf. Haenchen 307), the *Zuvorkommen Gottes*, and to be taken no more literally than our 'I had hardly started speaking when . . .'?

(*b*) and (*c*) The evidence will hardly accommodate either the second or the third of the Pentecostal arguments. Notice *when* the Spirit fell on Cornelius: it was while Peter was speaking of the forgiveness of sins which the believer receives (10.43f.). Peter had said nothing of the gift of the Spirit (as he did in Act 2.38), but had just begun to speak of belief and forgiveness. The natural implication is that Cornelius at that moment reached out in faith to God for *forgiveness* and received, as God's response, the *Holy Spirit* (cf. 11.17; 15.9), not instead of the promised forgiveness but as the bearer of it (cf. Gal. 3.2f.). The Spirit was not something additional to God's acceptance and forgiveness but constituted that acceptance and forgiveness. The Spirit thus given affected Cornelius in various ways, but it was the one gift.

Similarly in 11.14f. The obvious implication is that the gift of the Spirit is what effected the salvation of Cornelius; for the message, which Cornelius had been told would result in his salvation, in the event resulted in nothing other than the outpouring of the Spirit. With the outpouring of the Spirit comes eschatological salvation, for to possess the Spirit thus received is to live in 'the last days' and to know salvation both as a present experience and

---

[5] 10.15 and 11.9 are, of course, talking about *ritual* defilement. The cleansing of the heart takes place only during Peter's visit (15.8f.).

a future hope.[6] Significantly also, on hearing that God had given
the same gift to Cornelius as he had given to themselves, the
Judean Christians concluded: 'This means that God has granted
life-giving repentance to the Gentiles also' (11.18 NEB) – the gift
of the Spirit was also God's gift of μετάνοια εἰς ζωήν.[7] The meeting
with God, we might say, was divinely effected on both sides, and
the divine executor was the Spirit given to those who heard of
God's salvation and yearned after it. 11.14–18 concentrates exclusively on God's acceptance of Cornelius; Cornelius was saved,
was baptized in the Spirit, was given the Spirit, was granted repentance unto life – all synonymous ways of saying: Cornelius
became a Christian. The baptism in the Spirit therefore was not
the consequence of a further step of faith on Cornelius's part, for
he knew only of belief unto salvation; but when he thus believed
he received the saving, life-giving baptism in the Spirit. As elsewhere in Luke and Paul the order of salvation is commitment to
the Lord Jesus resulting in God's gift of the Spirit.

All this is confirmed by 15.8f. It is clear that the two verses are
synonymous:

> v. 8: ὁ θεὸς ἐμαρτύρησεν αὐτοῖς καθὼς καὶ ἡμῖν δοὺς τὸ πνεῦμα τὸ
> ἅγιον.
>
> v. 9: (ὁ θεὸς) οὐ διέκρινεν μεταξὺ ἡμῶν τε καὶ αὐτῶν καθαρίσας τὰς
> καρδίας αὐτῶν.

Peter is obviously saying the same thing in two ways. God's bearing witness is equivalent to his not discriminating; the outpouring
of the Spirit was both his testimony to Peter on behalf of Cornelius, and his dissolving of the difference between Peter and
Cornelius. By giving Cornelius the Spirit God himself accepted
Cornelius, and, by thus removing the decisive distinction between
the pious God-fearer and the Christian Jews, showed that they too
must accept him as one of themselves.[8] Likewise, God's giving of

---

[6] See Acts 2.17–21 and p. 150 below; also van Unnik, *NovTest* 4 (1960) 44–53.
[7] Note the equivalence of the expressions in vv. 17f.:

ὁ θεὸς ἔδωκεν αὐτοῖς τὴν ἴσην δωρεὰν ὡς καὶ ἡμῖν.
ὁ θεὸς ἔδωκεν τοῖς ἔθνεσιν καὶ τὴν μετάνοιαν εἰς ζωήν.

μετάνοια εἰς ζωήν has here a fuller sense than simply 'repentance': it embraces
the whole of Cornelius's conversion (see p. 91 below). TEV's 'God has given
to the Gentiles also the opportunity to repent' will not do.
[8] δοὺς and καθαρίσας are 'simultaneous' participles (cf. Bruce, *Book* 306 n.
25).

the Holy Spirit is equivalent to his cleansing of their hearts; these two are one – two ways of describing the same thing. God cleansed their hearts by giving the Spirit. God gave the Spirit to cleanse their hearts.[9]

Moreover, this gift of the Spirit was in response to faith: the faith of 15.9 is the saving faith of 10.43; 11.17; 15.7 to which God gives the Spirit of forgiveness and cleansing. The connection between vv. 7f. implies that God bore witness to Cornelius's *belief*; he who knows the heart saw that Cornelius had come to the point of faith (πίστευσαι – aorist), and testified to Peter and his companions that it was so by giving him the Spirit. Note also 15.14: what Peter spoke of was God's gift of the Spirit to Cornelius; it was in this way that God 'visited the Gentiles to take out of them a people for his name'.

In short then, Cornelius is a prize example of one who had responded to God as far as it was possible for him to respond, but was not yet a Christian. His repentance and faith had not yet reached that level or been turned to that object, which would enable Luke to call them μετάνοια εἰς ζωήν and πίστις εἰς Χριστὸν Ἰησοῦν; and so he was without the forgiveness and salvation they bring. He only entered into this Christian experience when he received the Spirit. This experience was to him what Pentecost was to the 120 – the entry into the new age and covenant, into the people of God.[10] And it was this experience which Luke once again specifically designates 'the baptism in the Spirit'. Here at least, therefore, the baptism in the Spirit is God's act of acceptance, of forgiveness, cleansing and salvation, and not something separate from and beyond that which made Cornelius a Christian.

[9] Cf. Bruce, *Book* 306 n. 25; Carter and Earle 148.
[10] Note how frequently the parallel between Pentecost and Caesarea is reiterated – no less than four times in the six verses which cover Peter's report of the incident (10.47; 11.15, 17; 15.8). It was the same faith, the same Holy Spirit, the same baptism in the Spirit, the same manner of his outpouring, the same manifestations of his coming, the same results.

# VIII

## THE 'DISCIPLES' AT EPHESUS

ACTS 19.1–7 is the other foundational passage for Pentecostal theology of Spirit-baptism. A strong case would contain three major strands:

(a) The twelve Ephesians were Christians (μαθηταί, οἱ πιστεύσαντες) before Paul met them – Christians, that is, who had not received the Holy Spirit.[1]

(b) Paul's question in 19.2 seems to imply that for Paul one could be a Christian and yet not have (received) the Spirit.[2]

(c) The time interval between the Ephesians' baptism and Paul's laying on of hands means that there was a time interval between conversion (which precedes baptism) and the coming of the Spirit (which followed the laying on of hands).[3]

(a) Did Luke regard the twelve Ephesians as already Christians before their encounter with Paul? Their ignorance of the Holy Spirit and about Jesus, and the fact that Paul did not count their earlier baptism sufficient but had them undergo baptism in the name of the Lord Jesus, indicates a negative answer. But what of

[1] E. C. Miller, *Pentecost Examined* (1936) 51; H. G. Hathaway, *A Sound from Heaven* (1947) 32; Horton 5; Pierson 126–8. That μαθηταί means 'Christians' is widely agreed by commentators; see e.g. Käsemann 136, and the authors cited by him (136 n.3). The equivalent Catholic interpretation is that the twelve were Christians who lacked 'this completion of Christian life' (Rackham 346).

[2] Harper, *Power* 29; Prince, *Jordan* 69f.; Riggs 54; Stiles 8; Lindsay 35; in Holiness teaching see e.g. Cumming 143f. The Pentecostal exposition has the weighty support of Lake, *Beginnings* V 57 and W. L. Knox, *Acts* 88 at this point. For an equivalent Catholic interpretation in terms of Confirmation, see Chase 32.

[3] Prince, *Jordan* 70; Harper, *Power* 29; Ervin 103f. For equivalent Calvinist interpretation in support of their polemic against any hint of baptismal regeneration see Stonehouse 13; and for equivalent Catholic interpretation in favour of Confirmation see Mason 26; Leeming 217.

Luke's description of them as μαθηταί? It is true that in Acts μαθηταί usually equals 'Christians', but the 19.1 usage is unique: it is the *only* time that μαθηταί is not preceded by the definite article. Now οἱ μαθηταί used absolutely always has the sense in Acts of the *whole* Christian community of the city or area referred to, not just 'Christians' generally, but the whole body of disciples as a single entity: for example, οἱ μαθηταὶ ἐν Ιερουσαλημ (6.7); οἱ ἐν Δαμασκῷ μαθηταί (9.19); οἱ μαθηταὶ [ἐν 'Ιόππῃ] (9.38); οἱ μαθηταὶ ἀπὸ Καισαρίας (21.16). οἱ μαθηταί is almost a technical term for Luke. 'The disciples' act as one (19.30), are ministered to and consulted as one (20.1), are one as the target for the false teachers (20.30), are one so far as the decisions of the council affect them (neck – singular – 15.10). When he wishes to speak of a smaller group than the whole body, Luke either qualifies his description of οἱ μαθηταί precisely (as in 9.25) or else he speaks of '*some* of *the* disciples' (καὶ τῶν μαθητῶν – 21.16). Luke's description of the twelve as τινες μαθηταί therefore probably implies that the twelve did *not* belong to 'the disciples' in Ephesus – a fact confirmed by their ignorance of basic Christian matters. Indeed, I would suggest that Luke deliberately describes them in this way in order to indicate their relation, or rather, lack of relation to the church at Ephesus. Nor need the πιστεύσαντες mean any more than a mistaken (or charitable) presumption on Paul's part[4] – a mistake which Paul quickly discovered and rectified by putting them through the complete initiation procedure, as with all new converts. On the other hand, we may not simply dub them 'disciples of John the Baptist';[5] the use of μαθηταί requires some connection with Christianity, and presumably Paul must have had some reason for addressing them as οἱ πιστεύσαντες.

That they had received 'the baptism of John' hardly proves that they were disciples of the Baptist. It is probably a generic name for the rite originated by John and taken over by others including Jesus and his disciples (Marsh 156; cf. Lake and Cadbury, *Beginnings* IV 231, 238; Kraeling 208f.). On the question of whether there was a group of Baptist disciples at Ephesus see especially J. A. T. Robinson, *Studies* 49–51 n. 49.

In the natural course of events there must have been many

---

[4] But see below.
[5] Contra Rengstorf, *TDNT* IV 456f.; Käsemann 136; Haenchen 498; Williams 220; Scobie, *Baptist* 188; Schütz 105,130.

people who had some contact with John or Jesus only at a certain point in their ministries. They had heard enough to be deeply impressed and received 'the baptism of John'. But soon afterwards they had to leave the area where John or Jesus was working and lost contact with the whole movement. There would inevitably be a very wide spectrum covering all who had responded in some way and at some time to the gospel. For example, there would be those who knew only the repentance baptism of John; those who knew and believed in no more than John's teaching; those who knew Jesus only at some particular point in his ministry and through some particular incident; those who knew Jesus only in the flesh and had not yet realized the significance of his death or heard of his resurrection; those who knew only the early preaching and teaching of the first few days after Pentecost; and those whose faith was developing and deepening in different directions. And when we include the others won by the teaching of these groups, with some stressing one aspect of the message above the rest and others ignoring or forgetting important parts of the message (not to mention interaction among the different groups) the spectrum covers an infinite variety. This inherently probable speculation is strongly supported by the evidence of Mark 9.38–40; Matt. 7.22f.; Acts 19.13–16;[6] and from what Luke says of them – their description, their baptism, their (lack of) knowledge – the twelve Ephesians are most naturally seen as coming from this context. Paul's question – hardly his opening gambit in every and any conversation – is intelligible only against such a background; he rightly presupposes an act of commitment at some stage in the past. In short, they are disciples, but do not yet belong to *the* disciples; that is, they are not yet Christians.

μαθητής must have been used with greater or less strictness by different groups, and so long as there were people still alive who had known or known about Jesus, and who looked up to him with some degree of loyalty, μαθητής must have been a rather loose term. By confining οἱ μαθηταί to Christian communities Luke precisely delimits Christians from other groups; and by his unique use of μαθηταί here he is able to preserve the distinctive Christian title while at the same time acknowledging the (albeit imperfect) discipleship of others who were literally 'behind the times'.

(*b*) This argument assumes that Paul thought he was dealing

[6] Cf. Dibelius, *Täufer* 95f.

with Christians, and so asked a question appropriate to Christians. But this assumption is not firmly grounded. For the Paul of the Epistles it was impossible for a man to be a Christian unless he had received the Spirit (Rom. 8.9). The Paul of Acts 19 is no different, for his second question implies that the Spirit is received in connection with baptism; it was inconceivable to him that a Christian, one who had committed himself to Jesus as Lord in baptism in his name, could be yet without the Spirit. This is why the twelve had to go through the full initiation procedure. It was not that Paul accepted them as Christians with an incomplete experience; it is rather that they were not Christians at all. The absence of the Spirit indicated that they had not even begun the Christian life. And the Paul who would not accept Spirit-less disciples and believers as Christians could hardly be said to have anticipated meeting Spirit-less Christians. He who believes that only those are Christians who have the Spirit will not go round asking Christians whether they have received the Spirit.

This implies that Paul's opening question was one of suspicion and surprise, a suggestion which is borne out by Luke's description of the twelve and by the form of the question itself. The τινες μαθηταί did not belong to the Christian group (οἱ μαθηταί) at Ephesus. Paul knew of no Christians who were outside the body of the Christian community in any place, and therefore was puzzled: what sort of believers were they? So he straightaway pinpointed the question which would show whether they were Christians or not. He assumed (on what grounds Luke does not say) their commitment, but he queries whether it was Christian commitment. The question itself indicates a tone of surprise, for πνεῦμα ἅγιον is in the position of emphasis: 'Did you receive the *Holy Spirit* when you believed?' There was no evidence in their own bearing or in their company that they had the Spirit;[7] was then their act of faith that which resulted in the gift of the Spirit? Their answer quickly confirmed his suspicions: they were not Christians. In short, in 19.2 Paul is not asking Christians whether they have received the Spirit (a necessary but optional extra); rather he is asking twelve 'disciples' who profess belief whether they are Christians.

The argument that the *aorist* participle πιστεύσαντες indicates an action prior to the λαμβάνειν (Riggs 53f.; Stiles 8; Miller 49; cf. Ervin

[7] Cf. Schweizer, *TWNT* VI 408.

102 n. 47) betrays an inadequate grasp of Greek grammar. 'The action denoted by the Aorist Participle may be . . . antecedent to, coincident with, or subsequent to the action of the principal verb' (E. de W. Burton, *New Testament Moods and Tenses* [1898] 59f.). Examples of the aorist participle expressing action identical with that of the main verb are Matt. 19.27; 27.4; I Cor. 15.18; Eph. 1.9, 20; Heb. 7.27 (and the numerous instances of the phrase ἀποκρίθεις εἶπεν). In Acts see 1.8; 10.33; 27.3. As most commentators recognize, πιστεύσαντες in 19.2 is a coincident aorist; it is Paul's doctrine that a man receives the Spirit *when* he believes.

(*c*) The argument that vv. 5f. relate two quite separate procedures fails to recognize the fact that baptism and the laying on of hands here are the *one* ceremony. When Paul learned that they had not received the Spirit he immediately inquired after their baptism, not their faith, and *not* any other ceremony. Verse 3 therefore implies a very close connection between baptism and receiving the Spirit. Moreover, although the twelve were μαθηταί and their essential lack was the Spirit, Paul did not simply lay hands on them, but first baptized them.[8] The laying on of hands in v. 6 must therefore be the climax of a single ceremony whose most important element is baptism, and whose object is the reception of the Spirit. This is borne out by the form of vv. 5f., which could be translated: '. . . they were baptized in the name of the Lord Jesus and, Paul having laid hands on them, the Holy Spirit came on them.' The laying on of hands is almost parenthetical; the sequence of events is 'baptism (resulting in) . . . Spirit'. Certainly the one action leads into and reaches its conclusion in the other with no discernible break.[9]

Nor can we compartmentalize the experience of the twelve or distinguish different operations of the Spirit. It was a single (conversion) experience,[10] the high points of which were their commitment to the Lord Jesus in baptism and their reception of the Spirit

[8] Barth's attempt to equate John's baptism with Christian baptism (*Taufe* 165–72; also *SJT* 12 (1959) 36f.) is inadmissible. Baptism 'in the name of the Lord Jesus' signifies that the water-rite is related to Jesus in a manner impossible before his coming (and exaltation). J. K. Parratt's attempt to equate the two is rather more acceptable, but still fails to grasp the significance of the specifically Christian (= post-Pentecost) formula (*ExpT* 79 [1967–68] 182f.).

[9] Cf. Wilkens, *TZ* 23 (1967) 42. So today in many Protestant Churches the conclusion to the ceremony of admission to full membership is the giving and receiving of 'the right hand of fellowship'.

[10] In the next chapter I shall take up the Pentecostal reply that the twelve

– the only coming (upon) of the Spirit that we read of here. Only with the reception of the Spirit did the μαθηταί become Christians.[11]

The twelve Ephesians are therefore further examples of men who were not far short of Christianity, but were not yet Christians because they lacked the vital factor – the Holy Spirit. The issue facing Paul (and the reason presumably for Luke's inclusion of the narrative) was: 'How are such groups to be merged with the main stream of Christianity?' Paul's answer was to point to what was for him the final and absolute criterion: only those who had received the Spirit were Christians.[12] And when he discovered that the Spirit was lacking, all his energies were directed towards the object of bringing the twelve into the Christian experience of the Spirit.

The parallel case of Apollos is very instructive. He too 'knew only the baptism of John' and needed fuller instruction about 'the way of God' (18.25f.). But unlike the twelve μαθηταί he was not re-baptized,[13] for he differed from them in one, *the* one crucial respect: he already possessed the Spirit (18.25), whereas they did not.

ζέων τῷ πνεύματι stands between two phrases which describe Apollos as a disciple of Jesus. It is presumably therefore itself a description of Apollos as a Christian, and πνεῦμα must be taken as (Holy) Spirit rather than (human) spirit. Käsemann adds that Rom. 12.11 implies that the phrase was current in the language of Christian edification to indicate inspiration by the Spirit (143). See also Weiss 316; Dibelius, *Täufer* 95; Preisker 301; Lake and Cadbury, *Beginnings* IV 233; Lampe in *Studies* 198; also in *Peake* 796f.; Conzelmann, *Apg.* 109; Beasley-Murray 110; Stählin 250, 252; Flender 128; Bieder 47, 49. Haenchen notes that to interpret the phrase in terms of 'a fiery temperament' is a very unusual use of πνεῦμα (491 n. 10).

---

were converted and regenerate *before* their baptism, so that no matter how closely connected were the two ritual acts, the gift of the Spirit must have been subsequent to their conversion.

[11] Cf. the experience of Jesus at Jordan, and that of the Ethiopian eunuch (8.39 – should the Western text be original).

[12] Perhaps it was with the memory of such a group as these twelve, or even this very group, that Paul wrote Rom. 8.9. G. C. Darton has argued that Luke's method 'is always to convey the large momentous lesson by the small particular story about real people' (*St John the Baptist and the Kingdom of Heaven* [1961] 39f.).

[13] Dibelius, *Täufer* 95f.; H. Preisker, *ZNW* 30 (1931) 302; Flemington 41; Conzelmann, *Apg.* 109; Beasley-Murray 112; Bieder 49.

As with the disciples at Pentecost, the promise of Apollos's Johannine baptism had been fulfilled by the gift of the Spirit, and so he did not need Christian water-baptism; but the twelve disciples' Johannine baptism counted for nothing because they had not received the Spirit, and so they had to undergo the complete Christian initiation, just like all other such disciples of John and the earthly Jesus who had heard and experienced nothing of Pentecost.[14] Luke has clearly juxtaposed these two narratives to highlight the point he is making: namely, that 'in the beginning the Spirit was the decisive factor in early Christianity'.[15] On this single point both stories turn; this single issue determines whether they are Christians who need fuller instruction, or non-Christians who must be treated as new enquirers.

[14] This interpretation goes back to Dibelius, *Täufer* 95f. It was most strongly expressed by Preisker 301–4, and it has recently been championed by Beasley-Murray 110–12. See also Bieder 49, and cf. Schweizer's thesis about Luke's (mis)understanding of the Apollos narrative (*EvTh* 15 [1955] 247–54).

[15] Preisker 304. These two episodes show us 'a stage of early Christianity where neither cult nor office is decisive, but where the possession of the Spirit is everything' (303). On Käsemann's attempt to refute Preisker here see pp. 90ff. and n. 32. In forcing through his *Una sancta* thesis and dismissing 18.25c as 'a Lukan fabrication' (144) Käsemann has missed Luke's real point.

# IX

## CONVERSION-INITIATION IN THE ACTS OF THE APOSTLES

THERE are few problems so puzzling in NT theology as that posed by Acts in its treatment of conversion-initiation. The relation between the gift of the Spirit and water-baptism is particularly confusing – sometimes sharply contrasted (1.5; 11.16), sometimes quite unconnected (2.4; 8.16f.; 18.25), sometimes in natural sequence (2.38; 19.5f.), sometimes the other way about (9.17f.(?); 10.44–48). The role and significance of both John's baptism and the laying on of hands are complicating factors. Our study so far has suggested a solution to this problem, and to complete our treatment of Acts we must enlarge upon it a little more fully.

Our discussion will start from Acts 2.38 which I have left till now since it raises issues which can be best dealt with in a broader treatment than the debate with Pentecostalism has so far permitted. Moreover, Luke probably intends Acts 2.38 to establish the pattern and norm for Christian conversion-initiation in his presentation of Christianity's beginnings. At the close of the first Christian sermon the leading apostle sets the precedent for the instruction of enquirers.[1]

Peter is the one who breaks the new ground (10.1–11.18), and his lead is followed in the decisive issues of missionary outreach (15.7–11, 14ff.). In Acts 3.19f., the second Christian sermon, the pattern is repeated in equivalent terms, since the καιροὶ ἀναψύξεως are best understood as the period of respite and blessing prior to and culminating in the parousia, that is, the last days which the Spirit ushers in and into and which lead up to the last day; cf. also 5.32. If these statements and the numbers converted are historical, it also means that the great majority of the first Christians had been received into the Church in accordance

---

[1] See Stählin 53; Hull 88,95; and cf. Dodd, *Apostolic Preaching* 23.

with this pattern. And having found it effective themselves they would see in it the pattern to be copied when they in turn did the work of evangelists (e.g. 8.4). The sermon in Acts 2 may also be intended to be a pattern for kerygmatic preaching (Lampe in *Studies* 159).

Furthermore, it is the only verse in Acts which directly relates to one another the three most important elements in conversion-initiation: repentance, water-baptism, and the gift of the Spirit – repentance and faith being the opposite sides of the same coin.

The three principal words used by Luke to describe man's act of faith are μετανοεῖν, ἐπιστρέφειν and πιστεύειν. Each describes the act from a different angle: μετανοεῖν always has the sense of turning away from (ἀπό) sin; ἐπιστρέφειν always has the sense of turning to (ἐπί) God; and πιστεύειν has essentially the sense of commitment to (εἰς) Christ. They can be used singly, when they may have a fuller sense (e.g. 2.38; 9.35; 11.18; 16.31), or they may be used in pairs (e.g. 3.19; 26.20; 2.38 with 2.44; 20.21; 11.21; 26.18). In the former cases they obviously often comprehend the whole act of faith; in the latter, their sense is more restricted in the way already suggested. (ἀπο)δέχεσθαι (2.41; 8.14; 11.1; 17.11) and προσέχειν (8.6, 11; 16.14) also describe the response to the preached word (λόγος).

Of these three elements only one each can properly be said to be performed by each of the three parties involved: the initiate, the Christian community, and God.[2] In normal Christian conversion-initiation each of these parties plays a distinctive role, and unless each party plays its part the conversion-initiation is incomplete. μετανοήσατε (imperative active) is what the enquirers must do themselves; βαπτισθήτω (imperative passive) is what must be done to the enquirer by the community; λήμψεσθε (future indicative active) is the unqualified promise (the only two conditions have been named) of what the enquirer will receive from God. Those who repent and are baptized will receive the gift of the Spirit. It should be noted that no possibility of delay is envisaged here.[3] As with the command and promise of 16.31, the act of obedience to the command receives the promised result.

(*a*) Of the three elements the most important is the gift of the Spirit. In 2.38 it is the climax of the total event of conversion-initiation: of the two things offered – forgiveness of sins and the Holy Spirit – it is the positive gift which Peter emphasizes, that

---

[2] Cf. L. Cerfaux, *The Church in the Theology of St Paul* (ET 1959) 163.
[3] Contra Stiles 8; Harper, *Power* 25.

which first attracted the crowd, and that which is the essence of the new age and covenant (2.39). The Spirit is the bearer of salvation, for the promise of 2.38 must include the promise of 2.21 (and 16.31). This is confirmed by the fact that 2.39c clearly alludes to the close of Joel 2.32, the very verse at which the quotation of Acts 2.17–21 left off;[4] the deliverance 'in those days' Peter interprets of eschatological salvation in 2.21 and of the gift of the Spirit in 2.38f. We have already seen that for Luke as for Paul the gift of the Spirit is the means whereby men enter into the blessing of Abraham. Also, in so far as Jesus' experience at Jordan is at this stage (of Luke's writing) consciously a type of Christian conversion-initiation, we must recall that there the anointing of the Spirit was the most important element, with baptism filling only a preliminary role.

That the gift of the Spirit is for Luke the most important element in Christian conversion-initiation is also shown by four of the incidents we have examined. With the 120, it is the gift of the Spirit which ushered them into the new age and covenant; water-baptism by John may be presupposed, but it does not feature at all in their actual entry into the age of the Spirit. With the Samaritans, Christian water-baptism had been administered, but it did not amount to a full or valid conversion-initiation, and in the absence of the Spirit its significance was much reduced; in the event it was the coming of the Spirit which was sought above all else. With Cornelius, it was the reception of the Spirit which brought salvation, forgiveness and cleansing of heart; it was that which settled the question of his acceptance by the Christian community (water-baptism is not even mentioned in 11.14–18); water-baptism was simply man's catching up with and acknowledgment of the prior decisive act of God. With Apollos and the Ephesians, it was possession or absence of the Spirit which decided whether their Johannine baptism was sufficient; for the one, Christian baptism was unnecessary, for his possession of the Spirit indicated that he was already a Christian; for the others, Christian baptism was necessary, for the absence of the Spirit indicated that they were not Christians.

In Paul's conversion it is naturally his unique encounter with the risen Jesus (cf. I Cor. 15.8) which commands the centre of the stage.

[4] Bruce, *Acts* 99; also *Book* 78; Haenchen 152; Stählin 54; Conzelmann, *Apg.* 31.

We may assume that all the other examples of conversion-initiation recorded by Luke follow the pattern of Acts 2.38. The gift of the Spirit need not be mentioned – though it may be implied by the 'rejoicing' of the Ethiopian eunuch and the Philippian jailor (Lampe in *Studies* 198) – since fulfilment of the conditions (repentance/belief and baptism) results in the Spirit being given and received. It was only because the majority did receive the Spirit at the time of their water-baptism or immediately after, that water-baptism later became the sacrament of the gift of the Spirit. In a similar way baptism need not be mentioned but can be assumed (e.g. 9.42; 11.21; 17.34).

It has become evident, in fact, that one of Luke's purposes in recording these unusual instances is to show that the one thing which makes a man a Christian is the gift of the Spirit. Men can have been for a long time in Jesus' company, can have made profession of faith and been baptized in the name of the Lord Jesus, can be wholly 'clean' and acceptable to God, can even be 'disciples', and *yet not be Christians*, because they lack and until they receive the Holy Spirit. In the last analysis the only thing that matters in deciding whether a man is a Christian or not is whether he has received the Spirit or not.

(*b*) It is important to grasp the relation between faith, the act of believing into (πιστεῦσαι εἰς) Christ, and the gift of the Spirit. Much of our argument so far may have failed to convince Pentecostals, most of whom seem to hold what to them is the classic Reformed view of the order of salvation, namely, that the Spirit works in or with a person prior to his conversion, enabling him to repent and believe, at which point he receives Jesus into his heart and life. To these two distinct works of grace the Pentecostal adds a third in his theology of the baptism in the Spirit.[5] Thus in such cases as 2.38, 19.5f., the Pentecostal believes his case to be sound because baptism is a confession of a conversion which has already taken place, and conversion indicates that the Spirit is already operative in a man's life, so that the Spirit received at or after

[5] An extreme example would be the Blessed Trinity Society's pamphlet *Why* . . .: 'Once we have accepted the Lord Jesus Christ, there is a further step which is necessary to receive the full promise of God, and that is the acceptance of the Gift of the Holy Spirit' (cited in *The Churchman* 80 [1966] 304); cf. Ervin 93 n. 15. In Holiness teaching see A. B. Simpson, *The Holy Spirit or Power from on High* (1896) II 28; and on the Catholic side see the quotations from F. H. Elpis and H. Cooper in Lampe, *Seal* xxiiif.; cf. Rackham 116; Dix, *The Shape of the Liturgy* (1945) 260; Thornton 173.

baptism is a work of grace distinct from and subsequent to conversion.[6]

Many conservative theologians take the classic Reformed position to be that in the *ordo salutis* regeneration precedes conversion and is that which enables a man to convert. Thus e.g. Smeaton quotes Wesley with approval: '. . . every man, *in order to believe* unto salvation, must receive the Holy Ghost' (199, from Wesley's *Works* VIII 49, my italics). See also A. Kuyper, *The Work of the Holy Spirit* (1900, reprinted 1956) 283–353, especially 295ff.; E. H. Palmer, *The Holy Spirit* (1958) 79, 83; J. H. Gerstner, *The Biblical Expositor* (ed. C. F. H. Henry 1960) 217. This initial reception of the Spirit is distinguished from his later coming to bestow charismata (Lambert 133, 144; Warfield 122f.; Stonehouse 82; Lenski 431, 780; Gerstner 218; J. K. Parratt, *The Seal of the Spirit in the New Testament Teaching* (London University dissertation 1965); cf. p. 57 n. 8, and the sacramentalist interpretation of Acts 10 which distinguishes the 'ecstatic Spirit' from the 'baptismal Spirit' – Haenchen 307 n. 4; Schlier, *Zeit* 115f.; Kuss 102f.; see also Oulton 239f., and cf. Foakes-Jackson 95). Parratt seems to distinguish a third reception of the Spirit – before, in and after the act of faith (72, 74f., 163f.). Lenski falls into the same inconsistency in his interpretation of Acts 10 (431, 434). Barth's last work shows a somewhat similar confusion as to whether water-baptism is the human response to the divine initiative of Spirit-baptism, or Spirit-baptism the divine response to the human petition of water-baptism; see e.g. his comment on Acts 10.46f. (*Dogmatik* IV/4 85).

I do not deny that the Christian theologian may quite properly speak of the convicting work of the Spirit prior to and leading up to conversion (even if John 16.8–11, and perhaps I Cor. 14.24f., are about the only passages which can be quoted in support).[7] However, I affirm most emphatically that for the NT writers who speak on this matter, the gift of saving grace which the individual receives in conversion, that is, on believing, is the Holy Spirit. The decisive gift of the Spirit which makes a man a Christian and

[6] E.g., Riggs, 51f., 55, 58f.; Miller 50f.; Horton 13, 18; Harper, *Walk in the Spirit* (1968) 15; also *Fire* 21f.

[7] Robinson, *Spirit* 209; Schweizer, *TWNT* VI 425. Contrast Bultmann, who denies that Paul ever attributes faith to the Spirit (*Theology of the New Testament* [ET 1952] I 330). In Acts it would be more precise to say that faith is stirred up through the (inspired) proclamation of the Gospel. This will become evident in our study of Paul. In Acts it is enough to notice the prominence of λόγος – used about thirty-six times for the proclaimed Gospel. As Büchsel points out: reception of the Spirit without a prior preaching of the Gospel is unknown to Luke (256–63); cf. Barrett, *Luke* 68.

without which he is no Christian comes neither before nor after conversion but *in* conversion. The NT knows of no prior reception.[8] So far as Paul is concerned, Rom. 8.9 rules out the possibility both of a *non*-Christian possessing the Spirit and of a Christian *not* possessing the Spirit: only the reception and consequent possession of the Spirit makes a man a Christian. For John, spiritual birth means being born of the Spirit who comes from above, not of a Spirit already present (3.3–8), for the πνεῦμα is the breath of God (20.22) which brings life and is life (cf. 4.10; 6.63; 7.38f.). All that the believer receives in conversion – salvation, forgiveness, justification, sonship, etc. – he receives because he receives the Spirit (cf. ch. VII).

The Pentecostal attempt to evade the NT emphasis by distinguishing the acceptance of Jesus at conversion from the later gift of the Spirit is in fact a departure from NT teaching. For the NT *nowhere* speaks of conversion as 'receiving Christ' (despite the frequent use of this phrase in popular evangelism). John 1.12 refers primarily to the historical welcome which a few of 'his own' gave him, in contrast to the rejection of the many (1.11f.; cf. 5.43; 6.21; 13.20). In Col. 2.6 the word used is παραλαμβάνω which properly means the receiving of a heritage or tradition; Paul reminds the Colossians how they received the proclamation of Jesus as Lord (Arndt and Gingrich) – 'since Jesus was delivered to you as Christ and Lord' (NEB). Rev. 3.20, although much beloved as an evangelistic illustration, is written, of course, to Christians. Paul and John do speak of Christ indwelling a person and of a Christian 'having Christ', but the more precise way of speaking is that Christ indwells the believer in and by his Spirit and the Christian has the Spirit of Christ. For the Spirit from the ascension onwards is peculiarly the Spirit of Jesus (Acts 16.7; Rom. 8.9; Gal. 4.6; Phil. 1.19). What one receives at conversion is the Spirit and life of the risen exalted Christ.

Cf. also John's talk of the Spirit as the ἄλλος παράκλητος with 14.18–24. Note I Cor. 15.45 and the way in which Paul can use the terms 'Spirit', 'Spirit of God', 'Spirit of Christ', and 'Christ' interchangeably in Rom. 8.9f. M. Bouttier, *En Christ* (1962) has shown that on balance Paul prefers to speak of I/we in Christ and the Spirit in me/us, rather than Christ in me/us and I/we in the Spirit (see Moule, *Phenomenon* 24–26). He can only speak interchangeably of 'Christ in the believer' and

[8] See further, p. 120 below.

'the Spirit in the believer' because these two phrases mean precisely the
same thing. He does not simply identify Christ and the Spirit – only in
experience. The equivalence lies in the total phrases – Christ's life *in the
believer* is effected by his Spirit. See pp. 148f. below.

To become a Christian, in short, is to receive the Spirit of
Christ, the Holy Spirit. What the Pentecostal attempts to separate
into two works of God is in fact one single divine act. For Luke
the relation between faith and the Spirit can be expressed simply
thus: in conversion one believes, commits oneself to Christ, and
receives the Spirit from Christ. Man's act in conversion is to repent,
to turn and to believe;[9] God's act is to give the Spirit to man on
believing (Acts 2.38; 11.17; 15.9; 19.2; cf. John 7.39; Gal. 3.2).
The two together are the essential components of conversion, but
in the last analysis it is God's gift which alone counts. Faith would
not justify if God did not give his Spirit. Faith is only the reaching
out of an empty hand to receive; it is what is received which alone
ultimately counts. If, then, Bruner is correct in saying that 'the
truth of Pentecostalism's doctrine of the Spirit rests or falls on the
exegesis of the knotty pneumatic passages in Acts' (43), our conclusion can only be that the doctrine falls.

(*c*) If one cannot separate the act of faith from the gift of the
Spirit, what is the role of baptism within the event of conversion-
initiation? First we must examine the relation between faith-
repentance and baptism. In Acts faith and baptism are normally
closely linked (2.38, 41; 8.12f.; 8.37f. (D); 16.14f., 31–33; 18.8).
In the case of the Ephesians the sequence of Paul's questions
indicates that πιστεῦσαι and βαπτισθῆναι are interchangeable ways
of describing the act of faith: baptism was the necessary expression
of commitment, without which they could not be said to have
truly 'believed'.[10] This is also implied by the use of Christ's name
in the rite. Enquirers on the day of Pentecost were baptized ἐπί or
ἐν τῷ ὀνόματι Ἰησοῦ Χριστοῦ. ἐπί probably means that the baptisand
in water-baptism called upon the name of the Lord (2.21; 22.16),
and ἐν that the name was named over the baptisand (this being the
formula and technique in healing miracles and exorcisms – 3.6;

[9] See p. 91 above. These words always describe man's act away from sin
and towards God. God does not perform these operations – though we may
say they are God's doing (see 3.26; 5.31; 11.18; 16.14; cf. 4.12; 11.14; 2.41,
47; 11.24; cf. A. Weiser, *TWNT* VI 187).

[10] 'The idea of an unbaptized Christian is simply not entertained in NT'
(Bruce, *Book* 77); cf. Käsemann 144.

4.7, 10; 19.13–15). Water-baptism is therefore to be regarded as the occasion on which the initiate called upon the Lord for mercy, and the means by which he committed himself to the one whose name was named over him. Properly administered water-baptism must have been the climax and act of faith, the expression of repentance and the vehicle of commitment.[11]

As we have seen, Paul's water-baptism must have been the moment of surrender and death for the old self and entry into the new life of the Spirit (cf. Rom. 7.6 with 6.4). Hull, however, has argued that the conditions to be fulfilled for the gift of the Spirit, both for Peter and Luke, were repentance, faith in Jesus, and the *readiness to be baptized* (93ff.). This does not really square with the importance of baptism, even for Luke.

At the same time, while recognizing that one cannot say 'faith' without also saying 'water-baptism', we must recognize that of the two it is the former which is the significant element. Baptism gives expression to faith, but without faith baptism is meaningless, an empty symbol. It is false to say that water-baptism conveys, confers or effects forgiveness of sins.[12] It may symbolize cleansing, but it is the faith and repentance which receives the forgiveness, and the Holy Spirit who conveys, confers and effects it. Luke never mentions water-baptism by itself as the condition of or means to receiving forgiveness; he mentions it only in connection with some other attitude (repentance – Luke 3.3; Acts 2.38) or act (calling on his name – Acts 22.16). But whereas water-baptism is never spoken of as the sole prerequisite to receiving forgiveness, Luke on a number of occasions speaks of repentance or faith as the sole prerequisite (Luke 5.20; 24.47; Acts 3.19; 5.31; 10.43; 13.38; 26.18; cf. 4.4; 9.35, 42; 11.21; 13.48; 14.1; 16.31; 17.12, 34). In other words, water-baptism is neither the sole preliminary nor in itself an essential preliminary to receiving forgiveness.

Moreover, we have already seen in chapter I that in Luke where repentance is joined to water-baptism it is the former alone which is really decisive for forgiveness. So in 2.38, 'Peter's basic and

[11] Beasley-Murray 102, and his quotation from von Baer (121); see also R. P. Martin, *Worship in the Early Church* (1964) 100; White 134f.
[12] Contra e.g. Lake and Cadbury, *Beginnings* IV 26; Rackham lxxvi; Wikenhauser 53f.; Bultmann, *Theology* I 140; J. G. Davies, *The Spirit, the Church and the Sacraments* (1954) 128f.; Dewar 53; Kuss 121, 122, 132, 148; Delling, *Taufe* 62. The view lands in confusion in the case of Cornelius (cf. Mason 38; Schlier, *Zeit* 115f.).

primary demand is for repentance';[13] the forgiveness of sins can be promised to the baptisand only because his baptism is his act and expression of repentance.[14] Likewise in 22.16, the other favourite verse of the sacramentalist in Acts, the washing away of sins is achieved on the human side not by water but by the calling upon the name of the Lord; not the rite itself but the attitude and commitment (for which it gave occasion and to which it gave expression) made the decisive contact with the Lord which resulted in cleansing.

The ἐπικαλεσάμενος τὸ ὄνομα αὐτοῦ goes principally with the ἀπόλουσαι τὰς ἁμαρτίας σου, as the balance of the sentence also suggests – ἀναστὰς . . . βάπτισαι, ἀπόλουσαι, ἐπικαλεσάμενος. Acts 22.16 shows that βαπτίζειν and ἀπολούειν are not synonyms. Nor is there any requirement in the text itself to take the two actions described by these verbs as causally related = be baptized and (in and by that action) have your sins washed away. They are co-ordinate actions, related through the ἐπικαλεσάμενος κτλ. In fact, we have once again the three elements of conversion–initiation – water-baptism, the Spirit's cleansing, and the individual's appeal of faith.

Finally we may note that in Acts Christians are called 'those who have believed in the Lord', and 'those who call upon the name of the Lord', but never 'the baptized'.[15] The essential characteristic of the Christian and that which matters on the human side is in the last analysis faith and not water-baptism. The sacrament 'acts on' faith, but only faith 'acts on' God. Schweizer is therefore correct when he states: 'For Luke baptism is simply a natural episode in what he regards as much more important, namely conversion'.[16]

(*d*) Finally, what is the relation between baptism (which expresses faith) and Spirit (who is given to faith)? The sacrament and the heavenly gift must certainly not be identified.[17] As water-baptism

[13] Stonehouse 84; Bruce, *Book* 75. See also Lambert 89; Lake and Cadbury, *Beginnings* IV 26; Kittel 39–41.
[14] Cf. Kittel 40–42; Wilkens, *TZ* 23 (1967) 33f.     [15] Lambert 90.
[16] *TWNT* VI 411; cf. Munck, *Paul* 18 n. 1.
[17] 'All Christian baptism is baptism in the Holy Spirit' (Richardson 350; cf. Schlier, *Zeit* 114; von Allmen 32). It is fairly commonplace to say that water-baptism 'confers', 'gives', 'is the source of', 'mediates', 'communicates', 'procures', 'imparts', 'brings' or 'bestows' the Spirit – e.g., O. C. Quick, *The Christian Sacraments* (1927) 184; Marsh 154f.; *Confirmation Today* (1944) 9f.; Bornkamm 46, 48; Lampe, *Seal* 33, 66; Cullmann, *Baptism* 10; Kuss 104f.; Davies 104; Bultmann, *Theology* I 138; Beasley-Murray 112; Haenchen 498f.; Conzelmann, *Theology* 100; Wikenhauser 54.

does not convey forgiveness, so it does not convey the Spirit. There is absolutely no ground for saying that the Holy Spirit is given by or through water-baptism – especially in Luke. With Jesus the baptismal rite was only preparatory to his anointing with the Spirit, which took place after it was completed and while he was praying. If, as seems most likely, the Christian practice of water-baptism from the first was simply a continuation and adaptation of the Johannine rite,[18] and if, as also seems most likely, Jesus' own baptism was seen as the pattern, then it should be noted that the essentially preparatory nature of the Johannine baptism is carried over into Christian baptism. Although the fulfilment comes at once, because baptism in the name of the Lord Jesus expresses commitment to Jesus as Lord, the water-baptism itself does not effect entrance into the new age and Christian experience but only points forward and leads up to the messianic baptism in Spirit which alone effects that entrance, as John had said.

As John 3.22, 26; 4.2 indicate, Jesus' disciples seem to have continued John's baptism after joining Jesus, for a time at least. After Pentecost they would simply resume the practice, though with a deeper significance and as a rite of initiation. Although there is a high degree of continuity between the two rites they cannot simply be equated, otherwise the Samaritans' baptisms would have been repeated in Acts 8 as that of the Ephesians was in Acts 19. See also pp. 20f., 87 n. 8.

It is only when the emphasis is put in its proper place in the complex of conversion-initiation – viz. on the anointing with the Spirit – that the parallel between Christian conversion-initiation and Jesus' experience at Jordan becomes clear. *This* parallel seems to be drawn in the NT, whereas that between Christian baptism and Jesus' baptism is not (II Cor. 1.21; I John 2.20, 27; also the way in which sonship is closely linked with the reception of the Spirit in both – Rom. 8.15; Gal. 4.6). One becomes a Christian by sharing in the 'christing' of the Christ.

The preparatory nature of Christian baptism is clearly indicated by the fact that the baptism in the Spirit (with its purely metaphorical use of 'baptism') continues into the Christian era to be regarded as the fulfilment of John's water-baptism, and continues to be set

[18] 'Had John not baptized there would probably be no Christian baptism' (Büchsel 141). See further H. Mentz, *Taufe und Kirche in ihrem ursprünglichen Zusammenhang* (1960) 34, 41–52; and cf. G. Braumann, *Vorpaulinische Taufverkündigung bei Paulus* (1962) 30–50, 80f.

in contrast with the latter (Acts 1.5; 11.16).[19] That is to say, in Luke's view, the fulfilment of John's water-baptism is *not* Christian water-baptism,[20] far less that curious hybrid unknown to the NT, Christian water-and-Spirit baptism,[21] but Spirit-baptism.[22] And in the Christian era Christian water-baptism takes over the subsidiary and preparatory role previously filled by John's water-baptism – still a baptism of repentance, still a condition of receiving the Spirit (2.38).[23] In Acts the two baptisms remain distinct; for it is a striking fact that in no case is the Spirit given through water-baptism or even simultaneously with water-baptism. For Luke there are only two baptisms – water-baptism and Spirit-baptism (Luke 3.16; Acts 1.5; 11.16). In the former, 'baptism' means only the rite of immersion (or perhaps effusion) and nothing more; in the latter, it means only the (manifest) giving of the Spirit and nothing more. The view which regards 2.38 as proof that water-baptism is the vehicle of the Spirit is one which has no foundation except in the theology of later centuries. Baptism may be a necessary expression of faith, but God gives the Spirit directly to faith, as the case histories of the 120 and Cornelius make abundantly clear. The highly critical audience in 11.15–18 were not at all concerned with the issue of Cornelius's water-baptism. Only one baptism is mentioned – Spirit-baptism; God had baptized them, and that was all that mattered.

If Luke is to be our guide, therefore, water-baptism can properly be described as the vehicle of faith; but *not* as the vehicle of the Spirit. It enables man to approach God, and represents what God has done for men and still does in men, but otherwise it is not the channel of God's grace or the means of his giving the Spirit, as Acts 8 makes clear. We cannot divorce the Spirit from faith, nor (normally) water-baptism from faith; but if our understanding is to be clear and our teaching true (to Luke at least) we must distin-

---

[19] Cf. Wilkens, *TZ* 23 (1967) 32, 43f. The repeated contrast between John's water-baptism and Christ's Spirit-baptism in 11.16 coincides too closely with the distinction between Christian water-baptism and the outpouring of the Spirit in the Cornelius episode to be coincidental.

[20] Contra e.g. Foakes-Jackson 18; Bultmann, *History* 247; Oepke, *TDNT* I 543; Wilkens 105.

[21] Contra Williams 291; Rackham 30; S. Bailey, *Theology* 49 (1946) 11; Lampe, *Seal* 33; Clark 19; Richardson 357.

[22] This was why the 120 and Apollos did not need to receive Christian water-baptism.

[23] Cf. C. F. D. Moule, *Theology* 48 (1945) 247.

guish the Spirit from water-baptism. Faith reaches out to God in and through water-baptism; God reaches out to men and meets that faith in and through his Spirit.

Thus far on the purely individualistic level, but we must not forget the third party in the conversion-initiation event – the Christian community. Speaking in generalized terms, the Church, through its representative, plays a role in regard both to baptism and to the gift of the Spirit. On the one hand baptism is also to be seen as the rite of entry into the Christian community and means by which the community receives the initiate into its fellowship (2.41; 10.48). On the other hand, the community can play an important role in the gift and reception of the Spirit. Luke stresses that the Spirit comes directly from God (Acts 2.4, 33; 10.44; 11.17), but also notes that on some occasions the Spirit comes 'through' the action (which expressed the faith and acceptance) of men already Spirit-baptized (8.17; 19.6; cf. Luke 8.45–48). As Luke could not conceive of a Christian without the Spirit – the point of Acts 8 and 18.24–19.7 – so he could not conceive of a local Christian not in the company and fellowship of the Christian community gathered there. By the gift of the Spirit God accepted the individual into his Church and baptized him into the Body of Christ (in Pauline terms); by water-baptism (and sometimes the laying on of hands) the Christian community accepted the individual into the Church. In and by his water-baptism the individual committed himself both to Christ and to his people. Christian water-baptism, therefore, as Luke portrays it, was the means of entry into the Christian community, and, as the means of commitment to Christ, resulted in the reception of the Spirit. In that moment God, the Church, and the individual were all involved. As a result it can properly be said that the Spirit comes not only directly from God but also through the Church, in the sense that the love, welcome and prayer of the Church's representatives (however expressed) enables the individual the more fully to commit himself to the risen Christ and his cause and the more readily to receive his Spirit.

To sum up, if we are to understand the Lukan teaching, while recognizing that water-baptism has an essential role within conversion-initiation, and that it is (usually closely) related to Spirit-baptism through the faith which it expresses, we must nevertheless acknowledge both that Spirit-baptism and water-baptism are distinct entities and that the focus and nerve-centre of Christian conversion-initiation is the gift of the Spirit. At this point certainly Luke was no 'early Catholic', and the attention which theologians have devoted to water-baptism on the assumption (implicit or explicit) that it is the most important element in conversion-initiation and that the salvation gifts of God (including the Spirit) are somehow dependent on it, is to be regretted. Luke's writing rather reflects the early experience and practice of the Christian community when the touchstone of authenticity was not the still formless pattern of ritual but the Spirit unfettered by rite and ceremony. We may characterize that experience[24] and practice by noting that the *first* question Paul asked the twelve Ephesians was, 'Did you receive the Spirit when you believed?' *Only then* did he go on to ask, 'Into what were you baptized?' Had the first been answered in the affirmative, there would have been no need of the second. Preisker put the point well when he wrote, 'Early Christianity did not adjust itself in accordance with a cultic act, but in accordance with the act of God revealed in the giving of the Spirit.'[25]

[24] It goes without saying that in Acts the reception of the Spirit was a very vivid and 'concrete' experience (2.4; 8.17–19; 10.44–46; 19.6); see P. G. S. Hopwood, *The Religious Experience of the Primitive Church* (1936).

[25] Preisker 304; cf. Schweizer, *TWNT* VI 411; A. Schlatter, *Die Apostelgeschichte* (1948) 135; and especially Newbigin 95; see also Allen, *Spirit* 9.

# PART THREE

# X

## THE EARLY PAULINES

As we have seen, Pentecostalism is built foursquare on Acts. So far as its doctrine of Spirit-baptism is concerned Paul need not have written anything. Indeed Paul seems to be more of an embarrassment than an asset, so that time and again expositions of this doctrine conveniently ignore him, apart from a few face-saving references which are not always relevant to the doctrine as such. Two exceptions are usually I Cor. 12.13 and Eph. 1.13, which by means of often rather superficial exegesis are taken to confirm the doctrine already extracted from Acts. This means that while our primary task will be to examine the role of the Spirit and the gift of the Spirit in conversion-initiation, most of the actual debate will be not with Pentecostals but with sacramentalists, who, generally speaking, have found in Paul a richer, more consistent and more satisfying picture than the one presented by Luke.

An important methodological question must be resolved at the outset: How are we going to set about discovering Paul's mind on this subject? It would be easy to decide on a hypothesis, and then to begin with those passages which best support that hypothesis. The other, more 'difficult' and more 'obscure' passages ('difficult' and 'obscure' so far as the hypothesis is concerned, of course) can then be interpreted in the light of the 'clear' passages. For example, on the question of baptism, by starting with I Cor. 15.29 it can be argued that Paul's view of baptism was magical; or by giving central emphasis to I Cor. 1.14–17 it can be argued that Paul gave no weight whatsoever to baptism; or by making Rom. 6.1–11 determinative for Paul's theology of baptism a deeply mystical view of baptism can be formulated.

It is obvious that to treat evidence in this way is to prejudge the issue. What *a priori* grounds are there for assuming that any of these passages is the most characteristic of or has the maximum significance for Paul's thought on the subject? The possibility must be borne in mind that these passages stand at the extremes and not at the heart of his views on conversion-initiation; or again, that they are merely *ad hominem* arguments and do not lead us into the centre of Paul's own understanding.

A more serious defect of too many modern treatments of baptism is their failure to appreciate the fact that baptism is only one element in the total complex event of becoming a Christian. To focus attention on baptism, and to examine only those passages which have immediate bearing on baptism *necessarily* distorts the total picture. Most striking and most questionable is the way in which the gift of the Spirit is time and again subordinated to and interpreted in the light of baptism. Such treatments by their unbalanced approach immediately cause a question mark to be put against their conclusions.

Since Paul can speak of baptism with no mention of the Spirit and faith (e.g. Rom. 6.4), of faith with no mention of the Spirit and baptism (e.g. I Cor. 15.1–2), and of the gift of the Spirit with no mention of faith and baptism (e.g. II Cor. 1.21–22), it is needlessly misleading to speak of 'baptismal contexts' (or of Spirit- or faith-contexts for that matter). What we want are conversion-initiation contexts, whatever elements are present or absent. The most suitable approach, therefore, would seem to be to examine those passages which deal with conversion-initiation (from whatever angle) in a chronological order.[1] Although we can have no certainty about the chronological order of the Pauline letters, it so happens that the most important passages for our subject are to be found in those letters (and parts of letters) about whose chronological sequence there is wide agreement. Of course it would be a fallacy to expect that this approach will uncover a neat development in Paul's thought; but so long as we keep in mind the prime importance of circumstances (both of writer and readers) for the shape and statement of a theme, it would appear that this approach gives us the best chance of laying bare Paul's understanding of Christian conversion-initiation, and of detecting any developments and variations therein.

Since questions of date and authorship do not concern us here I will simply follow the sequence suggested by Kümmel in his

[1] I Cor. 15.29 cannot properly be regarded as a conversion-initiation

*Introduction to the New Testament* (ET 1966): Thessalonians, Galatians, I and II Corinthians, Romans, Colossians, Ephesians, Pastorals. We shall note and consider each passage which bears on conversion-initiation. In this way we should be able to discover what are the elements in conversion-initiation and what are their respective functions and relative importance, in so far as they can be viewed separately.

## I Thess. 1.5–9; 2.13

The elements in conversion-initiation of which Paul speaks here are: the Word preached, the response of faith, and the Holy Spirit. It is important to notice that the Spirit is active in both preachers and believers. It was its proclamation in the power of the Spirit which gave the Gospel its effect (and Paul his confidence), and the Thessalonians' reception of the Gospel was marked by their rejoicing in the Holy Spirit. Paul does not say how or when they received the Spirit, although the reception of the Spirit seems to be closely linked to the reception of the Word; but it was certainly a very vivid, perhaps even emotional, *experience* (v. 6).

## I Thess. 4.7f.

Here God is described as the one who is the giver of the Spirit.[2] εἰς ὑμᾶς implies that Paul regards the Spirit as in some sense possessing and the possession of each individual Christian at Thessalonica. He who lives an impure life disregards God by ignoring the Holy Spirit whose coming set him ἐν ἁγιασμῷ. Paul probably has the context of Ezek. 37 in mind in 4.8,[3] as well as the

---

passage. I take it to be an *ad hominem* argument referring to a practice of which Paul by no means approved. See Beasley-Murray 185–92; also Schnackenburg 95–102; Delling, *Taufe* 411.

[2] J. E. Frame, *Thessalonians* (ICC 1912) 156; G. Milligan, *St Paul's Epistles to the Thessalonians* (1908) 52; W. Pfister, *Das Leben im Geist nach Paulus* (1963) 15f. This is preferable to 'the Holy Spirit which God is giving you every day' (W. Neil, *Thessalonians* [Moffatt 1950] 84; so Lightfoot, *Notes on the Epistles of St Paul* [1895] 58; Swete 172; L. Morris, *The Epistles of Paul to the Thessalonians* [1959] 128), since Paul elsewhere thinks of the giving of the Spirit as a once-for-all action at conversion (Rom. 5.5; II Cor. 1.22; 5.5; [II Tim. 1.7]), and since it is almost certainly a reference to Ezek. 37.14 (καὶ δώσω τὸ πνεῦμα εἰς ὑμᾶς – see e.g. J. Grassi, *NTS* 11 [1964–65] 163). Cf. τὸν ῥυόμενον (1.10 – 'our deliverer' NEB); and τοῦ καλοῦντος (2.12). B. Rigaux, *Les Épîtres aux Thessaloniciens* (1956) prefers to read δόντα instead of διδόντα (514).

[3] Cf. Grassi, and the more general hypothesis of C. H. Dodd, *According to the Scriptures* (1952).

actual words of Ezek. 37.14 (hence the unusual εἰς); that is to say, he is thinking of God as the one who gives life to the (spiritually) dead by the gift of his Spirit – the Spirit being the breath of (spiritual) life (37.8–10, 14). We note also how closely God's call is linked with his giving of the Spirit. God's call is effectual[4] because it comes in the Word of God which the Spirit applies powerfully to the conscience and heart of man so that he responds to the call by receiving the Word and the Spirit.

## II Thess. 2.13f.

Here we have a passing mention of the way in which God brings to present effect his eternal election. It can be expressed in one of two ways: as God's effectual call through the Gospel; and as the Spirit's consecration, and their belief in the truth. In the latter case we see highlighted the two chief means to and elements in being saved: the operation of the Spirit in setting apart, and the operation of the individual in believing the truth proclaimed in the Gospel. There is no order of salvation here (ἁγιασμὸς πνεύματος, πίστις ἀληθείας), only an order of importance.

Water-baptism is entirely absent from Thessalonians. The call and the Word, the Spirit and belief are the important elements in conversion-initiation in what are probably Paul's earliest writings.

Braumann thinks that the statements about the resurrection and about redemption from the coming judgment correspond to the situation and proclamation of baptism (53); but, as we shall see, baptism in Paul is never associated directly with the thought of resurrection.

## Gal. 2.16–21

There is no doubt that we have here a conversion-initiation passage (2.16), but it is not an exposition of water-baptism.[5] Rather Paul is thinking of the spiritual transformation which is conversion. He recalls what becoming a Christian meant in his own case (ἐγώ – v. 19)[6] – it was an experience of spiritual death (to the law)

---

[4] See K. L. Schmidt, *TDNT* III 489; Milligan 26.

[5] Cf. P. Bonnard, *L'Épitre de Saint Paul aux Galates* (1953) 88f.; R. C. Tannehill, *Dying and Rising with Christ* (1967) 59; contra H. Schlier, *Der Brief an die Galater*[13] (1965) 99–103 (who even refers δικαιοῦν [2.16] to baptism [89f.]); Schnackenburg 62–65; E. Larsson, *Christus als Vorbild* (1962) 93–94; J. D. H. Downing in *Studia Evangelica* II Part 1 553f. See also pp. 115, 150 below.

[6] See H. Lietzmann, *Galaterbrief*[2] (HNT 1923) 16; A. Oepke, *Der Brief des Paulus an Galater*[2] (1957) 62; cf. E. de W. Burton, *Galatians* (ICC 1921) 132.

resulting in new life (centred on and determined by the indwelling Christ). It was not something which happened objectively 'outside of' Paul, operating externally on him; it was essentially a subjective experience, a spiritual transformation in the core of his personality. The experience may well have happened at, or better, included baptism; but to speak of it as sacramentally mediated (whatever that means) has no justification in the text.[7]

If water-baptism is not mentioned neither is the Spirit. Yet the work of the Spirit is implied more strongly than the rite of baptism. For one thing, 2.19f. is a development of the theme of justification by faith, not by works (v. 16) – a theme which Paul immediately takes up again in terms of the Spirit (3.2, 5). For another, the life which is 'Christ in me' is the same thing as the life of the Spirit in me (cf. 5.25).

For Paul ζωή is very much the result of the Spirit's operation (Gal. 3. 11–14; 5.25; 6.8; Rom. 8.2, 10; II Cor. 3.3, 6; cf. 5.4f.). The thought of Gal. 2.20 is closely parallel to that of Rom. 8.10 which is an alternative way of expressing 8.9 – 'the Spirit of God dwells in you'. Cf. H. N. Ridderbos, *The Epistle of Paul to the Churches of Galatia* (1953) 106. See pp. 95f., 105.

And for another, the crucifixion metaphor is taken up again in 5.24 as the conclusion to the exhortation: 'Walk by the Spirit and do not gratify the desires of the flesh' (5.16–24). The Spirit probably does not feature here because Paul wishes to put his primary emphasis on Christ;[8] but so far as the Pentecostal is concerned, it must be emphasized that the moment when Christ began to 'live in me' cannot be distinguished from the reception of the Spirit who is the life of 'Christ in me'.

As might be expected where justification is the underlying theme, faith is prominent as the means by which the individual receives this justification and lives out the life of 'Christ in me'.

## Gal. 3.1–5, 14

These verses are a crushing rejoinder to Pentecostal ideas about the reception of the Spirit.

(i) The reception of the Spirit is the beginning of the Christian

[7] Contra Schlier, *Galater* 99 n. 5. Cf. G. S. Duncan, *The Epistle to the Galatians* (Moffatt 1934) 71.
[8] Duncan 72.

life (vv. 2–5). ἐνάρχομαι cannot refer to anything other than the moment of becoming a Christian; the reception of the Spirit by faith is the beginning of God's good work which he will bring to completion by the same Spirit (Phil. 1.6).[9]

(ii) The gift of the Spirit and justification are two sides of the one coin.[10] The blessing of Abraham is equated with the latter in vv. 8f., and with the former in v. 14.[11] Both times the means given is faith.

(iii) The promised Spirit is what gives life.[12] The law had no power to bestow life (v. 21). Life and righteousness come by promise and faith, and the Spirit is the content of that promise[13] as experienced by man when received by faith (vv. 14–22).

(iv) It follows that the gift of the Spirit is what makes us sons of Abraham, sons of God and puts us ἐν Χριστῷ. For the promise to Abraham has a double fulfilment. It is fulfilled both in Christ as the promised seed (v. 16), and in the reception of the Spirit by individuals (v. 14). The two are complementary: the promise is fulfilled in the individual when he becomes ἐν Χριστῷ = when he receives the Spirit by faith. It is birth κατὰ πνεῦμα which gives participation in the covenant of promise, and makes the individual a child of promise (4.28f.), a son and an heir according to promise (3.18, 29; 4.7).

Becoming a Christian is therefore essentially a matter of receiving the Spirit. And the Spirit is received by the exercise of the faith which the message of Christ stirs up (ἐξ ἀκοῆς πίστεως – 3.2). The most significant thing about water-baptism here is that it is not mentioned.[14] Faith alone is the critical factor on the human side in

---

[9] Cf. C. H. Pinnock, *The Concept of Spirit in the Epistles of Paul* (University of Manchester Dissertation, 1963) 172f.; R. A. Cole, *The Epistle of Paul to the Galatians* (1965) 90. Phil. 1.6 is the only other place in the NT where both ἐνάρχομαι and the antithesis ἐνάρχομαι . . . ἐπιτελέω occur.

[10] Cf. Büchsel 428; Oepke, *Galater* 71.

[11] The two ἵνα-clauses do not express distinct, thoughts: the second expounds and explains the first (M.-J. Lagrange, *Épitre aux Galates*[2] [1926] 73; Oepke, *Galater* 76; Schlier, *Galater* 140; H. W. Beyer and P. Althaus, *Der Brief an die Galater*[9] [NTD 1962] 27; Ridderbos 128).

[12] NEB; Burton, *Galatians* 176; Schlier, *Galater* 140f. See p. 107 above.

[13] Schlier, *Galater* 141f.

[14] Cf. Bonnard 62f.; K. Stalder, *Das Werk des Geistes in der Heiligung bei Paulus* (1962) 79f. Flemington, among others, often calls attention to an aorist tense in such a context, as though that in itself implied baptism (so with reference to 3.2 [62]). Thornton calls ἐλάβετε 'a baptismal aorist' (9); so White 203; cf. A. Wikenhauser, *Pauline Mysticism* (ET 1960) 121. But there are more aorist actions in conversion-initiation than baptism, and the one which matters for Paul, here at least, is the reception of the Spirit.

the conversion complex which here revolves round preaching, faith and the Spirit.

ἀκοή can be used both for a message heard and passed on (Rom. 10.16f.; I Thess. 2.13) and for the act of hearing (I Cor. 12.17). The latter is the more appropriate sense here (Burton 147; Lagrange 58f.; Schlatter, *Erläuterungen zum Neuen Testament* 7 Teil [1928] 69f.; Ridderbos 113 n. 3): the emphasis is on the one who hears the message, and πίστις can hardly be the content of the message; moreover, the contrast with 'works of the law', the parallel with v. 14, and the καθώς in v. 6 ('As Abraham also believed') imply that vv. 2–5 are talking about the Galatians' act of faith – the response of those who heard the message.

J. K. Parratt, *ExpT* 79 (1967–68) suggests that ὁ ἐπιχορηγῶν τὸ πνεῦμα is not God or Christ but a particularly gifted individual who had the ability to bestow the charismatic Spirit – perhaps Paul himself – and that he conveyed the gift by the laying on of hands (152). But 'faith' in this context must be that of the Galatians, and it is very doubtful whether Paul would ever describe anyone other than God or Christ in such terms.

## Gal. 3.26f.

We now meet the important verb βαπτίζειν for the first time. In v. 27 Paul explains why he can speak of the Galatians as being ἐν Χριστῷ Ἰησοῦ. The reason is (γάρ) that 'as many of you as were baptized εἰς Χριστόν have put on Christ'.

Gal. 3.27 does describe the rite of water-baptism as a 'putting on Christ' or state that in baptism we put on Christ.[15] In my opinion βαπτίζεσθαι εἰς Χριστόν is simply a metaphor drawn from the rite of baptism to describe the entry of the believer into Christian experience – or, more precisely, the entry of the believer into the spiritual relationship of the Christian with Christ, which takes place in conversion-initiation.

ἐνδύσασθαι Χριστόν is obviously a metaphor.[16] It is drawn from

[15] Contra e.g. Lagrange 92; Lampe, *Seal* 112; Schnackenburg 61,106f., 205. K. Lake, *The Earlier Epistles of St Paul* (1911) thinks that this verse indicates an *ex opere operato* view of baptism (385).

[16] Beasley-Murray 147f.; cf. Schnackenburg 24. Christ is hardly thought of either as the water of baptism which the baptisand 'puts on' by being immersed (cf. R. T. Stamm, *IB* 10 [1935] 518f.; D. Mollat, and Y. B. Tremel in *BNT* 73, 192), or as the robe which the initiate puts on after his baptism. Flemington expounds: 'As they robed themselves again, it meant that *in that very moment* they "put on Christ"' (57, my italics). But it is highly unlikely that the initiate's action in re-robing had gained a formal ceremonial or sacramental significance at this early stage (Lightfoot, *Galatians*[10] [1890] 27; H. A. A.

Hebrew tradition where the figure of changing clothes to represent an inward and spiritual change was common (e.g. Isa. 61.10; Zech. 3.3ff.).[17] As the middle voice and the parallel uses (especially Rom. 13.14; Col. 3.10; Eph. 4.24) indicate, it signifies an act of the will – a responding to Christ and a commitment to Christ whereby the life and character (that is, the Spirit) of Jesus is received (henceforth to be manifested in a new way of life), and whereby participation in the καινὴ κτίσις (6.15), in the new humanity of Christ is granted (3.29). Quite possibly the metaphor was suggested by the baptisand's action of unclothing before and reclothing after baptism.[18] But it no more refers to water-baptism as such than it does in Romans, Colossians and Ephesians. ἐνδύσασθαι Χριστόν can be repeated; baptism is not – or was Paul requiring his Roman readers to be rebaptized? 'To put on Christ' is simply a figurative usage to describe more expressively the spiritual transformation which makes one a Christian. It neither describes a ritual act, nor does it say that a ritual act had this spiritual effect.

Beasley-Murray 147, and Oepke, *Galater* 89, are wrong to drive a wedge between the use of ἐνδύσασθαι here and elsewhere in Paul. The action by which a man commits himself to Christ, so that he becomes in Christ and begins to share the family likeness, is the same as the action by which he renews his commitment to Christ each day and so becomes more like Christ.

The spiritual reality of which Paul is thinking is probably the gift of the Spirit, and he would probably equate putting on Christ with receiving the Spirit of Christ.[19] (i) The coming of the Spirit in terms of an enclothing is found both in the OT and in early Christian thought.[20] (ii) Reception of the Spirit is prominent in the

---

Kennedy, *St Paul and the Mystery Religions* [1913] 188f.; W. L. Knox, *St Paul and the Church of the Gentiles* [1939] 138; Schnackenburg 25; Oepke, *Galater* 89; Delling, *Taufe* 120). All such interpretations suffer from a pedantic and unimaginative literalism.

[17] Beasley-Murray 148; see references in Lightfoot 150; Flemington 58.

[18] C. F. D. Moule, *Worship in the New Testament* (1961) 52; Beasley-Murray 148.

[19] Lampe, *Seal* 61; cf. Barth, *Taufe* 355–7. Lietzmann 23, and Ridderbos 148 n. 9, suggest that 'to put on Christ' is another expression for λαμβάνειν πνεῦμα υἱοθεσίας (Rom. 8.14f.); cf. A. Grail, *RB* 58 (1951) 508; J. Bligh, *Galatians* (1969) 325f.

[20] Judg. 6.34; I Chron. 12.18; II Chron. 24.20 – the Spirit 'put on' (ἐνέδυσεν) Gideon, Amasai, Zechariah; Luke 24.49; Herm. *Sim.* 9.24.2.

preceding context, and it is tied up with both sonship and inheritance (the twin themes of this section) in the conclusion (4.6f.) to the paragraph of which 3.26f. is a part. (iii) ὑμεῖς Χριστοῦ of 3.29 is very similar to Rom. 8.9: εἰ δέ τις πνεῦμα Χριστοῦ οὐκ ἔχει, οὗτος οὐκ ἔστιν αὐτοῦ.[21] (iv) For Paul, Christ is experienced by or as the πνεῦμα (cf. 2.20 and 4.6 – 'the Spirit of his Son').[22]

But if ἐνδύσασθαι Χριστόν is a metaphor, the same is true of βαπτίζεσθαι εἰς Χριστόν.

(i) The connection between v. 27a and v. 27b is so close that we must take the phrases as alternative and interchangeable expressions for the same reality:[23] to be baptized into Christ is to put on Christ. The sense is disrupted if we take one as a metaphor and one as a literal description of a physical act.

(ii) The context revolves round the contrast between the old covenant, where relationship with God is through the law and which is entered by an outward, physical rite, and the new covenant, where relationship with God is through the Spirit of Christ and which is entered by the act of believing; the contrast, in fact, between sonship κατὰ σάρκα and sonship κατὰ πνεῦμα (4.28f.).

(iii) Paul makes his contrast between circumcision and faith, *not* between circumcision and baptism. If baptism was an 'effective symbol' which achieved what circumcision could not achieve, Paul could have met his opponents by pointing out that in baptism all that they hoped to achieve by circumcision had already been achieved. But Paul's contrast is between circumcision and *faith*. He could not attack one material rite as he does here if at the same time he believed that another was necessary for the reception of the Spirit.[24] The Christian does not say to the Jew, 'Your rites are ineffective, but ours are effective.' He points rather to the cross and the resurrection, to faith and the Spirit.

(iv) The subject of the action denoted by ἐβαπτίσθητε is God, as comparison with I Cor. 12.13 and II Cor. 1.21 indicates. It is God who effects the incorporation into Christ, and he does it by

---

[21] So Schlier, *Galater* 175.

[22] See I. Hermann, *Kyrios und Pneuma* (1961); and pp. 95f., 107 above.

[23] L. Cerfaux, *Christ in the Theology of St Paul* (ET 1959) 336; cf. Beasley-Murray 148. Contrast Barth, *Taufe* 361.

[24] Cf. Bonnard 89. See J. Bligh, *The Heythrop Journal* 7 (1966) 61; also *Galatians* 323f.; Pinnock 173. Cf. also Dean Alford's warning in *Greek Testament* 11 122; Barth, *Dogmatik* IV/4 127.

baptizing ἐν πνεύματι, so that entry into the new relationship (καινὴ κτίσις – 6.15) is birth κατὰ πνεῦμα (4.29).[25]

(v) Whereas βαπτίζεσθαι εἰς τὸ ὄνομα refers primarily to the baptismal rite as such (see pp. 117f. below), βαπτίζεσθαι εἰς inevitably carries a local or incorporative significance. βαπτίζειν εἰς Χριστόν is a figurative way of describing the act of God which puts a man 'in Christ'.

On each of the three occasions which are decisive for its meaning the context requires βαπτίζεσθαι εἰς to bear the sense of 'baptized into' – baptized so as to become a member of the Second Adam (Rom. 6.3), of the Body of Christ (I Cor. 12.13), of Christ the sole seed of Abraham (Gal. 3.27). I Cor. 10 can hardly be determinative for the other occurrences, since it occurs in a midrashic allegory. Paul can speak of βαπτίζεσθαι εἰς τὸν Μωϋσῆν only because Moses is an allegory of Christ. See pp. 125ff. Bietenhard, *TWNT* V 274, Beasley-Murray 128f., and Schnackenburg 25, are wrong to equate the two phrases (cf. Moule, *Phenomenon* 38, 75).

In other words, to be baptized into Christ is the same thing as putting on Christ. These phrases belong to that whole series of metaphors on whose variety and richness Paul draws in an attempt to describe as fully as words permit the wonder and miracle of becoming a Christian, a son of God and offspring of Abraham.[26] None of them is to be taken literally. To focus attention on the baptismal rite is therefore to make the mistake of the child who remembers the illustration but pays too little heed to the moral drawn from it. The rite provides and lies behind the metaphor, but we cannot say from Gal. 3.26f. that it effects what it thus figuratively describes.

This does not mean that baptism was a 'bare symbol'. The fact that Paul can draw a metaphor from it indicates that the ritual act played an important role in the conversion-initiation of those addressed, and that its symbolism spoke to them in the moment of their initiation enabling them to yield the more fully to the incorporating action of God. It also clearly plays a role comple-

[25] Cf. Unger, *Bib.Sac.* 101 (1944) 244–7; J. F. Walvoord, *The Holy Spirit*[3] (1958) 139.
[26] The others are death and crucifixion (2.19f.), redemption from slavery (4.3, 5, 9,) and coming of age (4.2), birth (4.27–29) and creation (6.15). In fact, λαμβάνειν τὸ πνεῦμα is the only description of conversion which is not metaphorical.

mentary to the more important faith.[27] The balance of emphasis implies that baptism is to be understood as the expression of faith, as an 'act of faith',[28] and that only as such is it valid. But so far as this verse goes it is not possible to say that baptism plays a more important role than the putting on of clothes after baptism, for both actions equally provide metaphors for the one event of entering into spiritual union with Christ.

## Gal. 4.6f.

Strange though it may seem, Gal. 4.6, the only verse in Paul which provides strong support for Pentecostal theology, has only recently been pressed into service by the neo-Pentecostals,[29] though those who hold a high view of Confirmation have been quick to seize upon it.

What does Paul mean when he says, 'Because you are sons, God has sent the Spirit of his Son into your hearts . . .'? The suggestion that 4.6 refers either to the sense of assurance which God gives not at but after conversion,[30] or to a second stage of initiation = Confirmation,[31] must be rejected in view of what Paul has said in Gal. 3 and of the parallel in Rom. 8.14–16. As we have seen, the gift of the Spirit is for Paul the same as justification by faith; it is that which brings the individual into the covenant of promise, that which begins his Christian life (3.3, 14). It is clear that this reception of the Spirit was a conscious *experience* (3.2, 4); and Paul gives no indication that he is thinking in 4.6 of a different coming of the Spirit than that referred to in ch. 3. Rom. 8.15f. certainly cannot be understood of a later coming of the Spirit after conversion, for then 8.14 would become unintelligible.[32]

It is possible that ὅτι here has the declarative sense, 'that', or 'to

[27] In Gal. 3 faith is mentioned 15 times, βαπτίζεσθαι once. Paul might have said, 'You are all sons of God, through faith, in Christ Jesus; for as many as have *believed* into Christ have put on Christ.' Cf. Lambert 150–2; Kennedy 250.

[28] Lagrange 92.

[29] J. Baker, *Baptized in One Spirit* (1967) 13f.; Harper, *Fire* 16. But Riggs calls it 'a plain statement that the Holy Spirit comes into one's heart at conversion' (43)!

[30] Hermann 95f.; Burton, *Galatians* 222; Parratt, *EQ* 41 (1969) 165. Cf. Schlatter 104; Duncan 130; Bouttier, *Christianity according to Paul* (ET 1966) 51 n. 24; Barth, *Taufe* 325, 329; F. Prat, *Theology of St Paul* (ET 1945) II 134 n. 1.

[31] Thornton 11f., following Mason 45; Chase 87f.; Neunheuser 49f.

[32] Contra Hermann 95f.

prove that',[33] but even if we take ὅτι = 'because' the more plausible interpretation is that 4.6 refers to the gift of the Spirit at conversion-initiation whereby the objective fact of sonship accomplished by the coming (ἐξαπέστειλεν) of the Son becomes the individual's personal possession in his subjective experience.

(i) The sequence of thought in this section is logical, not chrono-logical. It is similar to the logical sequence, 'if . . . then' (v. 7). As it is the logical consequence of being a son that you should be an heir too, so it is the logical consequence of being a son that you should possess the Spirit.

Büchsel points out that Paul's use of ἐστέ (instead of ἦτε) indicates that he is not thinking of a chronological order of events (428 n. 5). If J. D. Hester, *Paul's Concept of Inheritance* (1968) is correct in thinking that Paul has in mind the Roman form of adoption with the Spirit sent to act as witness in the adoption 'transaction' (60–62), it would mean that the gift of the Spirit was part of that 'transaction'.

(ii) The chronological interpretation fails to grapple with the confusion of Paul's metaphors. In 4.1–7 Paul combines two meta-phors which do not really cohere. In the one he thinks of Christians as heirs before their conversion – only, heirs under age and no better than slaves; in fact, actually slaves to the elemental spirits of the universe. In the other he takes up the slavery metaphor: before their conversion they were slaves; Christ was sent to redeem them so that they might receive adoption to the status of sonship. In the first, becoming a Christian is seen in terms of the *heir coming of age*; in the second, it is seen in terms of the slave becoming an *adopted son*. But there is not a clean break between the two metaphors. For the idea of slavery is identified with that of minority (vv. 3f.). Thus the time of adoption is the same as the time when the son and heir comes of age. This entry upon the full rights and ex-perience of sonship is effected by the sending of the Spirit of the Son.

(iii) What unites the two metaphors is their application to the stages of salvation-history. That which is mirrored in the first metaphor and in the individual's conversion is the single break

---

[33] Lietzmann 25; Lagrange 103f; Lampe, *JTS* 6 (1955) 113; Moule, *Idiom Book* 147; J. Jeremias, *The Prayers of Jesus* (ET 1967) 65 n. 74; A. Duprez, *Recherches de Science Religieuse* 52 (1964) 421–31; NEB; JB; TEV; cf. Schweizer, *TWNT* VI 424 n. 624.

between the covenant of law and works, and the covenant of promise and faith. But the actual break between the two covenants was in two stages – the sending of the Son (ἐξαπέστειλεν – v. 4) at the incarnation, and the sending of the Spirit of the Son (ἐξαπέστειλεν – v. 6) at Pentecost.[34] And this is mirrored in the individual's conversion, in the twin aspects of adoption and the Spirit which he receives at that time.

Gal. 4.1–7 is therefore another conversion-initiation context, in which the metaphors used build up to the culminating thought of the reception of the Spirit, and the correlative concepts of sonship and inheritance.

## *Gal. 5.24f.*

This passage differs from 2.20 in two ways: the crucifixion of the flesh is self-inflicted, and the life is referred to the Spirit ('if the Spirit is the source of our life' – NEB). To become a Christian is to enter upon a life determined by the Spirit, and so determined from its first moments. If baptism is in mind,[35] the thought is of the individual's act of commitment by means of baptism. But again the Spirit is more prominent, as v. 25, the preceding context, and the parallel with Rom. 8[36] shows. Clearly for Paul and his converts there was no need to speak of baptism as such; it was much more simple to speak directly of their spiritual experience and commitment.

To sum up our study of Paul so far, we can affirm with confidence that in his early writing, the correlatives of the Spirit and faith were the dominant themes in his thought about conversion-initiation. There is no talk of a subsequent coming of the Spirit, and βαπτίζειν is used once as a metaphor for that entry into union with Christ which we otherwise call conversion.

[34] Cf. R. B. Hoyle, *The Holy Spirit in St Paul* (1927) 81.

[35] Schlier, *Galater* 263; Lietzmann 24; Oepke, *Galater* 143; Beyer-Althaus 49; Downing 553–6; E. Kamlah, *Die Form der katalogischen Paränese im Neuen Testament* (1964) 16.

[36] οἱ τοῦ Χριστοῦ: cf. Rom. 8.9; ἐσταύρωσαν τὴν σάρκα: cf. Rom. 8.13.

# XI

## THE CORINTHIAN LETTERS

THE Corinthian correspondence provides us with many conversion-initiation passages, including a number of key texts for both Pentecostal and sacramentalist.

### I Cor. 1.4–9

Here conversion is thought of in terms of a gift of grace, an enriching with spiritual gifts, a confirming of the message, a being called into the fellowship of Jesus Christ. All these terms are closely related to the Spirit.

(i) χάρις and πνεῦμα overlap in meaning where each has the sense of a concrete gift of God to man. In several places χάρις could be replaced by πνεῦμα without significant alteration of sense;[1] and in other passages χάρις is best seen as the 'clothing' with which the Spirit comes, as that whereby he manifests himself in charismata (Rom. 1.5; 15.15; I Cor. 3.10; Eph. 3.2, 8; 4.7). The latter link-up is more appropriate here since vv. 5–7, which expand and explain v. 4, speak of charismata in general and of two in particular – λόγος and γνῶσις.

(ii) The Spirit in his coming into the lives of the Corinthians enriched them with the spiritual gifts of λόγος and of γνῶσις by which he manifested himself, so that ever since they had had no lack of charismata in their assemblies (I Cor. 12.8; 14).

(iii) ἐβεβαιώθη refers to the assurance which the Spirit brings (cf. II Cor. 1.21), both within (cf. Rom. 8.15) and as a result of the charismata (cf. I Thess. 1.5f.; I Cor. 2.4f.).

(iv) The link with ἐκλήθητε (see p. 106 above) and κοινωνία (cf. II Cor. 13.14; Phil. 2.1) also suggests that the underlying

[1] See Bultmann, *Theology* I 290, also 156, 335; N. P. Williams, *The Grace of God* (1930) 110f.; Hoyle 39; cf. J. K. Mozley, *The Gospel Sacraments* (1933) 54.

thought in v. 9 is still centred on the Spirit; the gift of grace (v. 4) is the effectual call of God by means of the Gospel and the Spirit.

Thus again we see that in conversion-initiation where neither the Spirit nor baptism[2] is mentioned, it is the thought of the Spirit which lies nearest to the surface.

## I Cor. 1.10–17

This passage is a battlefield where both sacramentalists and their opponents claim the victory, v. 13 being the stronghold of the one, and v. 17 that of the other. What does it say about baptism?

(i) βαπτίζειν εἰς τὸ ὄνομα clearly means 'to baptize into allegiance to the person named' and indicates that baptism in the name of Christ is the formal act wherein and whereby the baptisand gives himself to Christ. For one thing, ἐγὼ δὲ Παύλου (v. 12) obviously means the same as ἐγὼ ἐβαπτίσθην εἰς τὸ ὄνομα Παύλου (v. 13).[3] Since the former describes the attitude of disciple to leader, the latter, to be a rebuke, must describe the action by which allegiance is given.[4] For another, the regular use of the phrase εἰς τὸ ὄνομα in contemporary transactions had the meaning, 'to the account of'.[5]

Since Corinth was a city whose very life depended on trade and commerce this meaning of the phrase must inevitably have coloured the Corinthians' understanding of vv. 13–15. Beasley-Murray and Schnackenburg follow Bietenhard in deriving the phrase from *l'šem*, but when they end up with the sense 'so as to belong to' (in discipleship) it rather indicates that *l'šem* ('for the sake of') has been influenced by εἰς τὸ ὄνομα (denoting a transference in ownership). Delling suggests that the phrase

---

[2] E. Dinkler in *Neotestamentica et Patristica* (O. Cullmann Festschrift 1962) 173–91, thinks that I Cor. 1.6f. refers implicitly to the event of baptism (177 n. 2). Schlier, *TDNT* I 603, similarly speaks of the 'baptismal terminology' of I Cor. 1.8; but Schlier looks at all such passages through baptismal spectacles.

[3] See RSV, NEB, TEV, and 3.23. Deissmann quotes the parallel where Καίσαρος means 'belonging to the Emperor' (*Light From the Ancient East* [ET 1927] 377). See also Lietzmann and Kümmel, *An die Korinther*[4] (HNT 1949) 7–8; H. Conzelmann, *Der erste Brief an die Korinther* (1969) 50.

[4] Cf. M. Goguel, *The Primitive Church* (ET 1964) 299.

[5] See Moulton and Milligan; Oepke, *TDNT* I 539f.; Prat II 465; E.-B. Allo, *Première Épître aux Corinthiens*[2] (1956) 11; E. Lohse, *Kerygma und Dogma* 11 (1965) 313 and n. 17; and particularly Heitmüller, *Im Namen Jesu* (1903) 100ff.; cf. A. D. Nock, *Early Gentile Christianity and its Hellenistic Background* (1964) 125; E. Best, *One Body in Christ* (1955) 66; Moule, *Worship* 53; A. M. Hunter, *Paul and his Predecessors*[2] (1961) 69; C. K. Barrett, *The First Epistle to the Corinthians* (1968) 47.

really means that the baptisand appropriates for himself the saving event of the cross (*Taufe* 115–18). But this is based on an overstrained interpretation of v. 13 (see below), and fails to do justice both to the phrase itself and to the context.

We need not press the actual phrase: what is important is the idea it conveys – of a change in ownership. Baptism is such a transaction, where the baptisand formally gives himself into the hands of a new Master. Paul therefore is challenging the Corinthians to remember that their baptism was performed in the name of Christ, and that thereby they are all committed to Christ and not to parties or apostles. He is the source and centre of their fellowship (v. 9) and his name is the banner under which he seeks to unite them (v. 10).

(ii) The fact that Paul fastens on the cross and baptism (as well as the unity of Christ) as sticks with which to belabour the Corinthians for their divisiveness and false partisanship, shows that the cross and baptism are in some senses determinative of the Christians' unitedly belonging to Christ. As such they are obviously related to each other. Baptism we have seen to be the means of commitment to Christ's lordship so as to belong to him. Jesus' death on the cross, on the other hand, was the purchase price (6.20; 7.23; cf. Gal. 3.13; 4.5).[6] The new owner takes possession of his property by sending his Spirit to dwell therein (6.19). The Spirit comes when the individual commits himself to Christ's lordship in baptism.

To deduce from v. 13 that Christian initiation gives the initiate a share in the salvation event of Calvary reads too much from the text and involves the more profound ideas of Rom. 6; and the different formulae ($\beta$. $\epsilon$ἰς τὸ ὄνομα as opposed to $\beta$. $\epsilon$ἰς) forbids us to go too far along this line. While the association of the two questions in v. 13 is suggestive, any link between the event of the cross and that of baptism must be based on firmer ground than 1.13 affords (contra Cullmann, *Baptism* 15; H.-W. Bartsch, *EvTh* 8 [1948–49] 91; Robinson, *Studies* 170; Delling, *Taufe* 115).

(iii) While baptism can play an important role in initiation, v. 17 makes it clear that we must not give it too much importance. For there the task of baptizing is contrasted with preaching. Now for Paul it is the preaching of the gospel which is the vital means to

---

[6] H. D. Wendland, *Die Briefe an die Korinther*[10] (NTD 1964) 48.

salvation.[7] And since he baptized only a handful, it must have been through his preaching (and their response to it) that he became the Corinthians' father (4.15) and they his workmanship and the seal of his apostleship (9.1–2), and it must have been by the gospel that he won men and sought to save men (9.19, 22; Rom. 1.16). For Paul, *the* vital element, on the human level, in winning men to Christ is the presentation of the gospel. In short, v. 17 sets water-baptism in antithesis with that through which the Spirit works to effect salvation.[8]

It has sometimes been argued that it is not baptism which Paul regards as a minor matter but the question of who performs it, since the essential thing in baptism is God's work and not the role of the baptizer.[9] But while there is some truth in this – in that the divisions in Corinth were based on who (or whose associates) had baptized whom – it must not be overlooked that this seems to have involved a false understanding of baptism itself (cf. 15.29).[10] This is why Paul contrasts not the 'performers' of baptism (God or man), but the work of baptizing itself (which had been divisive simply because it was so much the work of man), with the work of preaching (which is the instrument of God). And that is why Paul quickly points out that he has no interest in baptizing – his task is to preach the gospel; baptism is not at the heart of his salvation strategy – the key work there is given to the gospel. So, just as the abuse of circumcision led him to dispense with circumcision altogether and to exalt faith, in a similar way, when baptism was abused and its role misunderstood, he turned away from it and put its function in proper perspective by highlighting that which really mattered in the ministering and receiving of salvation. The gospel brought salvation to Corinth, but baptism brought division. Therefore Paul thanks God that he did not baptize, and directs attention away from that which had divided them towards that which had brought them all to the one Christ, pointing out that so far as his

[7] Rom. 1.16; 10.17; 15.18; I Cor. 1.21; 2.4f.; 4.15; 14.24f.; 15.1f.; II Cor. 2.14–17; 4.4–6; Gal. 3.2, 5; Eph. 5.26; 6.17; Col. 1.5f.; I Thess. 1.5; 2.13; II Thess. 3.1; (II Tim. 2.9). See also Friedrich, *TDNT* II 730–3.

[8] Cf. Hoyle 152f.

[9] Lietzmann-Kümmel 168; Wendland 15f.; Lampe, *Seal* 54; Schnackenburg 169; Delling, *Taufe* 118.

[10] Cf. J. Moffatt, *The First Epistle of Paul to the Corinthians* (Moffatt 1938) 11–12; Lietzmann-Kümmel 8; J. Héring, *The First Epistle of St Paul to the Corinthians* (ET 1962) 7; Lohse 314f., Kümmel, *Introduction* 201; Conzelmann 49f.

mission was concerned baptism had no indispensable role and only the gospel mattered.[11]

In brief, for Paul as for Luke, baptism appears to be a function of faith, man's means of response to the gospel of God. Baptism as an act εἰς τὸ ὄνομα Ἰησοῦ Χριστοῦ is man's way of accepting God's offer of salvation and of 'clinching the bargain' with God. When we look for God's means of effecting salvation we find them in the Spirit and the gospel. We can therefore say that he is the vehicle of God's saving grace as baptism is the vehicle of man's saving faith. I Cor. 1.17 may not merely be waved aside and the role it gives to baptism simply be discounted in favour of those passages which are amenable to a high doctrine of baptism. No doubt the verse comes at one extreme of Paul's doctrine of baptism, and his statement of it here has been determined by the circumstances he is addressing, but, nevertheless, it belongs to that doctrine, and unless we give it due weight we shall fail to reach the right understanding of Paul's total view of baptism.

## I Cor. 2.12

This sentence has been quoted in support of the view that there is a giving and receiving of the Spirit prior to faith in order to impart faith.[12] But in I Cor. 2.10–3.4 the basic contrast is between the Christian (πνευματικός in virtue of his reception of the Spirit) and the non-Christian (ψυχικός because he is 'devoid of the Spirit' – Jude 19). There is a distinction between Christians who are πνευματικοί in the sense of 'mature' and Christians who are yet σαρκικοί – but there is no thought of a non-Christian being πνευματικός (as having received the Spirit who then proceeds to impart faith).

Parratt also cites II Thess. 2.13; II Cor. 4.13; Gal. 5.5; I Cor. 12.3; Acts 6.5; 11.24. But II Thess. 2.13 gives the chief elements in conversion in order of importance, not in order or stages of salvation. On I Cor. 12.3 see p. 151. The other references are not relevant. The fact remains that the only reception of the Spirit which the NT talks about is the gift of the Spirit to the man who believes (πίστευσας), the gift which makes him a Christian. See p. 94 above.

## I Cor. 6.11

For most commentators this is 'a baptismal saying' by which

[11] Cf. W. Marxsen in *Apophoreta* (E. Haenchen Festschrift 1964) 173.
[12] Parratt, *Seal* 67.

many understand that baptism is the key to its interpretation. But in fact Paul is not talking about baptism at all – he speaks rather of the great spiritual transformation of conversion which turned the Corinthians' lives inside out and made immoral and impure men into saints, cleansed and justified by the authority and power of God. We may not assume that when Christians in the NT are recalled to the beginning of their Christian lives the reference is therefore to their baptism. Conversion-initiation was a much richer and fuller *experience* than the ritual act, and simply to refer all aorists which occur in such contexts to 'baptism' is quite unjustified. Converts knew that something had happened to them, not as a deduction from a ceremony performed 'according to the book', but immediately in their consciousness of the Spirit, of his cleansing, transforming power. In this total event baptism had a part, but did not play the key role. To start by asking the question, 'What does this passage teach about baptism?' is therefore to lead off on the wrong foot.

(i) ἀπελούσασθε is clearly to be understood of spiritual cleansing rather than of the washing of the body with baptismal water.[13] The decisive factor here is the context. The interpretation of ἀπελούσασθε cannot be divorced from the preceding list of vices: *these* are what have been washed away; and these are moral and spiritual matters. Whatever washes them away is a cleansing of the heart and conscience (cf. Mark 7.21f.; Acts 15.9; Heb. 9.14). ἀπελούσασθε, like ἡγιάσθητε and ἐδικαιώθητε, therefore deals primarily with matters of the heart and spiritual relationships and does not have its first reference to baptism,[14] although it may be implied that water-baptism was the occasion when this cleansing took place.

(ii) The other phrase which suggests the rite of water-baptism is ἐν τῷ ὀνόματι τοῦ κυρίου Ἰησοῦ Χριστοῦ. But in the Synoptics and Acts similar phrases are mostly used in connection with healings and exorcisms. The understanding underlying the use of the phrase ἐν τῷ ὀνόματι therefore is that the name is an expression of the power and authority of the person who bears it. To act 'in the name' of someone is to exercise his authority and power as his agent.[15] The same is true in Paul's use of the phrase (I Cor.

---

[13] Contra Flemington 56; Pfister 19; D. E. H. Whiteley, *The Theology of St Paul* (1964) 177. Cf. p. 98.
[14] Cf. Arndt and Gingrich; Barrett 141; Schnackenburg 3.
[15] See Bietenhard 270, 276f.

5.4; Eph. 5.20; Phil. 2.10; II Thess. 3.6). But in I Cor. 6.11 there
are two significant features. Firstly, it is the only time that Paul
uses it with passive verbs, where God is clearly the subject. The
thought is then not so much of *man* exercising Jesus' authority,
or of man coming to God by Jesus, but rather of *God* coming to
*man* by Jesus, by virtue of his position and power. Secondly, Paul
always uses the phrase with κύριος (including Phil. 2.10f., where
'the name' is κύριος). So here, Paul uses the name which was given
to Jesus at his exaltation as a result of his obedience to death.
Hence the thought in I Cor. 6.11 is that God acts to cleanse, sanctify and justify by the power of Jesus, crucified, raised and exalted,
by the virtue of that death, resurrection and exaltation, and by the
authority thereby won over sin, death and the worldly powers (cf.
John 14.26; 16.23; Acts 4.10; 10.43; I John 2.12). It follows therefore, that what Paul is really thinking of in his use of the phrase
ἐν τῷ ὀνόματι . . . is not the rite of baptism, but the work of God
exercising the authority and power which Jesus gained by his
victory on the cross over the sin that had so defiled the Corinthians.

(iii) The final phrase, ἐν τῷ πνεύματι τοῦ θεοῦ ἡμῶν, should probably be translated 'in the Spirit of our God'. The Spirit is then
seen as the agent and executor of God's action: he acts in (the
person of) or through (NEB) the Spirit, exercising the authority
of the Lord Jesus Christ to cleanse, sanctify and justify. It is the
Spirit who effects these things.[16] Whether he does so in conjunction with water-baptism is not in Paul's mind at this point. Paul
does not look through water-baptism to speak of the spiritual
transformation wrought in conversion-initiation. He looks directly
at the spiritual transformation itself.

All three verbs refer, of course, to the one event (of conversion-
initiation) and are all qualified by the two ἐν-phrases.[17] The
ἀπελούσασθε ἐν τῷ πνεύματι therefore speaks more or less directly of
the baptism in the Spirit[18] which effects the cleansing of the heart
(Acts 15.9) as well as incorporation into the Body of Christ (I Cor.
12.13). We see also that 'sanctification' is an initial work of the
Spirit at conversion, when he sets a man apart to live for God (cf.
II Thess. 2.13f.). That justification also takes place in the Spirit is

16 Cf. Schnackenburg 5, 29; Conzelmann 130 n. 46.
17 Contra Chase 77f.; C. A. A. Scott, *Christianity according to St Paul* (1927)
120; F. W. Grosheide, *Commentary on the First Epistle to the Corinthians* (1953)
141.
18 Cf. Braumann 37.

important, since it is such a prominent theme in Paul's letters.[19]
But it merely confirms what we found in Gal. 3.1–14. These facts
knock the Pentecostals' case on the head.

The link between the Spirit and justification is very strong: e.g.,
δωρεά in Paul is almost certainly to be confined in its sense to these two
meanings; see Gal. 3.1–5, 14; 5.5; II Cor. 3.8f.; Rom. 8.9f.; cf. Rom.
6.13–20 with 8, and Rom. 6.17 with II Thess. 2.13f.; also I Tim. 3.16;
Tit. 3.6f. With I Cor. 6.11 cf. Rom. 14.17.

We should not forget that faith is implied in the middle
ἀπελούσασθε,[20] and in the inclusion of ἐδικαιώθητε.[21] So here once
again we have tied together the three elements of conversion-
initiation which we found in Acts. The difference is that in Acts
Luke gives all three prominence but distinguishes them very clearly
from one another; whereas in his letters Paul does not bother to
distinguish them but puts all the emphasis on the spiritual transformation which God effects through the Spirit by the authority of
the Lord Jesus Christ.

## I Cor. 6.14–20

This is not really a conversion-initiation context, but it speaks
directly of the state and the relationship into which the believer
enters when he becomes a Christian. In particular, Pentecostals
should note:

(i) Verses 15 and 19 are obviously parallel and say the same
thing: to be a temple of the Holy Spirit is to be a member of Christ.
As in 12.13 the reception of the Spirit is what constitutes an
individual a member of Christ.

(ii) 6.17 is especially noteworthy, for here Paul speaks of becoming a Christian as equivalent, on the spiritual plane, to marriage or

---

[19] There are no really adequate reasons for taking δικαιόω in a sense different
from Paul's normal usage (Beasley-Murray 165; Barrett 142; Conzelmann 129;
contra Arndt and Gingrich; Bultmann, *Theology* I 136).

[20] Lightfoot, *Notes* 213; A. Robertson and A. Plummer, *I Corinthians*[2] (ICC
1914) 119; Beasley-Murray 164, 166; Barrett 141f.; Lambert 156; Kennedy
252–3; Prat II 251. But since occurrences of the passive are exceedingly rare
(Liddell and Scott, Moulton and Milligan, Arndt and Gingrich give no
examples; Lampe, *Patristic Lexicon*, gives only one, and that from the fourth
century AD) it suggests that the middle can serve for the passive. The sense is
simply, 'to let or allow oneself be . . .' (Blass-Debrunner-Funk 314, 317).

[21] Beasley-Murray 164, 166; Schrenk, *TDNT* II 216.

physical union on the physical plane.[22] Conversion-initiation unites the individual personally to Christ in such a close and intimate way, that in the resulting relationship of union they are one Spirit – not two spirits, the believer's and Christ's – just as in marriage the resulting union is one flesh. So close is the union of the Christian with his Lord that he shares the Spirit of Christ, he has the Spirit of Christ. As with physical union, there results 'a new creation that has its life only in their union'.[23] 6.17 therefore shows beyond dispute that the indwelling Spirit is inseparable from union with Christ,[24] and that the gift of the Spirit is what effects this union.

(iii) The connection of thought between vv. 19f. indicates that Christ's purchase of the individual (the purchase price being his death) is made effective by the Spirit. The Spirit is the steward who comes on behalf of the Lord Jesus to take possession of the property purchased on the cross; it is the Spirit who applies the salvation and redemption won by Jesus in his death and resurrection. This is what it means to become a Christian – to receive God's Spirit and thus come under Christ's lordship.

## *I Cor. 10.1–5*

This is usually taken as a warning against false sacramentalism: the Israelites had sacraments as we have,[25] and yet they did not preserve them from destruction; so let us beware. But this really misses the point: Paul is not saying that the Israelites had sacraments; nor is he saying that it is possible to partake of the Christian sacrament and yet be destroyed. What he is saying is that the Israelites had mighty experiences of redemption and of God's grace, and yet fell into idolatry and sin and were destroyed. These great redemptive acts of grace point to and are an allegory of the experience of redemption and grace in the Christian era and in Christ, and they warn us that there is always the possibility of those who have experienced that redemption and grace falling similarly

[22] Union with Christ 'is the eschatological fulfilment of Gen. 2.24' (N. A. Dahl, *BNTE* 439).

[23] Filson, on Matt. 19.4ff.; cf. L. Cerfaux, *The Christian in the Theology of St Paul* (ET 1967) 297.

[24] A. Schlatter, *Paulus der Bote Jesu*[3] (1962) 205. See also Percy, cited in Lietzmann-Kümmel 175.

[25] So Schweitzer 20f.; Moffatt 129; Wendland 70 (though see 73); Best, *Body* 72; W. E. Moore, *NTS* 10 (1963–64) 511; Barrett, 221–3. The great majority of commentators refer 10.1–5 directly to the Christian sacraments.

into sin and being rejected by Christ.[26] That is to say, the whole passage is an illustration (τύποι – v. 6) in an exhortation to discipline and perseverence based on (γάρ – v. 1) 9.24–27.[27]

The key to understanding this passage is to realize that Paul is using the events of the Exodus and the wilderness wanderings as an allegory of *Christian* experience.

(i) The Rock was Christ. He is not talking about Christ's pre-existence here.[28] Nor is he saying that Christ *was* the material rock or was in the rock, or provided the Israelites with water.[29] He is simply saying that Christ is the source of *our* spiritual sustenance. The equivalent in the wilderness wanderings was the Rock. Hence, to interpret the allegory he gives us the equation: the rock = Christ.

That he says 'The rock was (ἦν) Christ', and not '*is* (ἐστίν) Christ' (cf. Gal. 4.25; II Cor. 3.17) is not significant, since he makes no attempt to extend the figures of manna, rock, etc. into his own time, as he does with the figures of Hagar and the veil in Gal. 4.25 and II Cor. 3.14.

(ii) πνευματικὸν βρῶμα/πόμα. Paul is not saying that the Israelites partook of spiritual sustenance, nor that the manna and water were any more than manna and water. He is simply using the manna and water, the very real sustenance which the Israelites received from God, as an illustration of the spiritual sustenance Christians receive from Christ, their living Head.

The immediate reference of the allegory is not to the elements of the Lord's Supper, for then the equation would have been drawn between the βρῶμα and the πόμα on the one hand, and the body and blood of Christ on the other. But in v. 4 Christ is equated not with the spiritual food (cf. 12.12f.), rather with the *source* of the spiritual drink.

(iii) ἐβαπτίσαντο εἰς τὸν Μωϋσῆν. Again, Paul is not saying that the Israelites were really baptized, far less that they were baptized

[26] 'The real point of connection lay in the act of grace on God's part' (C. T. Craig, *IB* 10 [1953] 108).

[27] See Beasley-Murray 181–3; also J. C. Hurd, *The Origin of I Corinthians* (1965) 131–42.

[28] M. M. Bourke, *Studiorum Paulinorum Congressus Internationalis Catholicus 1961* (1963) I 373–5; contra Héring 85; Lietzmann-Kümmel 45; Wendland 70; Allo 231; Braumann 20; Barrett 223; Conzelmann 196.

[29] Contra H. J. Schoeps, *Paul* (ET 1961) 153; cf. Robertson-Plummer 201; Moffatt 130.

into Moses or into a relation with Moses[30] or a loyalty to Moses.[31] He is rather thinking of the Christian's baptism into Christ and using the Exodus as an illustration of the Christian's incorporation into Christ.[32]

The rationale behind this sort of Christian 'midrash'[33] is that OT events and sayings are viewed from the standpoint and in the light of the revelation brought and the redemption effected by Christ. The technique is also illustrated in Gal. 3.8; 4.21–31; I Cor. 9.8–10; II Cor. 3.7–18. Gal. 3.8: Abraham did not in fact hear the gospel itself. The words he heard can only be called 'gospel' when seen in the light of Christ; they draw their significance as gospel from Jesus and his redemptive acts. So with Isaac and Ishmael in Gal. 4: the meaning Paul sees in their births is entirely drawn from NT categories – κατὰ πνεῦμα and κατὰ σάρκα. Likewise the veil of Moses referred to in II Cor. 3 had none of the significance which Paul there sees in it for the old dispensation; its entire significance lies in the new dispensation (it is the *same* veil – 3.14). Paul might well have said of these passages what he says of the Mosaic law regarding oxen: it was not written for the sake of the oxen, but for ours; it was not really speaking about oxen, but about ministers of the gospel (I Cor. 9.8–10). So in Gal. 4 he is not really talking about Isaac and Ishmael as such, but about birth κατὰ πνεῦμα and birth κατὰ σάρκα. In II Cor. 3 he is not really talking about the veil of Moses, but about the veil over Israel's heart.

So in I Cor. 10 the Red Sea crossing and the wilderness experiences are only 'sacraments' because they are seen in the light of and draw their significance as 'sacraments' from the spiritual

---

[30] Contra Delling, *Taufe* 126.

[31] Contra Moffatt 129. This would have been expressed by εἰς τὸ ὄνομα τοῦ Μωϋσέως (see pp. 117f.).

[32] Cf. Beasley-Murray 185; Héring 86; Lietzmann-Kümmel 45; Barrett 221; Marsh 79f.; A. George in *BNT* 18; Tannehill 23f. βαπ. εἰς has its full sense (contra Schnackenburg 22f.; Delling, *Taufe* 112 n. 405); see p. 112 above. Both Moses and the Rock = Christ in the allegory; but that does not mean that the *Israelites* were baptized into Christ (contra Best, *Body* 72). One may not interpret the allegory so literally. Nor may we speak of two baptisms here, one in Spirit (cloud) prior to one in water (contra Dix, *Laying on of Hands* 9; J. Brooke, *Light on the Baptism of the Holy Spirit* [n.d.] 20), or of baptism in sea (Christian baptism) and baptism in cloud (Confirmation – before baptism!) (contra Lowther Clarke 13 n. 13). The cloud above and the sea on either side *together* constitute the Israelites' 'baptism' (see Lietzmann-Kümmel 44, 180; Schnackenburg 92f.).

[33] W. D. Davies, *Paul and Rabbinic Judaism*[2] (1955) 105; Wendland 69.

realities of the new age, the Christian era (hence they are written for *our* instruction, who live in eschatological days). In these verses Paul is not really talking about manna and water, but about the spiritual nourishment which *Christ* gives Christians; he is not really talking about a 'baptism' in the Red Sea to Moses, but of baptism in the Spirit into Christ.[34] For the Israelites these events were not sacraments; they were the events of deliverance naked and simple. But we can regard them as 'sacraments', in the same way as we can regard the Israelites as 'our fathers' (v. 1), because *their* concrete experience of (literal, physical) redemption is an allegory of *our* concrete experience of (spiritual) redemption. In the same way, *our* literal, physical immersion and eating of bread and wine are sacraments because they point to our redemption in Christ.

In short, Paul is not addressing those who *think* they are Christians because they have participated in the sacraments, but those who *are* Christians (who have been baptized into Christ and receive spiritual nourishment from Christ), and he is warning them that *they* may fall. He is contesting not so much a false sacramentalism as failure to persevere and endure.[35] As elsewhere, Paul thinks first and foremost of the redemption effected by the Spirit when he brings the believer into union with the greater Moses in his greater Exodus. Of this redemption both the Red Sea crossing and water-baptism are 'sacraments'. They are not to be equated with it, nor do they effect it. But they are superb allegories of it.

## I Cor. 12.13

As the one passage in Paul which speaks explicitly of baptism in the Spirit, I Cor. 12.13 is crucial for the Pentecostal. Various attempts have been made to bring this verse into line with his theology.

(i) Paul is here speaking neither of water-baptism nor of baptism in the Spirit, but of a third baptism – baptism *by* the Spirit, which is another name for conversion.[36] This is chiefly based on the RSV

---

[34] Paul may have mentioned the cloud first because he is thinking of the whole as baptism in the Spirit, since according to Ex. 13.21; 14.24 the Lord was in the cloud (cf. Lietzmann-Kummel 181; Wendland 71; Delling, *Taufe* 112 n. 405); Conzelmann 196. See p. 30 n. 29 above.

[35] 10.1–13 continues the warning and exhortation which began with τρέχετε – keep running – 9.24. Cf. the similar exhortation in Gal. 5.7.

[36] Riggs 58; D. J. du Plessis, *The Spirit Bade Me Go* (1963) 70; Lindsay 6; and see Bruner 40. The neo-Pentecostals have for the most part abandoned this interpretation.

translation, but the argument that ἐν has instrumental force is
supported by many scholars.[37] However, the interpretation is
almost certainly to be rejected. In the NT ἐν with βαπτίζειν never
designates the one who performs the baptism; on the contrary, it
always indicates the element in which the baptisand is immersed
(or with which he is deluged) – except, of course, when it is part
of a fuller phrase like ἐν τῇ ἐρήμῳ or ἐν τῷ ὀνόματι. And in each of
the six other passages which speak of Spirit-baptism (Matt. 3.11;
Mark 1.8; Luke 3.16; John 1.33; Acts 1.5; 11.16) the Spirit is the
element used in the Messiah's baptism in contrast to the water used
in John's baptism.

(ii) A more subtle argument is to give εἰς the force of 'in', 'for
(the sake of)', or 'with a view to'.[38] But while Luke often uses εἰς
instead of ἐν in a local sense, the confusion is rare in Paul, so that
we can always assume that in Paul it has the basic sense of '*motion
towards or into*' some goal.[39] In this case the goal is the one body,
and the effect of baptism in the Spirit is incorporation into the
Body, or alternatively union with Christ (so Gal. 3.27; Rom. 6.3f.).
Paul is talking about the operation and effect of Spirit baptism, not
the place of its performance. In no case can βαπτίζειν εἰς bear the
sense of 'to baptize (as *already*) in'.[40] Nor can we take εἰς = 'for'
here. The object of εἰς is a state not an action (as in Matt. 10.10),
and after a verb of motion like βαπτίζειν, εἰς can only have the sense
of movement towards so as to be in. There is no real parallel therefore with Matt. 10.10 and I Cor. 16.1.

Ervin, 44–47, recognizes the force of the εἰς, and admits that Paul's
statement cannot accommodate even an implicit (Pentecostal) distinc-

[37] E.g. Kennedy 239 f.; Oepke, *TDNT* I 539; Moffatt 186; Cullmann,
*Baptism* 30; Schnackenburg 28f.; Cerfaux, *Christian* 302; TEV. Those who
take ἐν = 'in' include Robertson-Plummer 272; Lietzmann-Kümmel 63;
Héring 129; J. J. Meuzelaar, *Der Leib des Messias* (1961) 90; Delling, *Taufe* 119;
Bieder 120; Barrett 288; NEB; JB; and the neo-Pentecostals Baker 7f,;
Harper, *Fire* 8; Ervin 42f.

[38] W. F. P. Burton, *My Personal Experience of Receiving the Holy Spirit* (n.d.);
K. Southworth, *The Pentecostal* I No. 3 (1965) 8–9; Prince, *Baptism* 8; also
Jordan 53–55; Baker 18–20; Harper, *Fire* 8f., 11f.; cf. Barth, *Taufe* 352.
Passages referred to for comparison are Matt. 3.11; 10.10; Acts 2.38; Rom.
6.4; I Cor. 16.1; Gal. 3.27.

[39] See Turner, *Grammar* III 255.

[40] It is the sense of 'baptized (as *already*) in' for which Prince is striving. He
has obviously forgotten Mark 1.9. He and Baker likewise misunderstand
Matt. 3.11 and the significance of NT baptism as the Rubicon step of committal without which faith and repentance were dead. See pp. 14f., 96f. above. On
Rom. 6.4 see p. 141 below.

tion between conversion and Spirit-baptism (contra Harper, *Power* 44f.; Baker 15; cf. B. Allen 8f.). In an attempt to safeguard his Pentecostal doctrine he is forced to argue that Paul's use of the phrase is quite different in meaning from that of the Gospels and Acts – an argument which undermines rather than supports that doctrine.

In short, once the initiatory and incorporative significance of the metaphor is grasped, the Pentecostal arguments fall to the ground. For Paul, to become a Christian and to become a member of the Body of Christ are synonymous. Thus, unless recourse is had to semantic sleight-of-hand with ἐν or εἰς, there is no alternative to the conclusion that the baptism in the Spirit is what made the Corinthians members of the Body of Christ, that is, Christians.[41]

On the other front, the most popular view of I Cor. 12.13 is that Paul is describing Christian water-baptism which conveys the Spirit and which incorporates the baptisand into the Body of Christ.[42] But βαπτίζειν in itself does not specify *water*-baptism.

If it invariably signified immersion *in water*, even in its metaphorical usage, we would have contradiction in sense in Mark 10.38; Luke 12.50; Acts 1.5; I Cor. 10.2 and here, and tautology in John 1.26, 31. J. Schneider's rendering of I Cor. 12.13 as, 'In one Spirit were we all (by means of baptism) baptized into one body' (*Baptism and Church in the New Testament* [ET 1957] 35) betrays his awareness that the verse cannot be presented as a straightforward reference to baptism as it stands, without the addition of some such phrase as he employs.

Paul is thinking of baptism in the Spirit; he is not speaking about water at all.[43] And to say that Paul did not distinguish outward rite and spiritual reality[44] completely ignores the fact that such a distinction lies at the heart of biblical piety from the prophets onwards,[45] a distinction of which Paul was very well aware (Rom.

---

[41] Cf. Moffatt 186; Flemington 57; Best, *Body* 69f.; Beasley-Murray 171; Schnackenburg 27; Kuss 139.

[42] Bultmann, *Theology* I 138, 333; Schlatter, *Paulus* 346; Héring 130; Beasley-Murray 169, 273; Schnackenburg 126; Käsemann 113; Clark 23; Hill 268; cf. J. Reiling, *BQ* 19 (1961–62) 343f. Surprisingly the neo-Pentecostal Christenson also refers v. 13a to water-baptism (40).

[43] Kittel 43; Wendland 97; Barth, *Taufe* 322, 328; Best, *Body* 73; Ervin 42. See also p. 18 above.

[44] Beasley-Murray 168; see also his *Baptism Today and Tomorrow* 56.

[45] Oepke, *TDNT* I 540; A. W. Argyle, *ExpT* 68 (1956–57) 196–9. See also pp. 15f. above. We can identify the two only if we say with Thornton that the Spirit acts upon and through the water of baptism (16).

2.28f.). It is their experience of the Spirit (not of water-baptism) which provides the jumping-off point for Paul's appeal to the Corinthians for a right attitude towards the exercise of spiritual gifts. It is their experience of the *one* Spirit (not water-baptism) which is the basis of their unity.[46] Paul must have been familiar with the idea of Spirit-baptism. The tradition is common to all four Gospels and prominent in the tradition of Pentecost. Rom. 5.5 (ἐκκέχυται – the 'Pentecost-word') and Titus 3.5–6 (ἐξέχεεν), if Pauline, strongly suggest that Paul was familiar with this tradition; I Cor. 6.11 (and probably 10.2) imply thought of baptism in the Spirit; and there are absolutely no grounds for denying that this is what he is talking about here.[47] This being so, it is very much to the point to remember that in the six other explicit references to Spirit-baptism the contrast is always made with the rite of the Baptist. Paul himself does not repeat the antithesis but speaks only of the Spirit-baptism which God or Christ administers.

Lampe argues that 'Pauline thought affords no ground for the modern theories which seem to effect a separation in the one action and to distinguish a "Spirit-baptism" and a "water-baptism", not as the inward and outward parts of the one sacrament, but as independent entities' (*Seal* 57). But what is the 'one action'? The 'modern theories' are as old as John the Baptist!

The fact is that for Paul βαπτίζειν has only two meanings, one literal and the other metaphorical: it describes either the water-rite pure and simple (I Cor. 1.13–17) or the spiritual transformation which puts the believer 'in Christ', and which is the effect of receiving the gift of the Spirit (hence 'baptism in the Spirit'). The metaphor is drawn from the rite, just as it was in the Baptist's (and Luke's) talk of Spirit-baptism and in Jesus' talk of a baptism of death. But neither here nor there does the metaphor include the ritual act within itself. In using the metaphor Paul is never concerned with the relation between water-baptism and the gift of the Spirit: he does not say how close or how distinct they are. Only in Rom. 6.4 and Col. 2.12 is the rite explicitly related to the reality.

That Paul is speaking of spiritual realities and spiritual relationships in metaphorical language is confirmed by 12.13c, where ποτίζειν also refers simply to the Corinthians' experience of the Spirit in conversion (aorist) – *not* to baptism, the Lord's Supper,

---

[46] Cf. Marsh 132.     [47] Cf. Beasley-Murray 203.

or confirmation, as most commentators seem to think.[48] ποτίζειν has two common meanings: to give to drink, and to water or irrigate. Paul knows both meanings (I Cor. 3.2, 6–8), and here he uses it in the second sense.

(i) In biblical Greek the passive occurs only three times, and on the other two occasions the land is the subject (Gen. 13.10; Ezek. 32.6). (ii) ποτίζειν is used with πνεῦμα on only one other occasion in biblical Greek (Isa. 29.10), and this is the only time that ποτίζειν is used to translate *nāsak*; but *nāsak* never has any other sense than 'to pour out'. (iii) In popular Greek ποτίζειν as a common agricultural term was its most frequent use (Moulton and Milligan). The use of an agricultural metaphor may seem crude to us, but it would not ring so harshly then. He has already used the same metaphor in I Cor. 3.6–8, and he may draw in another agricultural metaphor in Rom. 6.5, as he does in Rom. 11.17ff.

Evidently in v. 13c Paul is taking up the OT images where the golden age to come is seen in terms of a land and a people on whom the Spirit has been poured (Isa. 32.15; 44.3; Ezek. 39.29; Joel 2.28). As in Gal. 3.27 he switches from the metaphor of baptism to a second metaphor, almost as expressive in itself, and here even more expressive because of its OT associations. Conversion, for Paul and the Corinthians, was an experience of the Spirit which was like the outpouring of a sudden flood or rainstorm on a parched ground, and which made their lives like a well-watered garden (Jer. 31.12). This imagery would be perfectly comprehensible to Paul's readers; it is only when commentators begin trying to equate or square it with water-baptism that difficulties arise. There is no thought of water-baptism here whatsoever.

## II Cor. 1.21f.

This passage has been variously interpreted as a description either of baptism or the baptismal experience, of Confirmation or a post-baptismal experience, or of a combination of these. Once again the proper interpretation is of the experience of the Spirit in conversion-initiation. Water-baptism (far less Confirmation) does not enter the thought at all.[49]

---

[48] Cf. Lampe, *Seal* 56; Lambert 163; Kennedy 239; Schweizer, *TWNT* VI 424 n. 626.

[49] Cf. J. Héring, *The Second Epistle of St Paul to the Corinthians* (ET 1967) 12; P. E. Hughes, *Paul's Second Epistle to the Corinthians* (1962) 43–45. Contra H. Windisch, *Der zweite Korintherbrief*[9] (1924) 73; Wendland 148; Dinkler in *Neotestamentica et Patristica* (1962) 173–91.

(i) The dominant note of the passage is assurance – the certainty which is based on the faithfulness of God as expressed in Christ and in the guarantee of the Spirit.[50] This does not mean that the Corinthians received or revived their assurance by looking back to some ceremony, whether of water-baptism or of laying on of hands, or both. The experience of receiving the Spirit was vivid enough in itself, both in its external accompaniments (Gal. 3.5; I Cor. 1.4–9), moral transformation (II Thess. 2.13; I Cor. 6.9–11), enlightenment (I Cor. 2.12), joy (I Thess. 1.5–9), love (Gal. 5.22; Rom. 5.5), consciousness of sonship (Gal. 4.6; Rom. 8.15), sense of liberty and life (II Cor. 3.17; Rom. 8.2), and generally in the consciousness of his presence and power (I Thess. 1.5; 4.8; Gal. 3.1–5, 14; I Cor. 2.4f.; 6.17–19; etc). It is important to realize that for Paul (and John) one of the highest and best works of the Spirit is the assurance of salvation.[51] To refer the experience of assurance to any other source is to confess ignorance of the nature of NT Christian experience.

(ii) ὁ δὲ βεβαιῶν ἡμᾶς σὺν ὑμῖν εἰς Χριστόν. Some have argued that εἰς Χριστόν implies a reference to water-baptism.[52] On the contrary we must say that it speaks of Spirit-baptism (I Cor. 12.13) – of that act of God through the Spirit whereby he incorporates us into the Body of Christ (Gal. 3.27). The present tense implies that this union with Christ once effected at conversion is strengthened and made closer with the passing of time.[53] This process εἰς Χριστόν is best understood in terms of a growing likeness to Christ (Gal. 4.19; II Cor. 3.18). Our attachment to Christ is only made firm, and the downward pull of the flesh and sin overcome by our becoming more and more like Christ. And both the victory and the metamorphosis are the work of the Spirit (Gal. 5.16–25; Rom. 8.13; I Cor. 13; II Cor. 3.18). Therefore, we may say that as the Spirit confirms (ἐβεβαιώθη) the preaching of Christ to the heart (I Cor. 1.6; cf. 2.4f.), and is the means God uses to bring men into

---

[50] See W. C. van Unnik in *Studia Paulina* (J. de Zwaan Festschrift 1953) 215–34.

[51] D. von Dobschütz, *Monatsschrift für Pastoral Theologie* 20 (1924) 232.

[52] Flemington 67; J. C. Hindley, *Indian Journal of Theology* 9 (1960) 115. Dinkler claims that βεβαιοῦν is rooted in baptismal language, but all he cites in the NT are I Cor. 1.8 and the irrelevant II Thess. 2.17; Heb. 13.9 (179 n. 1).

[53] Cf. the idea of putting on Christ, which though accomplished at conversion-initiation (Gal. 3.27) has to be continually repeated (Rom. 13.14).

Christ (I Cor. 12.13), so he is God's instrument in establishing them into Christ.

(iii) καὶ χρίσας ἡμᾶς. Since χρίω elsewhere in the NT is used only of Jesus, Paul's choice of it here is no accident but a deliberate play on words – εἰς Χριστὸν καὶ χρίσας. Paul is almost certainly thinking of Jesus' anointing with the Spirit at Jordan (Luke 4.18; Acts 4.27; 10.38). The anointing of God which made Jesus the Christ is the same as the anointing of God which makes men Christians.[54] Since the anointing of Jesus is not to be equated with or made a part of Jesus' baptism, it follows that Paul in using χρίω is thinking of baptism in the Spirit, not water-baptism.[55]

(iv) ὁ καὶ σφραγισάμενος ἡμᾶς. In the light of Eph. 1.13; 4.30 this can only refer to the seal which is the Spirit. It is quite false to say that Paul understands the seal as water-baptism.[56] We must rather say with Schnackenburg that 'the actuality and fulness of the Spirit of God . . . dominates the Apostle's field of vision'.[57] Whatever the connection with water-baptism is, it does not feature in this passage.

That a seal implies an external mark (cf. Ezek. 9.4; Rev. 7.3) does not mean that Paul thought of baptism as the seal. Nor is the patristic usage any indication of the meaning here. I stress again that the reception of the Spirit in NT days was an event of which recipient and on-looker could not but be aware (I Thess. 1.5–9; Gal. 3.1–5; I Cor. 1.4–9; see also p. 102 n. 24; p. 132 above; John 3.8; and cf. Arndt and Gingrich, σφραγίζω; J. K. Parratt, *BQ* 23 [1969] 111–13). That the Spirit usually came at the event of baptism is probable, but it is on his coming alone that Paul fastens attention both here and in Eph. 1.13. It was only when the living consciousness and experience of the Spirit became less immediate and more a conclusion to be drawn from a ceremony rightly performed that the seal terminology came to be applied to the visible and public rite performed by men. The same is probably true of φωτισμός:

[54] ἡμᾶς refers to Christians generally, as in vv. 20 and 22. For a similar emphatic use of ἡμᾶς σὺν ὑμῖν where σύν means 'including' see 4.14.

[55] Cf. A. Plummer, *II Corinthians* (ICC 1915) 40; Delling, *Taufe* 107; contra Schlier, *TDNT* I 603; Lampe, *Seal* 52; Wendland 148; Hindley 115; Dinkler 173, 180–2.

[56] The Epistle of Barnabas (second century AD) is the first to use the seal imagery of baptism itself ( A. Benoit, *Le Baptême Chrétien au Second Siècle* [1953] 46).

[57] Schnackenburg 91. See also Delling, *Taufe* 105f.; Lohse 316 n. 25; Fitzer, *TWNT* VII 950. Cf. Lambert 166–8; Plummer 41; Lampe, *Seal* 5; Hindley 116f.; P. W. Evans, *BQ* 16 (1955–56) 172–4.

as something given by the πνεῦμα from God (Eph. 1.18 – where the clause containing πεφωτισμένους is a variant for the preceding clause – Beasley-Murray 245), and as the enlightening power of the gospel shining in our hearts with the glory of Christ (II Cor. 4.4, 6; cf. 3.18), it is closely connected in Paul's thought with the Holy Spirit. Likewise in Heb. 6.4 (cf. Acts 9.17f.; Eph. 3.3–5; 1QS 4.2; 1QH 12.11f.). χρίσμα in I John 2.20, 27 is the same. All three refer to reception of the Spirit and its effects.

Some refer the seal of the Spirit to Confirmation on the basis of the business parallel and Rom. 4.11.[58] But as to the latter, the seal of the Spirit is to be equated not with any external rite, but rather with the circumcision of the heart which was the token of the new covenant predicted by the prophets.[59] And the point about the seal in business transactions is that the transaction is not completed until the seal is affixed. Thus, in the 'transaction' of conversion-initiation it is impossible to say that the individual is a Christian until he has received the Spirit. The Spirit is the one who effects participation in the new covenant and in the Kingdom of the End – he marks the transition into the eschatological state.[60] His coming effects and marks the change in ownership and lordship – his presence protects God's property and makes it known as God's.

(v) Of the final phrase we need say no more than that the Spirit thus given is the guarantee and security for the full salvation still to come; that God's giving of his guarantee is his side of the 'transaction' of salvation; and that possession of the Spirit thus constitutes this salvation in so far as it can be enjoyed now – the first instalment, the 'down-payment'.[61]

It is the Spirit, then, and all that he effects by way of assurance and protection, transforming and empowering, who alone fills Paul's thought and terminology in these verses. Whether faith and baptism play any part in these events is quite immaterial to the thought and intention of this passage.

---

[58] Thornton 29–32. See also his *Confirmation Today* 7 and the authors cited by Lampe, *Seal* 3f.; Schnackenburg 91. Chase refers both χρίσας and σφ. to the outward sign of Confirmation (82), whereas Allo refers χρίσας to baptism and σφ. to Confirmation (*Seconde Épître aux Corinthiens²* [1956] 29–30); J. H. Crehan, however, suggests referring ἀρραβών and σφ. to baptism, and βεβ. and χρίσας to Confirmation (*A Catholic Dictionary of Theology* II [1967] 89)!

[59] Lampe, *Seal* 16,56; cf. Beasley-Murray 174.

[60] The eschatological connotation of σφραγίς is important; see Beasley-Murray 175f.

[61] See Moulton and Milligan, ἀρραβών.

## II Cor. 3

This is a crucial chapter in any attempt to understand Paul's pneumatology. It certainly cuts the ground away from under the feet of the Pentecostal.

(i) Verse 3. The Corinthians are manifestly a letter written by Christ with the Spirit of God on their hearts. From the way he speaks it is clear that Paul is thinking of the moral and manifest transformation wrought in the lives of the Corinthians by their conversion (I Cor. 6.9–11). It is this which proves that Paul's ministry and preaching is of God. Christ effected the transformation of the Corinthians by the agency of the Spirit through Paul's preaching. Unusually for Paul Christ is seen here as the giver of the Spirit.

(ii) Verses 3, 6. In his talk of a writing ἐν καρδίαις σαρκίναις and of a καινὴ διαθήκη, and in his contrast between the Mosaic law and the Spirit, Paul is obviously thinking of Jer. 31.31–33; Ezek. 36.26.[62] The new covenant is centred on the Spirit. As the written law was the foundation-stone and governing principle of the old covenant, so the Spirit is the basis and heart of the new covenant. Without the Spirit there is no new covenant. Without receiving the Spirit it is impossible to participate in the new covenant. Without the leading of the Spirit it is impossible to continue within the new covenant.

(iii) Verses 6f. The Spirit gives life. Without the Spirit there is no life. The gift of the Spirit is not an optional extra for Christians. Without him the individual is still under the law and in the dispensation of death; that is, he is no Christian. Comparison with Jer. 31.31–33 and Ezek. 36.26 makes it clear that not only is the Spirit the one who brings life, but he is himself that life.[63] He himself has replaced the law as the regulating principle of life.

(iv) Verse 8. Christianity exists in a completely *new* dispensation; Christians live in a time that is wholly different and miraculous – the time of the End.[64] This is because, and only because they have the Spirit. This is also the dispensation of righteousness (v. 9), which confirms what we have already concluded from Gal. 3: that possession of righteousness and possession of life = the Spirit, are

---

[62] Windisch 109; Lietzmann-Kümmel 111; Wendland 155; Allo 81; Héring 22; Schrenk, *TDNT* I 766; Behm, *TDNT* II 130.

[63] Cf. Windisch 106,110.

[64] Cf. Behm, *TDNT* III 449.

synonymous (Gal. 3.21). Justification is impossible without receiving the Spirit, for the gift of the Spirit effects the righteousness
which constitutes a right relationship with God.

(v) Verses 16f. It is by turning to the Spirit that the temporary
and deadly nature of the old covenant is recognized.

Verse 16 is a *pesher* citation of Ex. 34.34. Verse 17 is therefore best
interpreted as an explanatory note, expounding the passage cited, in
terms of the central theme of the chapter: 'Now "the Lord" in this
passage is the Spirit of vv. 3, 6, 8.' Of more recent commentators, see
particularly M. Dibelius, *Botschaft und Geschichte* II (1956) 128–33;
Lietzmann-Kümmel 200; J. Schildenberger in *Studiorum Paulinorum
Congressus* I 456–9; van Unnik, *NovTest* 6 (1963) 165. NEB's translation
is superb and excellently conveys Paul's meaning; so TEV. For a fuller
treatment see my article in *JTS* 21 (1970).

But even if we took κύριος = Christ and v. 17 = we cannot know
Christ except by means of the Spirit (Hermann), or together with the
Spirit (Schlatter), the result is the same for the Pentecostal. 'According
to II Cor. 3.17 the contact with the Lord is reception of the Spirit as
such' (Büchsel 428). 'For purposes of communicating redemption the
Lord and the Spirit are one' (N. Q. Hamilton, *The Holy Spirit and
Eschatology in Paul* [1957] 8). See pp. 95f. above.

It is by turning to the Spirit = receiving the Spirit,[65] that the
bondage of the law is left behind and the fullness of the Spirit
entered upon (cf. Gal. 4–5).[66] It is thus by receiving the Spirit that
a man becomes in Christ, for in this action he passes from the
dispensation of death and condemnation to the dispensation of the
Spirit and of righteousness so that the old covenant becomes
abrogated for him, something which takes place only in Christ (v.
14).[67]

In all this chapter, then, there is no thought of a second gift of
the Spirit. Indeed there cannot be. The Spirit is so much the essence
and all of the new covenant in its application to man that it is
impossible to conceive of the new covenant apart from the Spirit,
and impossible to experience the blessings of the new covenant
apart from the indwelling of the Spirit. As the Jews' experience of
the old covenant was wholly in terms of and wholly determined by
the law, so the Christians' experience of the new covenant is wholly

[65] Lietzmann-Kümmel 113.
[66] Cf. van Unnik 165f.
[67] Lietzmann-Kümmel 113; Hermann 35f.; Schildenberger 456; W.
Schmithals, *Die Gnosis in Korinth*[2] (1965) 299–308; NEB.

in terms of and wholly determined by the Spirit. As obedience to the external law was the means by which the Jew maintained his relationship with God, so obedience to the indwelling Spirit is the means by which the Christian maintains his relationship with God. To become a Jew was to take upon oneself the yoke of the law. To become a Christian is to receive the gift of the Spirit.[68]

On the other side, those who exalt the role of baptism in initiation should note that it is the gift of the Spirit which is pre-eminent in conversion-initiation.

(i) Once again we see that Paul held a very clear distinction between outward form and inward reality, for the theme of ch. 3 is the contrast between the covenant of external law and outward ceremony and the covenant of the indwelling Spirit – not between two complementary principles, but between two utterly opposed principles. The contrast would lose its force if in fact water-baptism played a determinative role in this life-giving ministry. For Paul the whole basis of religion had been radically changed, from that which operates on the external, physical plane to that which operates on the internal, spiritual plane.

(ii) Christ wrote the letter on their hearts with the Spirit; as Christ's postman, Paul delivered the letter through his ministry of preaching (vv. 3, 6).

(iii) Faith is implied in vv. 16f.: to become a Christian is a matter of turning to the Lord who is the Spirit.

(iv) Water-baptism is again absent. Its presence would add nothing to the argument or understanding. Its absence detracts not at all from the argument or understanding. On the contrary, to give it any prominence would destroy the central emphasis which Paul wishes to make. On the other hand, the concrete and vivid quality of these first Christians' experience of the Spirit is very striking. Only an overwhelming conviction and certainty could have enabled them to affirm the claim of this passage over against those who took their stand on things as they had always been. They could never have maintained their position and won adherents to it had the Spirit not been intensely real in their experience.[69]

To sum up, the foregoing exposition of the key passages in I and II Corinthians shows that neither Pentecostal nor sacramentalist can look for support here. The anointing of the Spirit is what makes a man a Christian (II. 1.21f.); the gift of the Spirit is what

[68] See also Cerfaux, *Christian* 261–89.    [69] See Hermann 29, 31, 49f., 57.

gives him participation in Christ and in the new covenant (I. 6.14–20; II. 3); the baptism in the Spirit is what incorporates him into the Body of Christ (I. 12.13). The verses which sacramentalists have referred to the rites of baptism and/or Confirmation we have found to refer to baptism in the Spirit (I. 6.11; 10.2; 12.13; II. 1.21f.). There are no grounds in these letters for identifying or conflating these two baptisms, rather the only (relevant) reference to the water-rite (I. 1.10–17) confirms if anything that Paul saw it as the expression of man's response to God and in his thought set it over against the instruments of God's saving grace – the Spirit and the Word. For the most part, however, when looking back to his readers' conversion-initiation, Paul ignores the rite and concentrates almost entirely on the often dramatic life-giving and life-transforming experience of Spirit-baptism.

# XII

## THE LETTER TO ROME

IF Romans is indeed 'the theological self-confession of Paul',[1] we may hope for still fuller insight into Paul's thought on our subject.

### Rom. 5.5

ἐκκέχυται, when connected with the Spirit, vividly recalls Pentecost. As the disciples began their Christian lives at Pentecost with the outpouring of Christ's Spirit and God's love in their hearts, so did each one begin his Christian life in these early days of Christianity. There is no question of distinguishing the initial experience of God's love, of which the perfect ἐκκέχυται speaks, from the initiating gift of the Holy Spirit. For Paul they are one. Christian conversion is nothing other than a being seized and overwhelmed by the love of God in the person of the Holy Spirit.

### Rom. 6.1–14

Paul now turns to check the antinomian *reductio ad absurdum* of the arguments he has used in the faith-works controversy. Where in the latter faith was naturally much emphasized, now in what follows the principal theme is that of death and life.

(i) It is important to grasp that the subject of Rom. 6 is not baptism but death to sin and the life which follows from it. Paul's text for 6 (if not 6–8) is given in the first words he speaks in reply to the objection of v. 1: 'By no means! How can we who have died to sin still live in it?' It is this theme, of death to sin and life to God, which Paul enlarges upon in the following twelve verses. Baptism affords the first strand of the exposition of this theme, but

[1] Kümmel, *Introduction* 221.

then he passes on from it to take up other ideas which illustrate
the central theme from different angles.[2]

Too many commentators speak as though v. 2 was not there (e.g.,
Delling confines his discussion to 6.3ff. – *Taufe* 125). On the contrary,
v. 2 is the key without which the meaning of the passage cannot be
unlocked and opened up (J. Denney, *Expositor's Greek Testament* [1900]
II 632; Lambert 171; cf. W. Sanday and A. C. Headlam, *The Epistle to
the Romans*[5] [ICC 1902] 156; J. Knox, *IB* 9 [1954] 473; J. Murray, *The
Epistle of Paul to the Romans* I [1960] 213ff.). The words βαπτίζειν and
βάπτισμα appear only in vv. 3f., and there is a break after v. 4 (RSV,
NEB, JB, TEV). Verses 3–10 as a whole are an exposition of v. 2, and
while v. 4 (οὖν) ties in closely with v. 3, it also revives the antithesis of
v. 2 (M.-J. Lagrange, *Épître aux Romains*[6] [1950] 145). The γάρ of v. 5
picks up the theme of death with Christ and death to sin, not of baptism,
and vv. 5 and 6 are further illustrations and expositions of the theme
of v. 2, not of baptism.

(ii) Paul is dealing with the spiritual reality of death to sin (and
life to God) and in vv. 3–6 he depicts this theme under a series of
different images.[3] The first metaphor we are already familiar with –
βαπτίζεσθαι εἰς Χριστὸν Ἰησοῦν.[4] It is drawn from baptism, but does
not itself describe baptism, or contain within itself the thought of
the water-rite, any more than did the synonymous metaphors of
putting on Christ (Gal. 3.27) and being drenched with the Spirit
(I Cor. 12.13). The first and only concrete reference to water-
baptism in Rom. 6 is the phrase διὰ τοῦ βαπτίσματος; this phrase
marks an extension of Paul's thought to embrace the water-rite, and
indicates the relation between the metaphors (of baptism and
burial) and the rite itself in the actual event of conversion-initiation,
as we shall see. But when βαπτίζειν is used in its metaphorical sense

[2] Cf. Mentz 30; Marxsen 172; E. Güttgemanns, *Der leidende Apostel und
sein Herr* (1966) 213 n. 14; Tannehill 7–10; Barth, Dogmatik IV/4 128f., 216;
N. Gäumann, *Taufe und Ethik: Studien zu Römer 6* (1967) 72, 126f.
[3] Cf. Schnackenburg 26, 33, 49, 54f.; O. Kuss, *Der Römerbrief* I (1957) II
(1959) 303; see also Barth, *Taufe* 245; G. Wagner, *Pauline Baptism and the Pagan
Mysteries* (ET 1967) 282.
[4] It is not to be equated with βαπτίζεσθαι εἰς τὸ ὄνομα Ἰησοῦ Χριστοῦ (contra
C. K. Barrett, *The Epistle to the Romans* [1957] 122; Barth, *Taufe* 223–6;
Larsson 55; Wagner 287 n. 121; Gäumann 74 n. 53). See p. 112 above. It is by
incorporation into the Second Adam, a corporate or inclusive personality
(5.12–21), that we share in the righteousness of Christ (cf. C. H. Dodd, *The
Epistle to the Romans* [Moffatt 1932] 86; O. Michel, *Der Brief an die Römer*[12]
[1963] 149; Beasley-Murray 135–8; Wagner 292f.; Grundmann, *TWNT* VII
789; Best, *Body* 66f.).

any element which is involved is the Spirit, and what it describes is the spiritual mystical reality of union with Christ effected by God. Union with Christ means union with his death. Of the completeness of this death the rite of baptism is an excellent symbol: the disappearance, however brief, below the surface of the water represents a burial rather well – and in this case, participation in the completeness and finality of Christ's death.

That burial cannot be separated from death is shown by E. Stommel, *Römische Quartalschrift* 49 (1954) 1–20 (cited by Schnackenburg 34): ' "The event of dying, of departure from this world, was first really concluded by burial": in the thought of the ancients, a dead man went fully into the realm of the dead only at this point.' This fact rules Barth's elaborate distinction out of court (e.g. *Taufe* 229; cf. Lambert 173; Delling, *Taufe* 128f.; Bieder 191f.).

The difficulty of taking βαπ. εἰς = βαπ. εἰς τὸ ὄνομα is clearly shown in v. 3b. It is quite inadequate to translate 'with reference to his death' (Beasley-Murray 130) or 'in the direction of his death' (Schnackenburg 34). Paul obviously means much more than that. See also Tannehill 22.

The second metaphor (v. 5) may be drawn from agriculture or horticulture: 'planted together in the likeness of his death' (AV); for in the popular speech of the day σύμφυτος had the meaning 'cultivated' or 'planted'.[5] But it is more probable that Paul has in mind the more general biological imagery of the physical and natural growth which, for example, unites in unbroken wholeness the broken edges of a wound or a bone.[6]

σύμφυτος is to be derived from συμφύομαι (to grow together) rather than συμφυτεύω (to plant together) – Grundmann, *TWNT* VII 786. We should therefore understand σύμφυτος in the sense 'grown together', 'united with'. Professor Moule suggests 'fused' as a good modern equivalent.

Our union with Christ, says Paul, was like the grafting of a branch on to the main stem so that they become one, or like the healing of

---

[5] Moulton and Milligan. Those who see a botanical metaphor here include Sanday and Headlam 157; F. J. Leenhardt, *The Epistle to the Romans* (ET 1961) 160; Cullmann, *Baptism* 13f., 30; H. Schwarzmann, *Zur Tauftheologie des hl. Paulus in Röm 6* (1950) 28–32, 103; Barth, *Taufe* 236–8; Wikenhauser 114–16; cf. Lagrange 145f.; Michel 154; Barrett 123; Bieder 193. That Paul could use such a metaphor is indicated by I Cor. 12.13c and Rom. 11.17ff.

[6] Liddell and Scott, συμφύω. See also Best, *Body* 51 n. 2.

a wound so that the body is whole; more precisely, it was the coming together of us and the ὁμοίωμα of Christ's death,[7] so that henceforth we were indivisibly united with it in continuing growth and development.

The third metaphor is quite independent of the other two – συνεσταυρώθη. It describes the negative side of coming to participate in the new creation – the complete breaking of the ties of the old creation (Gal. 2.19; 5.24; 6.14f.; II Cor. 5.14f., 17). It is only this divine operation on the spiritual plane which can effect the destruction of the body of sin, and thus end man's subjection to sin as a member of Adam and of the old order.

In short, each metaphor points directly to the spiritual reality and not to baptism, which is itself a metaphor.[8]

(iii) ὁμοίωμα is important for any understanding of Paul's thought here. It signifies neither complete identity ('that which is') nor mere similarity ('that which is similar to') but a very close likeness ('that which is precisely like').[9]

Rom. 1.23: not the image of man, but the exact *likeness* of that image. Rom. 5.14: precisely the same sin as that of Adam. Rom. 8.3; Phil. 2.7 best illustrate the point: Paul wants to stress Christ's humanity as strongly as possible; he was precisely like men, completely identified with fallen humanity.

Hence it refers neither to baptism itself[10] nor to the death of Christ itself,[11] but rather to the spiritual transformation which

[7] To supply αὐτῷ spoils the imagery. So Sanday and Headlam 157; H. Lietzmann, *An die Römer*[3] (HNT 1928) 68; Barrett 123f.; A. Schlatter, *Gottes Gerechtigkeit* (1935) 202; H. W. Schmidt, *Der Brief des Paulus an die Römer* (1963) 110; Kuss, *Römer* 299f.; also *Auslegung* 151–6; Best, *Body* 51; J. Schneider, *TDNT* V 192; Schnackenburg 36f. (who changed his mind between the first and second editions); Larsson 59f.; Beasley-Murray 134; Tannehill 30–32; Gäumann 79; F. Mussner, *Praesentia Salutis: Gesammelte Studien zu Fragen und Themen des Neuen Testamentes* (1967) 192. Cf. Rom. 8.29; Phil. 3.10. See also p. 150 below.

[8] See Kennedy 226f.; Güttgemanns 213 n. 214.

[9] Cf. Kuss, *Auslegung* 157–9; Mentz 99 n. 34; Delling, *Taufe* 130 n. 465.

[10] Contra Denney 633; Scott, *Paul* 118; K. E. Kirk, *The Epistle to the Romans* (1937) 200; K. Barth, *The Teaching of the Church Regarding Baptism* (ET 1948) 13; Bultmann, *TDNT* III 19 n. 80; Schwarzmann 33f.; Barrett 123; Schmidt 110; Neunheuser 26, 28; see also those referred to in Wagner 276 n. 79.

[11] Contra G. Bornkamm, *Early Christian Experience* (ET 1969) 76f.; cf. Beasley-Murray 134; Cullmann, *Baptisma* 113f.; Delling, *Taufe* 127f.; Tannehill 35–39 and *passim*. Otherwise Paul would simply have said εἰ γὰρ σύμφυτοι γεγόναμεν τῷ θανάτῳ αὐτοῦ (cf. Schwarzmann 38ff.).

takes place at conversion when we become united with a death to sin precisely like Christ's. That is to say, God operates on us to destroy us, in so far as we are in Adam and determined by sin. This is not something which we merely believe happens, or which happens sacramentally (whatever that means); so far as Paul is concerned there really takes place in the convert something which can be called a death, so that henceforth that which determines and motivates our conduct is no longer sin.[12] It is as real an event in our spiritual history and experience as our share in the future consummation will be. Both these events are ὁμοιώματα of Christ's death and resurrection. Both are patterned precisely on Christ's – hence the parallel between vv. 5–7 and vv. 8–10, the former affirming of the Christian what the latter affirm of Christ.[13]

So closely does our experience parallel Christ's that when we think in terms of union with Christ we can speak of both the past initiating death and the future consummating resurrection as σὺν Χριστῷ (vv. 5, 8). The tenses of v. 5 also rule out the equation of ὁμοίωμα with baptism: the individual continues in the ὁμοίωμα (γεγόναμεν), and he certainly does not continue in the baptismal water!; and ἐσόμεθα looks forward to the future somatical resurrection of Christians patterned precisely on Christ's (almost all commentators agree that grammar and sense require the repetition of ὁμοίωμα in v. 5b). The σὺν Χριστῷ of the believer's experience of Christ now is in essence no different from the σὺν Χριστῷ of his experience in the future (v. 8); as with ὁμοίωμα neither usage can be referred directly to baptism (contra Gäumann 57f.).

(iv) It is a striking fact that Paul does not link baptism with the idea of resurrection. One would think that it would be a natural extension of the symbolism of baptism to see emergence from the baptismal waters as a picture of resurrection. But v. 4b is surprising precisely because the balance of the sentence is disrupted by Paul's refusal to use this imagery.[14] For Paul at this point resurrection is still future, for the ὁμοίωμα of Christ's resurrection is the resurrection of the body (Rom. 8.11).[15] The new life in Christ in

---

[12] Cf. Gäumann 78.

[13] Bornkamm 74f.; Leenhardt, *Romans* 159f.

[14] P. Althaus, *Der Brief an die Römer*[10] (NTD 1966) 62; Mussner 191; Gäumann 48 n. 114, 75f.

[15] Verses 5, 8 cannot adequately be understood as logical futures (Michel 154; H. Conzelmann, *Grundriss der Theologie des Neuen Testament* [1967] 299; Tannehill 10–12; Mussner 192f.; Gäumann 48 n. 114, 74 n. 59).

its *present* experience (vv. 4b, 11, 13) is here a corollary to and consequence of the initiating experience of death, as it was with Christ (vv. 9–11), not of baptism.[16] Neither to this present experience of life nor to the future resurrection does Paul relate baptism, either symbolically or sacramentally. When he comes to think more fully of life in the present he does so entirely in terms of the Spirit (ch. 8).

This is the first time that baptism has been related to death in the manner of vv. 3f. It is probable, therefore, that this passage represents a development in Paul's theology of baptism and a step forward beyond the older ideas generally.[17] But he goes no further: he does not relate baptism to Christ's resurrection. The reason for this may be that for Paul at least both the sacraments were intended to speak primarily of death – of Christ's death for them and their death with Christ (see I Cor. 11.24–26). There was no need for reminders of Christ's resurrection and their life in Christ: the life of the Spirit was so real and apparent both in their own experience and in that of other Christians, that such reminders would have been superfluous. But sin was still so powerful and the flesh still so weak that there was constant need of reminding that they had died – died to sin, crucified with Christ. This is certainly the significance and lesson which Paul draws out from the symbolism in 6; whereas in vv. 4b, 11 and ch. 8 baptism has no place whatsoever.

(v) According to this passage water-baptism has two functions. First, the rite of baptism vividly depicts a burial. This is why Paul seizes upon the metaphor of baptism immediately in his exposition of the Christian as dead to sin – simply because it is the most obvious, most expressive, and most meaningful metaphor for those whose baptism marked the beginning of their Christian life. It is only one of the possible metaphors, and, as we have seen, Paul uses others to bring life and weight to his exhortation, but it is the best.

[16] Schnackenburg 58; Wagner 282f.; cf. Schlatter 203f.

[17] Cf. Kuss, *Auslegung* 183f. ἀγνοεῖτε of v. 3 is probably just the polite teacher's manner of passing on new knowledge (Kuss, *Römer* 297, citing Lietzmann on Rom. 7.1; Wagner 278). Certainly in Rom. 1.13; 11.25; I Cor. 10.1; 12.1; II Cor. 1.8; I Thess. 4.13 it conveys the idea of passing on information and teaching unknown before; and in Rom. 7.1; 10.3; II Cor. 2.11; 6.9; Gal. 1.22; I Tim. 1.13 ἀγνοέω has the sense 'to be ignorant of' rather than 'to ignore'. When he refers to past teaching or experience Paul elsewhere uses γινώσκω (v. 6) or οἶδα (I Cor. 6.19; etc.).

Second, whereas βαπτίζεσθαι εἰς has only a metaphorical significance βάπτισμα *also* and primarily refers to the water-rite itself.[18] Verse 4 indicates that the rite of water-baptism not only symbolizes burial with Christ, but also that it helps in some way to effect it (διὰ τοῦ βαπτίσματος).[19] On the testimony of Rom. 6 alone one would be justified in arguing that in Paul's view God operates 'through baptism' and by means of baptism to effect the spiritual transformation which the ceremony symbolizes.[20] But when we view Rom. 6 in the context of what Paul has said elsewhere, I am persuaded, though not without some hesitation, that we should take διὰ τοῦ βαπτίσματος as describing the believer's submission of faith to the action of God, parallel to his obedience in Christian living in response to Christ's resurrection (v. 4b). This is certainly Luke's view rather than the other, and it accords best with the teaching of I Peter 3.21, the nearest thing to a definition of baptism that the NT affords. There Noah's deliverance is described as δι' ὕδατος, the type of Christian baptism which also saves, but only in that it is the prayer or pledge of man to God. Moreover, in the preaching/faith nexus of salvation, baptism is better seen as the expression of response to the gospel than as that which makes the preaching effective. Paul could never have written I Cor. 1.17[21] or set faith so sharply against circumcision if he viewed baptism in terms of the latter alternative, and the instrumental role of baptism here (διὰ τοῦ βαπτίσματος) is parallel to that of faith in Col. 2.12b (διὰ τῆς πίστεως).[22] Baptism is best seen here, therefore, as the means and step of commitment to Christ which results in new life. Without renunciation of the old life and commitment to the new there is no death and no life. Baptism does not effect these, but it can be the vital vehicle of their expression: as the initiate surrenders himself to the baptizer, giving him control of his body so that the plunging beneath the surface of the water is wholly in his hands, so he surrenders himself to God for God to put to death and bury his old self.[23] We may even say that it is *in* and *by* the act of sur-

---

[18] Contra Leenhardt, *Baptême* 49.

[19] This phrase alone is sufficient to rule out the traditional anti-sacramentalist view: that baptism is a sign of a conversion which has *already* taken place (see e.g. Scott, *Paul* 118).

[20] So explicitly L. Fasekaš, *TZ* 22 (1966) 314f.

[21] See pp. 118f. above, and on Rom. 10 (pp. 150f.) below.

[22] Cf. Scott, *Spirit* 155. On the place of faith here see also Beasley-Murray 143ff.

[23] Cf. E. Brunner, *The Letter to the Romans* (ET 1959) 49f.

render to the baptizer that there comes to its necessary climactic expression the commitment to God which results in death and life.

### Rom. 2.28f.; 7.4-6

These two passages, closely related through the πνεῦμα/γράμμα antithesis, require a brief comment.

The teaching of 2.28f. can be put simply: external rites are not to be identified or confused with internal realities; external rites are futile and invalid, even though given by God, unless there is a corresponding internal reality (cf. v. 25); external rites and internal realities belong to distinct and even antithetical spheres, so that one cannot be said to be performed or effected by or through the other. Moreover, when we realize that Paul thinks of the circumcision of the heart in terms of the Spirit,[24] it is only a small step to parallel circumcision of the flesh and circumcision of the heart with baptism in water and baptism in the Spirit.

Rom. 7.4-6 forms a bridge between chs. 6 and 8. It is the conclusion to Paul's answer to the second objection regarding the Christian's relation to the law now that he is under grace (6.15-7.6).[25] The πνεῦμα/γράμμα contrast is therefore the climax and conclusion to Paul's reply, as it was in 2.28f.,[26] and would have led at once into ch. 8 had Paul not felt the need to explain the role of law in the life of the Christian in the light of what he has just said. In 7.4 he has taken up the marriage illustration and applied it to the Christian. The idea of dying with Christ is so important to Paul and to the preceding context that he sacrifices the exactness of the parallel in 7.1-4. The thought is therefore no different from that of 6.2-6, and what I said there applies here.

Note that the thought of union with Christ in his resurrection is still absent. It is almost as though Paul carefully steers round it; for he speaks of union with Christ in his death, and of (marriage) union with the risen Christ, but not of union with Christ in his resurrection. This confirms what we have already noted above.

The only other point to be made is that in both passages, as in II Cor. 3, his contrast between Judaism and Christianity centres

---

[24] As in II Cor. 3.6 the πνεῦμα of the γράμμα/πνεῦμα antithesis must be understood as the Holy Spirit, despite Barrett's hesitation (60) and contra Lagrange 57. See further on Col. 2.11f.

[25] For parallels see A. Nygren, *Commentary on Romans* (ET 1952) 268; Michel 166.

[26] Michel 93.

on the Spirit as the decisive new factor. It is the Spirit alone who brings life. There is no law that can give life. Nothing that can be subsumed under the head of γράμμα – no external obedience, no outward rites – can do that, only the Spirit. The Spirit is centre and heart of the new covenant, as he is by his coming its initiator. For the Christian, religion is no longer based on a set of external regulations and rites which demand subservience, but on the spontaneous driving force of sheer vitality outworking in obedience and love.

## Rom. 8.1–27

Rom. 8 is the climax of Paul's exposition of his text from Hab. 2.4. Having expounded the words ὁ δὲ δίκαιος ἐκ πίστεως in the first five chapters (and then met the objections which arose therefrom), he now turns to the word ζήσεται. The theme which was foreshadowed in 2.28f.; 5.5 and 7.6 now appears in all its splendour – the glorious unfolding of spiritual experience in Christ and of life κατὰ πνεῦμα.

Popular (Holiness) preachers have sometimes expounded Rom. 7–8 as though Paul for a long time in his Christian life experienced the defeat and despair of ch. 7; but then he discovered the secret of victory and in experience passed from the dark and depression of ch. 7 into the light and assurance of ch. 8, thereafter to enjoy it for the rest of his life. But rather we must say that conversion was the entry into man of a new principle and power, the law of the Spirit of life, which rose above and dethroned the old principle and power, the law of sin and death; conversion was the transfer from the old covenant to the new, from the realm of death to that of life (vv. 6, 13), from domination by the flesh to domination by the Spirit (cf. 2.28f.; 7.6). Only it is never so final as these clear-cut antitheses suggest, for the Christian is continually tempted to live κατὰ σάρκα – that is, to live towards God under the terms of the old covenant, severed from Christ, fallen from grace, and on the way to death once more (8.5–8, 12f.; cf. Gal. 3.3; 5.2–4, 16–18) – and all too often he succumbs to that temptation, with all the frustration and despair which it involves. He must discover the Spirit's liberating might ever anew in every new situation. He must learn not to live κατὰ σάρκα, but rather to put to death by the Spirit's strength the deeds of the body (v. 13). That is to say, the Christian life from start to finish is a matter of daily dependence on the Spirit who alone brings life.

This passage is also one of the NT's most crushing denials of Pentecostal (and 'Confirmationist') teaching.

(i) Notice how v. 2. defines and explains (γάρ) the 'no condemnation' for those in Christ, in terms of the Spirit of life and the liberation he brings. Moreover, vv. 3f. explain (γάρ) v. 2, plainly implying that the Spirit effects in experience what Christ effected by his death. Indeed, so closely connected are the Spirit and the new life which makes one a Christian (vv. 2, [5], 6) that it is no surprise when Paul equates them in v. 10 – the Spirit *is* life. Likewise, justification or right relationship and the Spirit are so closely connected for Paul – so close that each can be described as the result and outworking of the other (vv. 4, 10) – that we can draw up a similar equation: gift of Spirit = gift of righteousness.[27]

(ii) Verse 9 is the most embarrassing verse in the NT to the crude Pentecostal view (that conversion is a matter of receiving Christ and Spirit-baptism of receiving the Spirit – see p. 93 n. 5, above), for it states in the bluntest terms: If anyone does not have the Spirit of Christ he does not belong to Christ, or, as NEB puts it, 'he is no Christian'.

εἴπερ has the sense of 'if indeed', 'if after all', or 'provided that', as giving a necessary condition, but not a necessary and sufficient condition (εἰ). This distinction between εἰ and εἴπερ is clearly visible in v. 17. See Blass-Debrunner-Funk 454 (2). Paul is not doubting that his readers have the Spirit, but neither is he equating possession of the Spirit with obedience to the Spirit. A man may have the Spirit indwelling him (i.e., be a Christian), and yet not be living κατὰ πνεῦμα. We could paraphrase the second clause of v. 9 thus: 'I am assuming, of course, that the Spirit of God really is dwelling within you.'

The conclusion which Rom. 8.9–11; I Cor. 6.17; 12.4–6; 15.45 thrust upon us is unavoidable: that in Paul's experience Christ and the Spirit were one, and that Christ was experienced through the Spirit.[28] It is especially clear here where v. 10 takes up and repeats v. 9b, with the substitution of 'Christ' for 'the Spirit of Christ', and where v. 11 takes up and repeats the thought of the two preceding verses, only in terms of 'the Spirit of God'. These three phrases describe precisely the same fact and experience.

[27] Michel 191 n. 2; see also Stalder 427–30; Wendland, *TLZ* 77 (1952) 459; Büchsel 427f.
[28] Hermann; see pp. 95f. above; cf. Dodd 124; Hamilton 10f.; Pfister 91; J. Bonsirven, *Theology of the NT* (ET 1963) 294; contrast Murray, *Romans* 288.

A few Pentecostals have argued that πνεῦμα Χριστοῦ here does not mean the Holy Spirit but 'the Christlike life' (Brooke 27; I have had a similar suggestion put to me by a fairly well-known Pentecostal evangelist); cf. the distinction between the Spirit of God and Holy Spirit which Nels Ferré makes (cited by Hendry 47). But such a distinction is completely without foundation in the NT, and ignores the chief dispensational significance of the event of Christ: viz. that the Holy Spirit of God becomes so related to Jesus and the redemption he effects as to be called 'the Spirit of Christ' (see C. F. D. Moule, *The Holy Spirit in the Church,* cited by E. M. B. Green, *The Meaning of Salvation* [1965] 175f.). Fortunately such desperate shifts are rarely resorted to; see e.g., Riggs' entirely orthodox interpretation of 8.9 (13).

For the NT generally and Paul in particular the crux of conversion is the gift and reception of the Holy Spirit, who thereafter dwells within the Christian as the Spirit of Christ, giving the experience of 'Christ in me' (cf. Gal. 2.20 with 3.2–3; also Rom. 8.10 ['the Spirit is life'] with Col. 3.4 ['Christ who is our life']). This is especially clear here: since the non-Christian cannot 'have the Spirit' and only those who 'have the Spirit' are Christians, it is by coming into 'possession' of the Spirit that one becomes a Christian (8.9, 15). This has an important consequence, for it means that the thing which determines whether a man is a Christian is not his profession of faith in Christ but the presence of the Spirit. 'If anyone does not have the Spirit', says Paul, 'he is no Christian'; '*Only those* who are led by the Spirit of God are sons of God' (v. 14). He does not say, If you are Christ's you have the Spirit, or, If you are sons you have the Spirit, far less, If you have believed all the right things and/or have been baptized (and so are a Christian) you have the Spirit. In the earliest days of Christianity possession of the Spirit was a fact of *immediate* perception, not a logical conclusion to be drawn from the performance of an ecclesiastical rite. This, as we saw, is strongly emphasized in Acts.

(iii) It is evident from vv. 14–17 that it is the Spirit who effects sonship, not merely strengthens the consciousness of sonship. NEB quite properly translates πνεῦμα υἱοθεσίας as 'a Spirit that makes us sons', for unless the reception of the Spirit is the reception of sonship Paul could not have written v. 14. 'Paul specifically identifies the Spirit as the Spirit of adoption, thus equating possession of the Spirit with possession of sonship'.[29] To experience the Spirit is to

---

[29] Hester 64; see also Kuss, *Römer* 601; Pfister 79.

experience sonship, and this is simply because the Spirit is the Spirit of the Son (Gal. 4.6).

(iv) Finally, we should note v. 23: the Spirit is the ἀπαρχή of the future consummation – ἡ ἀπολύτρωσις τοῦ σώματος ἡμῶν. The redemption is in two stages: the redemption of the inner man and the redemption of the body. Both are effected by God through his Spirit, and both involve an experience of death. The former is a once-for-all sharing in Christ's death resulting in a sharing in his resurrection life, that is, his Spirit (Rom. 8.2, 9, 10). The latter is a life-long experience of Christ's death – a wasting away of the body of death until, with its final destruction at death or the parousia, it is transformed into the resurrection body (II Cor. 4.7–5.10; Rom. 8.11, 13, 17, 23). So then, his coming at conversion makes us sons (8.15), and his life-long work brings our sonship to maturity and makes us perfect sons (8.23), not just with a hidden likeness to Christ and a life hidden with Christ in God, but with the very image of God himself and manifested in glory (8.29; II Cor. 3.18; Gal. 4.19; Phil. 3.21; cf. I John 3.2) – the culminating and final work of the Spirit. Thus the Spirit is himself the ἀπαρχή – not just the foreshadowing of it but the beginning of it – the beginnings of a harvest whose reaping proceeds slowly but surely until the final ingathering and rejoicing.

## Rom. 10.9–17

This passage is important for the light it sheds on Paul's understanding of the relation between belief and baptism.[30]

(i) The reversal of the order of the verbs in vv. 9f. shows that the two verbs are not to be thought of as distinct in time, but rather as simultaneous: the act of faith (= the act of commitment) *is* the act of confession. Faith does not reach its climactic point of committal without and until the act and moment of confession. In v. 10 the distinction between belief and confession is as rhetorical as that between justification and salvation.

(ii) That the act of belief (aorists in v. 9) = the act of confession, is also implied by the quotation from Joel in 10.13. ἐπικαλέσηται can be identified only with ὁμολογήσῃς in this context: it is the calling

---

[30] Most commentators rightly accept that the baptismal confession 'Jesus is Lord' is meant here, indicating that baptism is in the background of Paul's thought.

upon the name of the Lord in the public confession of faith (at baptism) which results in salvation.

(iii) This is not contradicted by v. 14 where there is a logical, not a *chrono*logical sequence. For Paul could not say that the act of belief results in salvation *prior* to the act of calling upon the Lord (v. 14), when he has just said that it is the latter act which results in salvation (v. 13). What we must rather say is that for Paul the act of faith is inseparable from the public confession of faith = the public act of committal = the public act of calling upon the Lord. Until that act there is no saving faith.

The clear implication of this is that baptism is properly to be regarded as the expression of response to the gospel and the vehicle of commitment to the Lord. Yet we must not ignore the fact that it is the faith confessed and the confession of faith which results in justification and salvation, not the circumstances or manner in which it was made.[31]

That 'Jesus is Lord' is a baptismal confession does not mean that Paul is thinking of the baptismal confession in I Cor. 12.3. For I Cor. 12 clearly shows that Paul is thinking of such utterances ('Jesus is accursed'; 'Jesus is Lord') being made in the context of Christian worship. He is obviously not thinking of the mere statement of a proposition (for anyone could say the words), but of an inspired or ecstatic utterance which did not originate in the individual's own rational consciousness. The baptismal confession, on the other hand, is the statement of a propositional belief which then becomes a confession of commitment in and by the act of baptism. T. M. Taylor's argument that ἀββά, ὁ πατήρ was a baptismal formula has a far from adequate foundation (*SJT* 11 [1958] 62–71).

To sum up, in Romans we see a development in Paul's explicit thought about baptism, in that he relates it to the Christian's burial with Christ (6.4). Romans has also confirmed that Paul distinguished clearly between ritual and reality (2.28f.; 7.6), between metaphor (βαπτίζεσθαι) and rite (βάπτισμα) (6.2–4), and that in Paul's eyes baptism was essentially the expression of commitment to the risen Lord (10.9–17; 6.4). As baptism speaks of faith and death, so the Spirit means grace and life. The Pentecostal outpouring of the Spirit is what makes a man a Christian (5.5) and what sets his feet on the way of life – the beginning of the way to life (8.1–27).

[31] Cf. Schnackenburg 82.

# XIII

## THE LATER PAULINES

In turning to Colossians, Ephesians and the Pastorals we enter the most disputed part of the Pauline corpus. They include a number of passages which both Pentecostal and sacramentalist have sought to interpret to their own advantage.

### Col. 1.13

Paul throughout Colossians refrains from ascribing any salvific work to the Spirit – no doubt because in the circumstances he wants to give all possible prominence to Christ. But that the Spirit is the agent of God's redemptive act in the spiritual transfer from the dimension of darkness to the kingdom of the Son is implied: (i) by the similarity of the prayer in vv. 9–14 with that of Eph. 1.17ff.,[1] and the mention of σύνεσις πνευματική (Col. 1.9); (ii) by the ideas of bearing fruit (cf. Gal. 5.22f.), δύναμις, δόξα (cf. II Cor. 3.8, 18) and χαρά (cf. I Thess. 1.6; Rom. 14.17; 15.13); and (iii) by the descriptions of the spiritual transformation in terms of inheritance (cf. Rom. 8.15–17; Gal. 4.6f.) and light (cf. II Cor. 3.16–4.6), and of the spiritual deliverance in terms of βασιλεία and ἀπολύτρωσις. The thought is very close to that of Eph. 1.13f., where again occur the ideas of inheritance and ἀπολύτρωσις in close connection with the Spirit. This work of God (through the Spirit) takes place wholly on the spiritual plane – any relation it has to baptism is purely subsidiary to the thought here.

μετέστησεν is a conversion aorist, not specifically a baptismal aorist. That 'baptism represents a gulf between the two spheres of power such that only a μεταστῆναι can bring man out of the one into the other'

[1] πνεῦμα in Eph. 1.17 is the Holy Spirit referred to in the same way as in Rom. 8.15.

(Käsemann 160; cf. E. Lohse, *Die Briefe an die Kolosser und an Philemon* [1968] 74; *Confirmation Today* [1944] 10; Mollat in *BNT* 63) is a fine picture, but I question whether it was present to the mind of the author.

## Col. 2.11–13

With his usual variety of metaphors Paul once again describes Christian conversion-initiation.

(i) Verse 11. The first metaphor is circumcision. Paul is not speaking here of baptism under the figure of circumcision; he is speaking directly of the circumcision of the heart (Jer. 4.4; Deut. 10.16; 30.6).[2] He is expounding the radical nature of the spiritual transformation which takes place at conversion; as the rite of circumcision was a stripping away of part of the physical body, so the spiritual circumcision of the heart (= conversion = incorporation into Christ) is a total stripping away of the body of flesh (= the body of sin [Rom. 6.6] = the body of death [Rom. 7. 24]).This spiritual circumcision experienced by the initiate when he becomes a Christian is a participation in the circumcision of Christ – that is, most likely, in the death of Christ.[3]

Delling argues that the three ἐν-phrases in vv. 11–12a are parallel and really identical. But there is no real parallelism. The first two ἐν-phrases, ἐν τῇ ἀπεκδύσει and ἐν τῇ περιτομῇ, stand very close together as one phrase dependent on περιετμήθητε; whereas ἐν τῷ βαπτίσματι stands in a separate, though closely related clause, governed by συνταφέντες. Secondly, the first of the three instances of ἐν has an instrumental sense, whereas the other two have a more local sense. And, thirdly, the ἀπέκδυσις and the περιτομή cannot be identified with the βάπτισμα.

That Paul is thinking of spiritual realities, and is making a very clear distinction between inward and outward, spiritual reality and physical rite, is shown by his use of ἀχειροποίητος. This operation which takes place in the innermost being of man and affects his total personality is 'purely spiritual' and 'invisible'.[4] It is the work

[2] Lightfoot, *Colossians and Philemon* (1875) 181; Lampe, *Seal* 56; Beasley-Murray 158. As Beasley-Murray points out, the baptismal language does not really begin until v. 12a (153).
[3] See C. F. D. Moule, *The Epistles to the Colossians and to Philemon* (1962) 94–96.
[4] E. F. Scott, *The Epistles of Paul to the Colossians, to Philemon and to the Ephesians* (Moffatt 1930) 44; E. Lohmeyer, *Die Briefe an die Philipper, Kolosser und an Philemon*13 (1964) 108; F. W. Beare, *IB* 11 (1955) 196; so Lambert 180; Beasley-Murray 153 n.1; Bieder 59; H. Martin, *BQ* 14 (1951–52) 220.

of God, not of man. It is deliberately contrasted with the physical, external, visible rite of circumcision. It is not baptism which is so contrasted with circumcision: Paul never says to his Jewish opponents, Our baptism is a more effective ceremony than your circumcision; rather he contrasts an outward rite with its corresponding inward reality. So here it is the spiritual, internal, invisible work of God in the heart of man on which Paul focuses.[5]

(ii) Verse 12a. The second metaphor is that of burial in baptism. συνταφέντες like ἀπέκδυσις can be nothing other than a metaphor, and βάπτισμα can be nothing more than the rite of water-baptism as such, seen in its symbolical significance. Immersion, that is to say, symbolizes burial, and so the completeness of the death experienced by the Christian by his participation in Christ's death.[6] Of course, he is thinking of a baptismal rite which was actually performed, whereas the rite of circumcision was not performed on Christians; yet his attention is focused primarily on what they *both* symbolize. As he had distinguished between inward and outward, spiritual and ritual with the one, so a similar distinction is implicit in his use of the other. βάπτισμα indicates that the rite of baptism is here taken up; the whole phrase indicates that it is the spiritual reality which baptism symbolizes which is at the centre of the thought.

(iii) Verse 12b. The third metaphor is resurrection. This is a new metaphor independent of the previous two. They described the negative side of becoming a Christian – the stripping away and burial of the individual in his bondage to the flesh. The third metaphor describes the converse, the positive side of this change – participation in Christ's resurrection. Paul is not still thinking in terms of baptism; nor is he thinking of emergence from the baptismal waters as a resurrection or as symbolical of resurrection. The ἐν ᾧ which begins v. 12b should not be referred to baptism but to Christ – 'in whom', not 'in which'.[7]

---

[5] See also Argyle 198.    [6] See pp. 141, 144 above.

[7] This is the normal view among the chief Continental expositors: M. Dibelius and H. Greeven, *An die Kolosser, Epheser an Philemon*[3] (HNT 1953) 31; Lohmeyer 111; Schlatter, *Erläuterungen* 7 Teil 278; C. Masson, *L'Épître de Saint Paul aux Colossiens* (1950) 126 n. 4; Kuss, *Auslegung* 153 n. 14; Schnackenburg 68; Delling, *Taufe* 124; Barth, *Taufe* 259; W. Marxsen, *Introduction to the New Testament* (ET 1968) 182; Lohse, *Kolosser* 156 n. 4; English-speaking exegetes however usually refer ἐν ᾧ to baptism (T. K. Abbott, *Ephesians and Colossians* [ICC 1897] 251f.; Scott 45; Flemington 62; Beasley-Murray 153f.; F. F. Bruce, *The Epistle to the Colossians* [1957] 234 [more doubtfully]; RSV; NEB; TEV).

To explain more fully: vv. 9–12 is a single unit in the long sentence vv. 8–15. Christ is the principal theme of this unit. Paul is meeting head on any attempt to disparage Christ or to diminish his role in redemption. The whole emphasis is therefore on Christ, and on the fact that redemption and fulfilment is accomplished *in Christ*.

ἐν αὐτῷ dwells the fullness of deity bodily;
ἐν αὐτῷ you have come to fullness of life;
ἐν ᾧ καὶ you were circumcised with a spiritual circumcision . . .
    being buried *with him* in baptism,
ἐν ᾧ καὶ you were raised through faith in the working of God who
    raised *him* from the dead.

We might say that vv. 11f. are an expansion of v. 10's ἐστὲ ἐν αὐτῷ πεπληρωμένοι; vv. 11–12a describes the negative side and v. 12b the positive side of that coming to fullness of life in Christ. Each time he stresses that it was *in him* that these things took place.

It is the ἐν ᾧ καὶ which is repeated, not the αὐτῷ. The inclusion of διὰ τῆς πίστεως also tells against a reference to baptism, since Paul nowhere else explicitly links faith and baptism so closely. To refer ἐν ᾧ to Christ does make for an awkwardness of thought since the verb following is a συν-compound, and so carries the sense of raised *with* him. But it is no more awkward than the precisely parallel passage in Eph. 2.4–6 – καὶ συνήγειρεν καὶ συνεκάθισεν ἐν τοῖς ἐπουρανίοις ἐν Χριστῷ Ἰησοῦ. The closeness of the parallel in fact tells in favour of taking ἐν ᾧ of Christ (whether it is the same author following the same line of thought or a disciple copying his teacher's idiosyncrasies). Nor can we say that this awkwardness of thought is one Paul would avoid – rather it is thrust upon him by his liking for the twin ideas of being ἐν Χριστῷ and of experiencing the saving events σὺν Χριστῷ. Cf. Masson 126 n. 5.

Both structure, theme and emphasis therefore demand that ἐν ᾧ be referred to Christ.

It is best, therefore, to follow Rom. 6 and to separate the idea of resurrection from that of baptism (though not, of course, from death with Christ). For Paul baptism symbolizes the finality of death in burial, and no more. He has advanced, at least in his explicit theology, from Rom. 6 in that he considers resurrection with Christ to be a thing of the past – to be part of the event of becoming a Christian (Col. 3.1).[8] But he has not yet come to the

---

[8] Contra Tannehill, who asserts, without sufficient proof, that Col. 2.11–13 is a more primitive form of the baptismal motif than Rom. 6 (10).

point where he sees baptism as symbolical of resurrection. The most he says here is that baptism symbolizes (and helps the baptisand to come to) the point of death with Christ. This participation in Christ's death has as its converse participation in his resurrection, so that the new Christian shares in Christ's resurrected life.

(iv) Verse 13. The fourth metaphor is again different. Where previously Paul had looked at conversion under the different aspects and figures of circumcision, burial and resurrection, now he sums up the event of becoming a Christian with one pregnant phrase – συνεζωοποίησεν ὑμᾶς σὺν αὐτῷ. It need hardly be said that baptism as a rite and symbol is not in his mind in this metaphor. His thought centres entirely on that first thrilling, never-to-be-forgotten experience when the risen life of Christ flooded his being and raised him from his darkness and death to newness of life in Christ.

Although the Spirit is not mentioned, the spiritual operation here spoken of cannot be understood apart from him or his work. He is God's agent in resurrection (Rom. 8.11) and in ζωοποίησις (Rom. 8.11; II Cor. 3.6; cf. I Cor. 15.45; Gal. 3.21), for he is himself the new life of the Christian (Rom. 7.6; 8.2, 10; I Thess. 4.8), and the risen life of Christ cannot be experienced or lived out except by or through the Spirit (Rom. 8.5–6, 13; Gal. 5.25). Spiritual circumcision also is the work of the Spirit and the gift of the Spirit. The circumcision which matters is the circumcision of the heart effected by the Spirit (Rom. 2.28f.). We are the circumcision, because we have been circumcised by the Spirit, and having thus received the Spirit, we worship by the Spirit of God (Phil. 3.3). There is also the link through the 'seal' metaphor. Circumcision was the seal (σφραγίς) of the righteousness of Abraham's faith (Rom. 4.11). The Spirit is God's seal on the Christian (II Cor. 1.21 – σφραγισάμενος; Eph. 1.13; 4.30 – ἐσφραγίσθητε). The gift of the Spirit is therefore to be equated with the circumcision of the heart (cf. Deut. 30.6 with Jer. 31.33 and Ezek. 36.26f.).

For the occasion when Judaism called circumcision a seal see Fitzer, *TWNT* VII 947. Barrett thinks the evidence too late to prove that the Jews spoke of circumcision as a seal in NT times, though it is a reasonable conjecture that they did so speak (*Romans* 92). The link between the circumcision of the heart and the Spirit in the Odes of Solomon is striking: 'My heart was circumcised . . . For the Most High circumcised me by his Holy Spirit . . . And his circumcision was my salvation' (11.1–3 – Bauer's translation in Hennecke-Schneemelcher, *NT Apokryphen* II [1964]). See also *The Gospel of Thomas*, Logion 53.

It is important to grasp this point: that the fulfilment of circumcision is *not* baptism but the gift of the Spirit. Neither does baptism fulfil the prophetic hope of spiritual circumcision; only the Spirit does that. Circumcision was not abrogated and set aside by Paul because a new rite of initiation had taken its place; he never and nowhere contrasts or compares the two. Circumcision has been set aside because that which it looked forward to and pictured has taken its place – the circumcision of Christ – not only on the cross but also in the hearts of believers. That is to say, baptism and circumcision are related not because baptism fulfils the hope of spiritual circumcision, but because both vividly depict Christ's death and the reality of the spiritual transformation effected by the Spirit in the heart of the convert.

It would be quite wrong to conclude that for Paul baptism was *only* symbolical. The συνταφέντες αὐτῷ ἐν τῷ βαπτίσματι indicates that baptism was also the occasion of the spiritual transformation depicted by burial (and circumcision), and to some extent the means of burial with Christ. The burial took place in the rite of water-baptism, and baptism was the occasion on which the individual was circumcised with the invisible circumcision of the Spirit. This does not mean that baptism effected that circumcision and that burial. It means simply that the baptisand surrendered himself to the cutting edge of the Spirit's knife by submitting himself to baptism. So we see that once again, as in Rom. 6, Paul uses βάπτισμα in two ways: first, for its symbolical significance – as circumcision's stripping away of the flesh images the stripping away of the body of flesh, so the sinking below the water's surface images the burial of the old nature; second, because it was the occasion and means towards the spiritual operation – the stripping away and burial took place 'in baptism', in the self-surrender of the individual at one and the same time, in one and the same action, both to the baptizer and to God, the water-baptizer and the Spirit-baptizer respectively. We have no justification for giving ἐν τῷ βαπτίσματι a deeper significance than this.[9]

[9] Even if the ἐν ᾧ is referred to baptism in v. 12b, the ἐν can be given only local significance, since the instrumental function is attributed to faith.

*Col. 2.20–3.14*

As with 1.13 some commentators like to believe that the aorists
of 2.20; 3.1, 3, 9f. refer to baptism.[10] This again makes the mistake
of externalizing what is primarily a spiritual transaction. Baptism
may play a part in it, but baptism is not at all the focus of attention.
For one thing, the idea of burial does not appear – and, as we have
seen, it is to the idea of burial that Paul usually links baptism as a
rite.[11] And for another, the fact that he can urge them to repeat
what they did once at the beginning of their Christian lives
(ἐνδύσασθε – v. 12; ἐνδυσάμενοι – v. 10) implies that the putting off
and putting on at conversion-initiation was essentially a spiritual
act of self-renunciation and commitment (cf. 3.5 with Rom. 8.13).
How it was expressed is not relevant here – for he is certainly not
asking them to repeat their baptism. Paul's mind is wholly on the
spiritual change which can be represented under the different
figures of death and resurrection, disrobing and enclothing, not on
baptism.[12]

If 3.5–17 is an example of a primitive Christian catechism, the recognized form of teaching given to inquirers seeking baptism (see e.g.
Moule, *Colossians* 113f.; Kamlah 36), we should note that the important
thing in what is required of the initiate is not baptism itself (which is
not mentioned) but the commitment expressed in it. The import of the
instruction to the initiate was that he should not go forward to baptism,
unless in and by that act he put off the old man and put on the new.
However, the metaphors are so common and natural that I am not
convinced of the necessity to refer them to a common source or
occasion.

*Eph. 1.13f.; 4.30*

Eph. 1.13 is one of the few Pauline(?) verses much used by
Pentecostals in defending their theology of Spirit-baptism: '. . .
after that ye believed, ye were sealed with that Holy Spirit of
promise' (AV – with the 'after' emphasized).[13] But this sort of

---

[10] Lightfoot 200, 206f.; Abbott 272, 278; Masson 135, 143; Beare 208ff.;
Lohse, *Kolosser* 180, 205f.; Mollat 74; Beasley-Murray, *Baptism Today and
Tomorrow* 6f.; Schweizer, *NTS* 14 (1967–68) 3; cf. Bruce 258, 272.
[11] See also Schnackenburg 72.
[12] Cf. Dibelius-Greeven 40; Scott, *Colossians* 62. See also pp. 109f. above.
[13] Riggs 54, 61; Horton 13; Brooke 21f.; Prince, *Jordan* 7of.; B. Allen 9;
but cf. Harper, *Power* 44. For the equivalent interpretation in Holiness
teaching see e.g. Cumming 145.

exegesis, as we have already noted, is based on a fundamental misunderstanding of Greek grammar.[14] The aorist participle does in fact usually express antecedent action, but it is the context, not the grammatical form, which determines this.[15] And the context here indicates that we should take the two verbs as the two sides of the one event: it was when they believed that God sealed them with the Spirit. As in Gal. 3.2, the step of faith is met by the gift of the Spirit.

(i) The whole section vv. 3–14 is a unity. It is based on v. 3, and the rest of the verses describe what are the blessings of the heavenly realm.[16] The whole sentence revolves round and reverberates with ἐν Χριστῷ (vv. 3, 4, 6, 7, 9, 10, 10, 11, 12, 13, 13). These are the blessings with which the individual is blessed when he becomes a Christian, that is, when he comes to be ἐν Χριστῷ. And the chief of these is the gift of the Holy Spirit, for the whole sentence moves forward majestically to the climax of vv. 13f., so that all the blessings can be rightly described as belonging to and coming from the Holy Spirit.[17]

(ii) Words like ἐπαγγελία, κληρονομία, περιποίησις show how much Paul is thinking of the Christian Church as the new Israel.[18] The Spirit is the essence of the new covenant of promise (as in Gal. 3.14). He is the eschatological seal who marks out Christians as the people of the End-time. It is only by receiving the Spirit that one becomes a member of the new Israel, the new covenant, the new age.

(iii) The Spirit is only the ἀρραβών of the Christian's inheritance. That is to say, the gift of the Spirit is the first instalment of that fullness of eternal life to which the Christian looks forward – the ἀπολύτρωσις τῆς περιποιήσεως. As the part- or down-payment, the ἀρραβών is part of and the same as the whole. In other words, the Spirit is the initial gift of salvation. He not only guarantees the completion of salvation (which ἀρραβών also signifies); he is himself the beginning of that salvation. It is only when he is received that the individual begins to be saved.

[14] See pp. 86f. above.
[15] Burton, *Moods and Tenses* 61.
[16] H. Schlier, *Der Brief an die Epheser* (1957) 39.
[17] Schlier 66.
[18] B. F. Westcott, *St Paul's Epistle to the Ephesians* (1906) 14–16; J. A. Robinson, *St Paul's Epistle to the Ephesians*[2] (1904) 36, 146; Scott, *Ephesians* 149f.; Schlier, *Epheser* 66f.

(iv) Since the Spirit is God's seal, the 'transaction' of conversion-initiation is completed only when God gives a man the Spirit and thus marks him as henceforth his property alone, marks him out for the day of final liberation (4.30 NEB).

In short, to receive the Spirit by faith is to become a Christian.

On the other front, any identification of the seal of the Spirit with baptism[19] or confirmation[20] is to be rejected. The thought centres wholly and solely on the Spirit given by God as his own distinctive seal. But notice once again the old Pauline link-up between hearing the Gospel, believing, and receiving the Spirit. So far as Paul is concerned, these are the indispensable elements in the nexus of conversion-initiation. In particular, the emphasis on faith is rather striking. Instead of writing simply ἐν ᾧ καὶ ἐσφραγίσθητε, Paul obviously thinks it important to insert πιστεύσαντες, even though the net result is a very awkward clause. This is no doubt because faith for Paul is the only, but also the vital prerequisite for receiving the Spirit (cf. 1.15, 19; 2.8; 3.12 with 2.18).

### *Eph.* 2.4–6

Some maintain that Paul is speaking of baptism here,[21] principally on the grounds of the undoubtedly close parallel between 2.5 and Col. 2.13. But this thesis cannot be sustained.

(i) Col. 2.13, as we saw, completely changed the metaphor from that to which baptism was attached. There is nothing of burial here, and the death spoken of is a pre-Christian state, not part of the conversion event. συνήγειρεν recalls Col. 2.12b, but that too was detached from βάπτισμα; and here it is yoked with συνκάθιζεν which is hardly a suitable figure for baptism.

---

[19] Most recently by G. Johnston: 'Those who accept it are "sealed", baptized, in water; in and through this water the Spirit of God floods their life' (*Ephesians, Philippians, Colossians and Philemon* [1967] 11); and Kirby 153f. Scott makes the astounding claim that 'frequently in the NT baptism is called a seal' (*Ephesians* 148). But see p. 133 above.

[20] Westcott 16; Schlier, *Epheser* 70; cf. *The Theology of Christian Initiation* 23; Thornton, *Confirmation Today* 9; and see p. 134 n. 58 above. Schlier's discussion at this point is typical of his sacramentalism.

[21] Schlier, *Epheser* 109–11; Schnackenburg 73–78. See also Larsson 106; Bieder 225–7; and those cited by Kümmel who contend that Ephesians is 'a "post-baptismal mystery discourse" addressed to recently baptized Christians to remind them of their baptism' (*Introduction* 251); cf. Bultmann, *Theology* I 142f.; Bouttier, *Paul* 39; Kirby 154ff. Schlier even thinks that Paul understands baptism as a heavenly journey (111), presumably with Reitzenstein's exposition of the meaning of Mandaean baptism in mind (see Wagner 21f.).

(ii) The thought is all upon the spiritual transition (σὺν Χριστῷ and ἐν Χριστῷ) from the aeon of death to that of life, effected by the divine ζωοποίησις. This is the work of the Spirit (Rom. 8.6, 10; II Cor. 3.6).

(iii) Their becoming Christians is summed up by the two key words – χάρις and πίστις – grace on God's side, faith on man's (2.5, 8). It is the interaction of these which effects salvation, though we may say that the Spirit is always the embodiment and vehicle of the one, while baptism is properly the embodiment and vehicle of the other.

## *Eph. 4.1–6*

This passage appears to indicate the respective roles of the Spirit and baptism in Christian conversion-initiation.[22] The principal thought is that of unity, as it is of the whole epistle. But before elaborating on the theme he designates it as unity of the Spirit – unity which is the work and gift of the Spirit. Unity is determined by the Spirit and maintained by the Spirit (I Cor. 12.12f.; Phil. 2.1; Eph. 2.18).

The unity of the Spirit is then elaborated in terms of seven great unities. These are to be grouped in a 3:3:1 scheme, as the balance of the sentence and the εἷς, μία, ἕν formula of the second triad indicates.[23] This means that πνεῦμα is in the middle of the first triad. And this is not accidental, for otherwise we would have expected πνεῦμα to come first, so that the first member of each of the three lines would give the climax ἓν πνεῦμα, εἷς κύριος, εἷς θεός. Moreover, it is evident that it is the Spirit which binds the other two members of the triad together. The unity of the body is effected and maintained by the Spirit (v. 3); and the Spirit is the substance and ground of the Christian's hope, for 1.18 identifies the hope with the κληρονομία of which the Spirit is the guarantee (1.14).

This probably implies that the same holds true of the second triad; that is, it is faith which binds together κύριος and βάπτισμα. Faith is one because it is directed to the one Lord, and has the one Lord as its ground and content.[24] And baptism is one because it

---

[22] The absence of any mention of the Lord's Supper implies that Paul is thinking about the initial conditions of the Christian life (Westcott 58f.; Schlier, *Epheser* 158 n. 2).

[23] Abbott 107; Robinson, *Ephesians* 93; Dibelius-Greeven 79; Schlier, *Epheser* 185.

[24] Schlatter, *Erläuterungen* 7 Teil 202.

expresses the one faith. The thought is essentially of the one Lord confessed in baptism (cf. Rom. 10.9f.). Thus we might well say that as the Spirit brings into union with the one Body and makes valid the one hope, so faith brings into union with the one Lord, and makes valid the one baptism.

Paul is not talking here about subjective experiences or spiritual transformations – not even when he speaks of faith and hope: they are both seen objectively and concretely (C. Masson, *L'Épître de Saint Paul aux Éphésiens* [1953] 186; Beasley-Murray 200). This confirms that in the Pauline use βάπτισμα is the external act of water-baptism as such and nothing more.

The fact that baptism is linked here with faith confirms that the water-rite stands on the side of man's faith rather than on the side of God's grace.[25] The fact that baptism is included in the list implies that baptism was regarded as the only legitimate way for faith to come to (initial) visible expression. But the position baptism is given shows that it was only important because of the faith it expressed, and because it was the act of commitment to the one Lord. The one God's response is to give the one Spirit who incorporates into the one Body and gives the one hope. And thus is established the unity of the Spirit.

## *Eph. 5.25–27*

The primary reference here is once again to the spiritual cleansing and sanctification which is the work of the Spirit, and as such the essence of conversion-initiation. Most think that the explicit mention of water can only be explained by a reference to water-baptism, though a few refer the phrase to Christ's death on the cross.[26] But the λουτρὸν τοῦ ὕδατος refers rather, in the first instance, to the customary pre-nuptial bridal bath, as the context clearly shows.

The thought of vv. 25–27 is entirely centred on the bridal analogy. Verse 25 regards the relation of Christ to the Christian in terms of husband and wife, and v. 27 thinks of the parousia as a wedding: 'in order that he might present (παραστήσῃ) the Church (as a bride) to

[25] The first triad consists of elements given by God; the second triad of elements in man's response.

[26] Kittel, who emended ῥήματι to αἵματι; Robinson, *Studies* 169; Barth, *Taufe* 472; Church of Scotland, *Biblical Doctrine* 38.

himself in glory' (Reicke, *TWNT* V 839; Schlier, *Epheser* 258; and cf. II Cor. 11.2). Verse 27 indicates the purpose of the action described in v. 26: the washing has the purpose of making the bride clean for her wedding (the second ἵνα-clause is *immediately* dependent on v. 26, but ultimately, of course, on v. 25). It is surely most natural and most in keeping with the analogy, therefore, to see the λουτρὸν τοῦ ὕδατος as part of the analogy, that is, as the bridal bath which precedes and prepares for the wedding. The other alternative is to say that he takes up the marriage metaphor in v. 25, drops it in v. 26, and takes it up again in v. 27. But this is a far less plausible interpretation. Moreover, the bride-analogy is common in Scripture: Matt. 25.1; Mark 2.20; John 3.29; Rom. 7.2-4; I Cor. 6.17; II Cor. 11.2; Rev. 19.9; 21.2; 22.17; in the OT see Isa. 54.4f.; 62.5; Hos. 2.14-17, 19f.; also Jer. 3.8; Ezek. 16.8-13. If indeed Ezek. 16.8-14 is the background of this passage (J. A. T. Robinson, *The Body* [1952] 82 n. 1) it is not at all surprising that the author extended the analogy to include the bridal bath, since Ezek. 16.8 explicitly speaks of washing ἐν ὕδατι. Those who accept the reference to the bridal bath include Kennedy 251; Cerfaux, *Christ* 310; see also those cited in Schnackenburg 5; Delling, *Taufe* n. 375.

The question then becomes: If the wedding equals the parousia in the analogy, to what does the bridal bath refer? Some would reply, 'To baptism'; but we should rather refer the image directly to the inner cleansing and sanctifying operation of the Spirit.[27]

(i) The spots and wrinkles etc. (v. 27) depict the blemishes and ravages of sin. As the bridal bath washes away all dirt and spots, so God's cleansing washes away all sin.

(ii) It is Christ who effects the washing, and his instrument of cleansing is not water but that which water so often signifies in Scripture – the Spirit.

(iii) The bride is the Church. To say that *the Church* is literally washed in water is rather artificial;[28] it is much easier to think of the Church, as Church, cleansed and sanctified by the Spirit (cf. 4.4). That is to say, we must go immediately from the figure of the bridal bath to the spiritual reality of cleansing, and not via water-baptism. It is in and by the Spirit's incorporation into the Body,

[27] Cf. E. K. Simpson, *The Epistle to the Ephesians* (1957) 121-32. Those who think baptism is probably referred to under the image of the bridal bath include Westcott 84; Abbott 168; Lambert 178; Prat II 216 n. 2; Masson 212; F. W. Beare, *IB* 10 (1953) 722-3; N. A. Dahl, *Kurze Auslegung des Epheser-briefes* (1965) 70; Bieder 166; cf. F. Foulkes, *The Epistle of Paul to the Ephesians* (1963) 158f. Beasley-Murray is uncertain (201).

[28] H. Conzelmann, *Der Brief an die Epheser*[10] (NTD 1965) 87.

the Church, that one participates in the Spirit's cleansing and sancti-fying of the Church (cf. I Cor. 12.13).

(iv) The verb which describes the cleansing (καθαρίζειν) has long since left the cultic sphere of ritual purity, and in NT religion it stands for a spiritual and moral cleansing and purifying.[29] It is the word which breaks down the old barriers between clean and un-clean (Mark 7.19; Matt. 23.25f.; Luke 11.39; Acts 10.15; 11.9), so that Peter's defence of his conduct with regard to Cornelius is that God cleansed (καθάρισας) their hearts by faith (Acts 15.9). It appears only three times in the Pauline literature. Titus 2.14 shows the sense clearly, and again in II Cor. 7.1 a moral cleansing is in view.

(v) Likewise ἁγιάζειν can only be referred to a spiritual opera-tion. In Paul ἁγιάζειν is one of the *Holy* Spirit's great works (Rom. 15.16; I Cor. 6.11; I Thess. 4.7f.; II Thess. 2.13; I Cor. 3.16f.) – the one whereby he sets aside the convert for God; and that takes place not on the cross nor at Confirmation, but in conversion-initiation, for it is that which makes one a Christian.[30]

(vi) Contrary to the opinion of most exegetes, ῥῆμα means 'preaching (of the gospel)',[31] not a baptismal confession, far less a baptismal formula. The determinative Pauline passages are Rom. 10.8, 17: there τὸ ῥῆμα of the Deut. 30.14 citation is defined as 'that which we preach'; and we are told that faith comes from the mes-sage, and the message through the proclamation of Christ (διὰ ῥήματος Χριστοῦ). This is the meaning of the two occurrences of ῥῆμα in Eph. 5.26; 6.17. It is preaching of God which the Spirit uses as his sword. And it is preaching which the Spirit uses to cleanse the heart of the believer (cf. James 1.18, 21; I Peter 1.23).[32]

ῥῆμα = 'preaching' is usually anarthrous in Paul. The article appears with ῥῆμα in Rom. 10.8 only because 'τὸ ῥῆμα' takes up the citation of Deut. 30.14 (the standard pesher technique). The absence or presence of Χριστοῦ or θεοῦ is immaterial to the sense. I question whether τὸ ῥῆμα should be regarded as the confession spoken of in Rom. 10.9. The most probable original text of 10.9 does not contain τὸ ῥῆμα. Paul has already interpreted τὸ ῥῆμα of Deut. 30.14 as 'that which we preach' (10.8). In

[29] Hauck, *TDNT* III 417, 423–6.
[30] See also Beasley-Murray's criticism of the Robinson-Barth interpreta-tion (201f.).
[31] Lambert 176f.; Meuzelaar 89 n. 2; Foulkes 158; cf. E. K. Simpson 131 n. 35.
[32] This accords well with the Pauline emphasis that preaching is a decisive factor in conversion (see p. 119 n. 7 above).

10.9 he proceeds to take up and interpret the latter phrases of Deut. 30.14, in typical pesher fashion, using them to define *the response to the* ῥῆμα rather than the ῥῆμα itself. Further, the absence of the article in Eph. 5.26 tells against referring ῥῆμα to the baptismal confession. For the confession seems to have had standard forms from very early on, and a reference to it would more likely be to '*the* confession' (as in Heb. 4.14; 10.23; cf. I Tim. 6.13); whereas preaching the gospel could take a great variety of forms, and could be referred to simply as '(a) proclamation (of the gospel)', as it is in Rom. 10.17 and Eph. 6.17. Only when Eph. 5.26 is referred directly to baptism as such does ἐν ῥήματι cause difficulty and have to be forced into speculative and less natural meanings – a fact worth noting in the context of this whole investigation.

(vii) Finally, we have seen that Paul uses baptism primarily as a metaphor and a symbol. His bridal analogy would be of little value if it only symbolized a symbol. But we have clearly seen so often how Paul goes straight from the metaphor to the reality; circumcision, for example, is not a picture of baptism, but of inner circumcision, the seal of the Spirit. So here, the bridal bath represents the inner cleansing and sanctifying of the Spirit. Its parallel in the real drama of initiation is water-baptism. But both point directly to the heart of the matter, not to each other.

## *Titus 3.5–7*

These verses could be cited in favour of the Pentecostal thesis, the ἀνακαίνωσις πνεύματος ἁγίου being detached from the λουτροῦ παλιγγενεσίας[33] and alone linked with the subsequent clause to describe the Pentecostal effusion of the Spirit;[34] further, the δικαιωθέντες could be regarded as chronologically prior to the γενηθῶμεν.[35] The net result would be:

[33] An old interpretation, going back to Theodoret, whereby λουτροῦ παλιγγενεσίας is referred to baptism and ἀνακαινώσεως πνεύματος ἁγίου to confirmation (see e.g. Chase 98–102; J. Coppens cited by Schnackenburg 86; also NEB and JB).

[34] Pastor L. F. Woodford of the Pentecostal assembly in Cambridge in 1965 drew my attention to the following parallels with the narrative of Pentecost and the other 'Pentecostal' passages in Acts: (i) ἐξέχεεν . . . πλουσίως – Acts 2.17, 18, 33; 10.45; (ii) ἐφ' ἡμᾶς – the emphatic ἐπί – Acts 2.17f.; 8.16; 10.44; 11.15; 19.6; Luke 24.49; (iii) διὰ Ἰησοῦ Χριστοῦ – Acts 2.33.

[35] Pastor Woodford cited Alford in support and referred also to the following translations: AV, RV, NEB, Weymouth, Darby, Rotherham, Conybeare. B. S. Easton speaks of 'a long exegetical tradition' which argues that ' "being justified" describes an event occurring *before* baptism' (*The Pastoral Epistles* 1948] 103). Cf. J. N. D. Kelly's translation in *The Pastoral Epistles* (1963) 248.

| Conversion | Baptism in the Spirit |
|---|---|
| he saved us through the washing of regeneration | and renewal of the Spirit which he poured out upon us richly through Jesus Christ our Saviour in order |
| that having been justified | we might become heirs in hope of eternal life. |

But this will hardly do.

(i) Verse 5. παλιγγενεσία and ἀνακαίνωσις are virtually synonymous. They can hardly be taken to signify two quite distinct and separate events and experiences. To be reborn *is* to be made anew. At most we can say that the two phrases describe the same transformation from slightly different angles.[36] Moreover, both phrases, λουτ. παλ. and ἀνακ. πν. ἁγ., are governed by the one διά. If the ideas had been distinct and the events involved separate, it would have been natural to repeat the διά. The NEB margin is therefore to be preferred: 'the water of rebirth and of renewal by . . .', with both παλ. and ἀνακ. being taken as dependent on λουτροῦ.[37] Again, just as it is difficult to distinguish παλ. from ἀνακ., so it is difficult to separate παλ. from πνεῦμα ἅγιον as the Spirit of regeneration. 'Rebirth is effected by the Holy Spirit.'[38] ἔσωσεν therefore describes the saving act of God in which he effects regeneration by the renewing power of the Holy Spirit – one act with different aspects, not a series of acts.

(ii) Verse 6. The manner in which the Holy Spirit comes for this regenerating and renewing operation is further described in the next clause, for here the outpouring of the Spirit is obviously what effects the (rebirth and) renewal of the Spirit, so that the ἐξέχεεν must describe the same event as the ἔσωσεν. The clear allusion to the tradition of Pentecost (ἐκχέω is used with the Spirit in the NT only here and in Acts 2.17, 18, 33) is a decisive check to Pentecostal ideas both of conversion and Spirit-baptism. For here it is the Pentecostal outpouring of the Spirit – the baptism in the Spirit – which effects the regeneration and renewal of salvation. Pentecost *is* regeneration and renewal.

[36] So most commentators. See especially Lampe, *Seal* 59f.; Schnackenburg 10f.; E. F. Scott, *The Pastoral Epistles* (Moffatt 1936) 175.

[37] So most; see especially Lampe, *Seal* 59f.; C. K. Barrett, *The Pastoral Epistles* (1963) 142.

[38] Barrett 142; see also Lampe, *Seal* 60.

(iii) With δικαιωθέντες we have once again a coincident aorist participle, for no Paulinist would think to distinguish the event of being justified[39] from that of becoming an heir 'in hope of eternal life', or either from the event of becoming a Christian; such passages as Rom. 3.24; 8.17; I Cor. 6.9–11; Gal. 4.5–7; Eph. 1.11 make that plain enough. Nor may we separate this δικαιωθέντες from what precedes it: the ἵνα-clause describes the purpose of the Pentecostal outpouring as well as of the ἔσωσεν.[40] The saving purpose of God, which is that we might be justified and become heirs, is effected by the baptism in the Spirit.

II Tim. 1.6 has sometimes been referred to Confirmation (e.g. Chase 35–41; Lowther Clarke 10), or to Spirit-baptism (O. Roberts, *The Baptism with the Holy Spirit* [1964] 46f.); but the much sounder interpretation refers this verse, together with I Tim. 4.14 (cf. also 1.18; 5.22), to a setting aside for particular work (equivalent to our 'ordination'), as χάρισμα (not δωρεά) in both passages, and the parallel in Acts 13.1–3 also suggest. I need do no more than refer to Barrett's excellent treatment and the articles by Daube and Jeremias which he also mentions (71f., 93, also 47, 81). II Tim. 1.7 has a wider reference to all Christians and to the gift of the Spirit at conversion – cf. Rom. 8.15.

It is evident, therefore, that Paul is describing the one event of becoming a Christian in as rich and full a way as possible. The outpouring of the Spirit is not something distinct from the renewal nor the renewal from the regeneration; neither is the becoming heirs distinct from the being justified, nor any of those from the being saved. God's purpose in the act of salvation is our justification and adoption; the means by which he achieves that purpose is 'the washing of regeneration and renewal in the Holy Spirit which he poured upon us richly through our Lord Jesus Christ'.

For the Spirit as the agent of spiritual 'begetting' in Paul see Gal. 4.29 and I Cor. 4.15 with 2.4; cf. II Cor. 3.6; on the Spirit and justification see pp. 108, 135f., 148 above; and on the link between the Spirit and κληρονομία see Rom. 8.15–17; I Cor. 6.9–11; Gal. 3.14, 18; 4.6f.; Eph. 1.13f.

[39] Any distinction between δικαιόω here and justification in the certain Paulines rather presupposes the distinction of authors than proves it. See Beasley-Murray 215f.; Kelly 253f.; J. Jeremias, *Die Briefe an Timotheus und Titus*[8] (NTD 1963) 67; Barrett 143; cf. M. Dibelius and H. Conzelmann, *Die Pastoralbriefe*[4] (HNT 1966) 113.

[40] Cf. C. Spicq, *Les Épîtres Pastorales*[2] (1947) 280.

But what is this λουτρόν? Most commentators unhesitatingly accept that the primary reference is to baptism. But once again I believe that we must see here a spiritual washing which is effected by the Spirit. λουτρόν is better understood as the act of washing (or the water used therein), than the receptacle used for washing.[41]

'Washing' is the sense we find in the four other occurrences in biblical Greek (S. of S. 4.2; 6.6; Ecclus. 34.25; Eph. 5.26). Aquila uses λουτρόν in Ps. 61.8; 107.9 for 'washpot', but Aquila's version is dated AD 130. The earlier we date the 'faithful saying' the more likely it is that the biblical usage is determinative. On the other hand, the closer we link the λουτρὸν παλιγγενεσίας with contemporary pagan terminology the more likely it is that λουτρόν has the sense of 'bath'. Yet this latter link is more open to question, for while παλιγγενεσία is probably borrowed from contemporary religious terminology, in the Mystery cults generally the idea of rebirth had not been linked to the introductory bath, which was simply a bath of cleansing (Schnackenburg 14; Wagner 259f., 270).

Moreover, since παλιγγενεσίας *and* ἀνακαινώσεως are both dependent on λουτροῦ, and neither can be independent of or separated from the Spirit, it is best to take 'regeneration and renewal' as a single concept describing the washing of the Holy Spirit – the washing, of regeneration and renewal, which the Holy Spirit effects.[42] This, though cumbersome, is, I suggest, confirmed by the ἐξέχεεν of v. 6: the writer speaks of the Spirit as 'poured out' because he is thinking of the Spirit's regenerative and renewing activity in terms of water and washing: it is the cleansing and purifying we experience when the Spirit is poured out upon us which brings about our regeneration and renewal.[43] The more definite is the conscious allusion to Pentecost, the stronger this suggestion becomes, for the outpouring of the Spirit at Pentecost was symbolized by (the washing of John's) baptism, but was wholly independent of the water-rite. Of water-baptism as such there is here no mention, though it may be implicit in the thought that water-baptism, which depicts this washing, was also the occasion when it took place.

This would certainly more accord with the picture of conversion which we have drawn out from Paul and Luke, than one where

[41] See Robinson, *Ephesians* 205f.; Simpson, *Pastorals* 114f.
[42] Cf. TEV; R. F. Horton, *The Pastoral Epistles* (1911).
[43] Cf. Kittel 43f.; Barth, *Dogmatik* IV/4 126; and see Schnackenburg 13. For the idea of spiritual cleansing cf. II Tim. 2.21; Titus 2.14.

baptism as such was described in terms of regeneration and renewal. And if we could be sure that this 'faithful saying' was written or dictated by Paul himself the matter would be settled. Alternatively, if Luke either was Paul's amanuensis and co-author, or framed Paul's thought in his own words after the latter's death,[44] the allusion to Pentecost would be all the more definite and the 'washing of the Spirit' interpretation all the more sure. We must, however, allow for the possibility that here we have a different theologian at work, one whose ideas are more akin to the theology (perhaps) of John 3.5. In that case there would be more to be said for the translation: 'the bath of the regeneration and renewal which the Holy Spirit effects'. Baptism would be not only the occasion of regeneration, but the rite itself would be characterized by the regeneration and renewal which took place in it. Not only so, but water-baptism would also be given a functional role in the event of salvation: 'he saved us . . . *through* (διά) the bath . . .'. It does not follow, however, that we can speak of baptism here as effecting regeneration or conveying the Holy Spirit – the genitive πνεύματος ἁγίου indicates not dependence on λουτροῦ but the agency which effects the παλιγγενεσία καὶ ἀνακαίνωσις, and the Spirit is poured out not διὰ λουτροῦ but διὰ Ἰησοῦ Χριστοῦ. The way would then be open to interpret the functional role of baptism in terms of faith, as we have so far been doing, and we would have to opt for one or other of the two translations offered by Beasley-Murray: 'the washing *characterized by* the regeneration and renewal wrought by the Holy Spirit', or 'the washing *wherein* the Holy Spirit wrought regeneration and renewal'.[45] On the evidence of the undisputed Pauline letters this cannot be regarded as typical of his theology of conversion-initiation. On the other hand, it is not altogether un-Pauline in its context.

If I Tim. 6.12f. refers to the baptismal confession, as is most probable (see Beasley-Murray 204–6), we should only note that it is to this that Timothy is recalled, and not to some sacramental efficacy of baptism such as some find reflected in the exhortations of Col. 3.

II Tim. 2.11–12 is not to be referred to baptism (contra Schneider, *Baptism* 34f.; Beasley-Murray 207–9), but it includes a reference to the

---

[44] Cf. C. F. D. Moule, *Bulletin of the John Rylands Library* 47 (1965) No. 2, 430–52; A. Strobel, *NTS* 15 (1968–69) 191–210.
[45] Beasley-Murray 211, 214f. (my italics); cf. Bultmann, *Theology* I 101; Schweizer, *TWNT* VI 444.

death with Christ experienced at conversion-initiation. The echo of
Rom. 6.8 confirms this since, as we saw, the thought there had passed
on from the sacrament mentioned in v. 4. (Notice that once again death
lies in the past while life lies in the future; it is a poetical antithesis, of
course, but it is certainly in line with Paul's thought in Rom. 6.1–11.)
To expound the rest of the hymn in terms of 'living out the baptismal
life' (Beasley-Murray 208; a frequent phrase in Moss) introduces an idea
foreign to the NT. For Paul at any rate the thought is rather of living
out life κατὰ πνεῦμα.

Once again, then, we have seen how Paul in an effort to describe
the richness and variety of the experience of conversion-initiation
has pressed into service metaphors and analogies drawn, for example, from the business world (Eph. 1.13f.), or from the significant events of human life, like birth (Titus 3.5), marriage (Eph.
5.25–27) and death (Col. 2.11f., 20; 3.3). In every case the thought
has centred wholly on the spiritual realities and inward work of
the Spirit rather than, and even as distinct from some outward rite.
There has never been any real question of a second stage such as
that argued for by Pentecostals and 'Confirmationists'; and baptism
has been clearly presented as the occasion of the Spirit's life-giving
coming (Col. 2.12; Titus 3.5f. [?]) and the expression of faith (Eph.
4.5), but as nothing more.

### CONCLUSION

Throughout Part Three we have continued our debate with Pentecostals on the one hand and sacramentalists on the other. So far
as Pentecostal theology is concerned, our task has been to look for
a reception of the Spirit which Paul distinguishes from conversion-
initiation. Most Pentecostals recognize the force of Rom. 8.9 and
agree that to be a Christian one must have received the Spirit in
some sense. But for them the focus of attention falls on a *second*
reception of the Spirit which they attempt to find as often as possible in Paul, identifying it with such terms as anointing, sealing,
and promise. Our study has shown: that Paul knows of only one
reception of the Spirit, not two; that the concepts of anointing,
sealing, outpouring, promise, gift, etc., all refer to that one coming
of the Spirit; that this coming of the Spirit is the very heart and
essence of conversion-initiation; and that even their own title
of 'baptism in the Spirit' is used by Paul to describe nothing

other than God's means of incorporating the convert into Christ.

There are a few passages which could be taken to imply frequent comings of the Spirit (I Thess. 4.8; Gal. 3.5; Phil. 1.19; Eph. 5.18). However, the first two are best taken as describing the continuing activity of God as more and more become Christians (cf. John 1.33), rather than a continual giving of the Spirit to individuals (see p. 105 n. 2 above). Phil. 1.19 is best taken as 'the supply afforded by the Spirit' (M. R. Vincent, *Philippians and Philemon* [ICC 1897] 24; F. W. Beare, *The Epistle to the Philippians* [1959] 62). The more probable interpretation of Eph. 5.18 does allow for repeated fillings with the Spirit (contra Ervin 74–78 – since the prohibition is against a repeated action and not a continuous state [μεθύσκω not μεθύω] it suggests that the exhortation should be understood similarly). Yet this cannot provide any support for the Pentecostal. For this is the same distinction as appears in Acts: repeated experiences of being filled (i.e. taken over or controlled) by the Spirit on the part of an individual or individuals who had already been once-and-for-all baptized in the Spirit. Of a special once-and-for-all *second* giving of or filling with the Spirit Paul knows nothing.

So far as sacramentalist theology is concerned, it is clear that the classification of many passages in Paul as 'baptismal' rests on a fundamental misunderstanding of Paul's thought. The failure to appreciate the concreteness and vitality of spiritual experience in NT times has too often led to the exaltation of the peripheral and secondary to a position of central and primary importance. Exposition has proceeded beyond the limits of Paul's theology without sufficient care for the context and caution of Paul's thought, and 'obvious' corollaries have been drawn out without checking whether they were obvious to Paul.

In particular, it is necessary to reaffirm that βαπτίζειν does not in and of itself mean 'to baptize in water' or necessarily include a reference to water-baptism; that βαπτίζεσθαι εἰς is not the same as βαπτίζεσθαι εἰς τὸ ὄνομα, the latter describing the operation and significance of the water-rite, the former being one of the many metaphors used by Paul to describe the Spirit's coming to the individual as God's gift of new life in response to faith; that βάπτισμα is the water-rite as such and symbolizes burial (not resurrection), ever a reminder of the finality of the initiate's break with the old self-centred way of life; and that inward, spiritual experience in general cannot be related to outward, material ceremonies, either by way of equation or of direct dependence.

The initial refusal to use 'baptism' as a blanket term or concertina word has been amply justified, even though Paul does not
sharpen his distinction between water-baptism and Spirit-baptism
in the way Luke does. The vivid experience of receiving the Spirit
(not baptism) and the effect of his coming (not baptism) is ever to
the forefront of Paul's thought both in his reminiscing and his
theologizing. Water-baptism is the means whereby the individual
expresses his faith and commits himself to Jesus as Lord. But it
may not be described as the means whereby God accepts him or
conveys to him the Spirit.[46] For Paul it is the Spirit who is the mark
of God's acceptance, and God's instruments of saving grace are the
Spirit and the gospel; the decisive act of grace is the gift of the
Spirit to the faith expressed in baptism.

It is sometimes argued that the reason why baptism is so seldom
mentioned in Paul is because it was common ground to all Christians
and its role could be assumed without explicit reference (e.g. Lake,
*Earlier Epistles* 384). But precisely the same could be said of preaching,
believing and receiving the Spirit. Yet Paul mentions them frequently.
This suggests that for Paul it was just these three elements which were
decisive in conversion. Baptism, while important, was nevertheless subsidiary to these three. It would seem, therefore, to be a misinterpreta-
tion of Paul's thought to give the water-rite the determinative and
dominant role in the event or theology of conversion-initiation; and it
is certainly quite without foundation to speak of Paul making baptism
'the corner stone of his Christ-related doctrine of salvation' (contra
Schnackenburg 21), or to describe the whole of his theology as an
exposition of baptism (contra A. R. C. Leaney, *SJT* 15 [1962] 394–9;
Lohse, *Kerygma und Dogma* 11 [1965] 318; E. Fuchs, *Studies in the Historical
Jesus* [ET 1964] 173).

In short, where the sacramentalist might say, God incorporates
us into Christ and bestows on us the Spirit *in and by baptism*, Paul
would say, We give ourselves *in and by baptism* to Christ, who gives
himself to us in and through the Spirit, and only thus unites us
with himself and with his people.

[46] Cf. Büchsel 426f.; Schneider, *Taufe* 70; Stalder 79.

# PART FOUR

## XIV

## THE JOHANNINE PENTECOST?

For the Pentecostal the Fourth Gospel is especially important
since it shows him clearly that the disciples were regenerate before
Pentecost and had received the Spirit before Pentecost. In particular, the impartation of the Spirit on the evening of resurrection
Sunday (20.22) seems to indicate beyond reasonable doubt that the
baptism in the Spirit fifty days later was at least a second and
distinct work of the Spirit in the lives of the disciples.[1]

The basic weakness in this argument is one I have already
touched on briefly in chapter IV. It is the assumption that John
and Luke-Acts are more or less narrative histories of the same sort,
so uniform in their manner of presenting facts and events that they
can immediately be dovetailed into each other in a straightforward
chronological fashion (Acts 2, for example, being the fulfilment of
John 7.38f.). But such an assumption ignores the basic questions:
What is the truth John and Luke wish to convey? and, How do
they attempt to convey it? The fact is that the first five books of the
NT are not a flat plain of homogeneous historicity. Theological
mountains (and molehills) break that flatness, and it is a mistake
to think that when we climb one of these mountains we are moving
forward historically at the same pace as when we traverse the level
plain.

John's treatment of Jesus' death is one of these mountains. To
put it simply, John wishes to demonstrate the unity of the decisive
events in the climax of Jesus' ministry – death, resurrection, ascension, gift of the Spirit – a fact most clearly seen by his use of the
words δοξάζειν and ὑψοῦν. Every so often the reader is pointed
forward to the event of Jesus' glorification (7.39; 12.16, 23; 13.31;
17.1), the decisive hour (ὥρα) of divine action (2.4; 7.30; 8.20;

---

[1] e.g. Harper, *Power* 19; Prince, *Jordan* 66. See pp. 38f. above.

173

12.23, 27; 13.1; 17.1),[2] which embraces not only Jesus' resurrection and ascension, and not merely his death, but all these together. John does not want to think of them as separate events, but rather as a single act of glorification.

Thus in 12.23f.; 13.31 it is primarily death which is in mind (cf. 21.19); in 12.32 and 17.5 it is the thought of ascension which is most prominent; and in 7.39 and 12.16 it is the event which results in the giving of the Spirit and quickening of memory (also the work of the Spirit – 14.26) which is foremost. In every case (except one) δοξάζειν refers not to one *or* other, but to all as a single hour of glorification. And even where two separate acts of glorification are envisaged (13.31f.) John is careful to add εὐθύς.

Similarly with ὑψόω (3.14; 8.28; 12.32, 34). As most recent commentators recognize, John uses this word not only for Jesus' lifting up on the cross, but also for his lifting up to heaven, that is, his ascension: the one word includes what are chronologically distinct events in the one action.[3] In short, John presents as a unitary conceptual whole the Son of Man's redemptive acts in dying rising, ascending and giving the Spirit. The decisive act of salvation is not complete until the Son of Man has ascended and bestowed the Spirit.

How does this fact – that John treats the redemption-effecting events theologically as well as chronologically – bear upon the crucial passage, John 20.22? There is some reason for believing that at this point John is concerned more with the theological unity of these events than their chronological separateness. For one thing, 20.17 seems to imply that the ascension was the immediate consequence of the resurrection and had in some sense taken place between 20.17 and 20.19.[4] This would simply mean that John shares with Luke and Paul the belief that it is only the Exalted One who bestows the Spirit, the divine gift being the immediate consequence of his ascension.

[2] See also καιρός (7.6, 8) and νῦν (12.31; 13.31; cf. 4.23; 5.25).

[3] See especially Brown 145f.

[4] See e.g. Bauer 181f.; Macgregor 359f.; R. H. Strachan, *The Fourth Gospel*[3] (1941) 328; W. Michaelis, *Die Erscheinungen des Auferstandenen* (1944); Dodd 442f.; Lightfoot 331; W. Wilkens, *Die Entstehungsgeschichte des vierten Evangeliums* (1958) 88–90; F.-M. Braun, *Jean le Théologien* III (1966) 225–8; J. Marsh, *St John* (1968) 639f.; and especially Archimandrite Cassien, *La Pentecôte Johannique* (1939) 9–91.

John's pneumatology seems to bear out this interpretation. In the conversation with Nicodemus the new life promised is described as ἄνωθεν (3.3, 7), ἐκ πνεύματος (3.5, 6, 8), and as the consequence of believing in the Son of Man lifted up (ὑψωθῆναι – 3.14), which is obviously closely linked to the immediately preceding thought of the Son of Man's ascending to heaven (3.13); this implies that birth ἐκ πνεύματος is the consequence of the Son of Man's ascension and of faith in him as thus exalted.

It is probable that John means us to read 3.5 in the light of 7.39 as well. In other words, the new birth by the Spirit was not possible till after the resurrection. John would not hesitate to write in the present tense since he is writing for his contemporaries, and since 7.39 is too explicit to allow any reference to the Spirit (apart from those relating to Jesus) to be understood of the time before his death.

The great discourse of John 6 concludes with a similar dovetailing of the ascension into the life-giving ministry of the Spirit (6.62f.); and the Johannine interpretation of the Tabernacles text clearly indicates that for John the gift of the Spirit was the consequence of Jesus' glorification in death-resurrection-ascension (7.39).

The Paraclete sayings are more complex, but the primary message is the same. The dominant theme is the continuity between the ministries of Jesus and the Paraclete.[5] The Spirit takes over as the ἄλλος παράκλητος where the first Paraclete leaves off. Indeed we might say that Jesus continues to be present with and in his disciples through the Paraclete. In other words, a purely spiritual relationship is to supersede what was also a physical one (14.18–23). This is why Jesus must go away in a little while = go to the Father = be lifted up in suffering and exaltation (14.28; 16.5, 16–24, 28), for only then can the Paraclete come (16.7).[6] As with 7.39, the coming of the Spirit awaits the ascension and is the immediate result of Jesus' departure in glory.

John has thus recorded a number of promises and prophecies of the Spirit's coming, but *only one coming*. Moreover, he has tied that coming to the unitary event of glorification and uplifting, both in the earlier forward-looking passages and in the actual event

[5] Barrett points out how the mission of the Spirit is closely parallel to that of the Son; cf. 15.26 with 8.42; 13.3; 16.27 (*Gospel* 402). See also R. E. Brown, *NTS* 13 (1966–67) 126–8.

[6] Cf. D. E. Holwerda, *The Holy Spirit and Eschatology in the Gospel of John* (1959) 18–21; C. F. D. Moule, *NovTest* 5 (1962) 178–80.

(20.22). It is quite natural, therefore, to say that John intended his readers to find the fulfilment of these earlier promises in the insufflation of 20.22, rather than in a later event which he does not record.[7] From this list of promises fulfilled in 20.22 we can hardly exclude the prophecy of John 1.33: Jesus' ministry as Baptizer in the Holy Spirit follows immediately from his ministry as Lamb of God (1.29). We could therefore say that in 20.22 John records the disciples' baptism in the Spirit.

If the conclusion stands the Pentecostal case at 20.22 falls. Yet I am not finally convinced that it is the conclusion John himself would draw out. Although we cannot deny John's concern to impress a theological scheme on a chronological sequence of events, it would not be true to say that the former completely ignores and suppresses the latter. The chronological separateness of the various events recorded in 20 (including the time-lapse between the death and resurrection of Jesus) is retained (20.1, 19, 26). Again, the argument that 20.17 indicates the theological unity of the ascension with the resurrection, and that the ascension followed immediately after Jesus' meeting with Mary is not entirely satisfactory. On any reckoning the οὔπω (20.17) preserves a clear enough time-lapse between resurrection and ascension.

Moule, *NovTest* 5 (1962) 175f., also explains the contrast between 20.17 and 20.27 as due to the different needs and circumstances of the two disciples concerned. The physical contact in each case was very different (μή μου ἅπτου – 'Do not cling to me' NEB), and there is no hint in the Thomas scene that the ascension was already past. All that is clearly implied is that Jesus can be seen and touched; and the blessing of 20.29 is for those who without being able to see and touch for themselves accept the testimony of those who have (cf. I John 1.1–3). The difference in the responses to the risen Jesus in vv. 16 and 28 probably has no significance at this point (contra Wilkens 88) in view of the identity of the responses in vv. 18 and 25. In a private communication Professor Moule also points out that the ἀναβαίνω comes in the message Mary has to tell the disciples, not as part of the reason why Mary should refrain from touching him. The οὔπω ἀναβέβηκα hardly implies that Jesus was at that moment in the process of ascending; and ἀναβαίνω can be translated, 'I am about to ascend' (Barrett, *Gospel* 470; Lagrange

---

[7] Those who think that the sending of the Paraclete refers to 20.22 include Bultmann, *Johannes* 536f.; Barrett, *Gospel* 474f.; H. Schlier in *Neutestamentliche Aufsätze* (J. Schmid Festschrift 1963) 234–6; O. Betz, *Der Paraklet* (1963) 169, as well as those cited in n. 4 above.

512), or 'I am going to ascend' (NEB margin). See also Sanders and Mastin 429.

Since John retains this distinct chronological separateness, nothing would be gained by placing the ascension before the vital resurrection appearances.[8] The theological point can still be made without disrupting or compressing the accepted sequence of events (as 20.1 shows).

Had the theology totally swamped the chronology we would have expected the ἀναβαίνω to come on Jesus' lips while he was still hanging on the cross. Some indeed think that 19.30 is deliberately phrased (παρέδωκεν τὸ πνεῦμα) to indicate that the gift of the Spirit is the immediate result of the Son of Man's being lifted up (Hoskyns 532; Lightfoot 319f.; Brown VI; Braun III 168); and 19.34, depicting both the death of Jesus and the outpouring of the Spirit (see pp. 187f.), certainly symbolizes perfectly the unity of the great redemptive acts (the life-giving Spirit comes only from the Crucified and as the immediate result of his glorification). But in that case 20.19–22 simply buttresses the fact that the theological point can be made without dispensing with the chronology. However, so far as 19.30 goes, Bultmann thinks that the phrase means nothing more than the ἀφῆκεν τὸ πνεῦμα of Matt. 27.50 and the ἐξέπνευσεν of Mark 15.37 (*Johannes* 523 n. 1), and for Barrett 20.22 allows no room for an earlier giving of the Spirit (*Gospel* 460; cf. Lagrange 497).

It may well be best, therefore, to interpret the Paraclete promises of 14.16, 26; 15.26 and 16.7 not of 20.22 (which is not naturally described as a 'sending' of the Spirit, especially by or from the Father), but of a later bestowal of the Spirit, following Jesus' final return to the Father after his various appearances to the disciples. John's account could then dovetail chronologically into the Acts narrative: John would know of two bestowals of the Spirit, though recording only one, and the promised baptism in the Spirit (1.33) could easily be referred to the unrecorded Pentecost.

It may however be that John wishes us to understand the two ministries of Jesus which the Baptist foretold as intimately related. That is to say, in the baptism in the Spirit Jesus conveys the cleansing and forgiveness of sin made possible by his sacrificial death as Lamb of God. 20.22

---

[8] John presumably shared the belief that the 'resurrection appearances' were something special (different from the later visions and revelations) and came to an end when Jesus returned once-for-all to the Father (so 20.29 implies).

would then be the disciples' baptism in the Spirit whereby they received the blessings newly won by Christ's lifting up and glorification.

To avoid the historical contrast between the 'Lukan Pentecost' and the 'Johannine Pentecost' it has been periodically argued that 20.22 does not depict an actual giving of the Spirit, but only points forward to Pentecost proleptically, as though Jesus was saying, 'When you hear the sound of the wind (= πνεῦμα = breath) then you will receive the Spirit.' This is an unsupported speculation which does too little justice to the text. Bultmann points out that the use of λαμβάνειν corresponds to the Christian community's terminology in Rom. 8.15; I Cor. 2.12; Acts 8.15ff., etc. (*Johannes* 476 n. 5).

I must confess that I am torn between these two interpretations. On the one hand, John's theological message is clear: the two great moments of redemption (crucifixion-resurrection and ascension-gift of the Spirit) are not independent of each other; the Spirit is the Spirit (breath) of Jesus, of Jesus exalted in death, resurrection and ascension, and the gift of the Spirit is the climax and conclusion of these decisive salvation-effecting events. On the other hand, it is equally plain that the theological motif can be adequately highlighted without obscuring the chronological outline, so that a lifting up to heaven can be thought of as a theological unity with the lifting up on the cross which took place at least three days, and probably as much as forty-three days earlier.[9]

Our conclusion thus far is simply that the Pentecostal thesis at this point cannot entirely be rejected: John may well have considered that the baptism in the Spirit was a second and distinct work of the Spirit in the spiritual experience of the first disciples. But the Pentecostal must argue for more than this: namely, that the experience of the apostles is, or can be a pattern which may be repeated in the lives of later Christians. It is with this further step that he definitely misses the way. For the chronological sequence of events in the lives of the apostles is unique and unrepeatable. The coming of the Son from the Father to dwell among men in human flesh was something which had never happened before and which has never happened since. Similarly the relation of Jesus' disciples to him in the period before Pentecost was one which simply cannot be known again.

This point deserves further amplification:

[9] Luke in fact is the only NT writer to distinguish carefully between Easter and Pentecost (S. M. Gilmour, *JBL* 81 [1962] 63).

(*a*) For the first Christians Jesus' ministry was the watershed between the dispensations: 'the law was given through Moses; grace and truth came through Jesus Christ' (1.17). Jesus fulfilled many of the messianic predictions and eschatological hopes of Moses and the prophets (1.45; 4.25f.; 5.39, 46; 6.31–35; 8.56).[10] He brought a radiancy of light that was not present before and set in motion the divine judgment (3.19 etc.). In so doing he altered the 'terms' of salvation: from then on eternal life was essentially a matter of believing in him (3.16–18, 36; 5.24 etc.) – what it could never have been before.

(*b*) It is important to realize that it was the total mission which effected this alteration – not just his life, but especially his death, resurrection and ascension. Saving belief for John is belief in Jesus as lifted up (3.14–16; 12.32). In particular, the Spirit could not be received from Jesus until Jesus had been glorified (in death and resurrection – 7.39); only then could those who believed in him receive the Spirit, who is the living water which becomes a spring of water welling up to eternal life (4.14). In other words, it is not until after Jesus' death and resurrection that it is possible even for the Pentecostal to speak of the disciples as 'genuine converted Christians' (Prince). However we understand the cleansing spoken of in 13.10f. and 15.3, it cannot be taken to mean Christian conversion.

The punctuation of 7.37f. is a well-known crux, and the issue is important since it almost certainly determines whether Jesus is the source of the rivers of living water or the believer (though see J. Blenkinsopp, *NTS* 6 [1959–60] 95–98). In my opinion the best interpretation is that which reads Jesus' words thus:

$$\dot{\epsilon}\acute{a}\nu \ \tau\iota\varsigma \ \delta\iota\psi\hat{a} \ \dot{\epsilon}\rho\chi\acute{\epsilon}\sigma\theta\omega \ \pi\rho\acute{o}\varsigma \ \mu\epsilon,$$
$$\kappa\alpha\grave{\iota} \ \pi\iota\nu\acute{\epsilon}\tau\omega \ \dot{o} \ \pi\iota\sigma\tau\epsilon\acute{\upsilon}\omega\nu \ \epsilon\dot{\iota}\varsigma \ \dot{\epsilon}\mu\acute{\epsilon}.$$
$$\kappa\alpha\theta\grave{\omega}\varsigma \ \epsilon\dot{\iota}\pi\epsilon\nu \ \dot{\eta} \ \gamma\rho\alpha\phi\acute{\eta} \ . \ . \ .$$

(so Lagrange, and the authors and western Fathers cited by him [214f.]; C. F. Burney, *The Aramaic Origin of the Fourth Gospel* [1922] 109ff.; Macgregor 207; C. C. Torrey, *Our Translated Gospels* [1936] 108–11; Hoskyns 321f.; W. F. Howard, *IB* 8 [1952] 588f.; Dodd 349; Bultmann, *Johannes* 228; G. D. Kilpatrick, *JTS* 11 [1960] 340–2; M. Black, *The New Testament Doctrine of the Spirit* [Hoyt Lectures, unpublished, 1963] Lecture 5; Mussner 139–42; Hill 199f., 291; Sanders and Mastin 213f.; NEB; JB; RSV margin; see especially W. Thüsing, *Die Erhöhung und*

---

[10] Bultmann, *Theology* II 37.

*Verherrlichung Jesu im Johannesevangelium* [1960] 160–5, and Brown, *Gospel* 320–7). In other words, the believer is invited to drink of the living water which flows from the body of Jesus when he is glorified (cf. 19.34); see pp. 187f.

(*c*) All that I have said is most clearly confirmed by 20.22 and John's use of ἐνεφύσησεν there. It is the word used in Gen. 2.7, Ezek. 37.9 and Wisd. 15.11[11] to describe the creation of man – the divine breath (πνεῦμα – in Gen. 2.7 πνοή) which brings life to what was otherwise a corpse. In other words, John presents the act of Jesus as a new creation: Jesus is the author of the new creation as he was of the old (1.3).[12] If Pentecostals look for the moment when the apostles[13] became regenerate they can find it only here and not before – only then was the spiritual life (breath) of the new creation communicated to them.

Since the Spirit-passages – 3.5–8; 4.10–14; 6.63; 7.37–39 – speak of the life-giving work of the Spirit, they are to be referred to 20.22 rather than to a later coming of the Spirit. The point must be stressed for 7.37–39, in view of the Pentecostal exposition which sees in these verses an invitation to the Christian to receive the Spirit (e.g. Roberts 25; Harper, *Walk* 16). This interpretation is excluded by the punctuation and interpretation adopted above. But even if the other punctuation is retained, the believing which results in the indwelling and overflowing of the Spirit is the same action as that described in 3.15, 16, 18, 36; 5.24; 6.47; 12.46; 20.31 – namely, the initial commitment of faith. The aorist of v. 39 shows that we cannot interpret the present of v. 38 in any other way.

The puzzling οὔπω ἦν πνεῦμα in 7.39 is not to be interpreted ontologically but functionally (as with 4.24). So far as the disciples' experience of the Spirit was concerned, until 20.22, the Spirit was not yet. They had not yet begun to experience that relation with Jesus through the Spirit which was only possible after his exaltation and ascension

[11] Gen. 2.7, Ezek. 37.9 are the only two occasions in the LXX when ἐμφυσάω is used to translate *nāpaḥ* (A has also Ezek. 22.20); these two passages plus Wisd. 15.11 are the only ones to link ἐμφυσάω with the divine creative breath.

[12] Macgregor 365; Hoskyns 544; Barrett, *Gospel* 474; Betz 165; Sanders and Mastin 433; Marsh 640, 643f.; Ervin 31f.

[13] We should probably understand the group of 'disciples' either as broader than the apostles (were Mary and the other women there? cf. Acts 1.14), or as representative of the broader circle of disciples (when did Thomas receive the Spirit?), or of believers in general (W. F. Howard, *Christianity according to St John* [1943] 141; Schweizer, *TWNT* VI 440 and n. 753; Käsemann, *RGG³* II 1278; Hill 287).

(Dodd 184; Barrett, *Gospel* 272; Brown, *Gospel* 324; H. F. Wodehouse, *Theology* 67 [1964] 310–12).

(*d*) While this substantiates the Pentecostals' principal claim – that the apostles were regenerate before Pentecost – it still does not justify them in taking the apostles' experience as *the* or even a *possible* pattern for experience today. For 20.22 has made it evident that the disciples' experience was determined by the process of salvation-history. God's unfolding plan of redemption was at a critical transition phase as a result of the incarnation; the old dispensation of law was giving way to the dispensation of (fuller) grace and truth; one stage of salvation-history was changing over to another. The disciples lived through this transition period, and during it their spiritual experience was limited to that which was appropriate and possible at each stage. Now, if we understand the significant events of John in a chronological scheme which links up with Acts, we have to say that the transition period between the dispensations lasted at least from Jesus' death to Pentecost, if not from the beginning of his ministry to Pentecost, if not from his birth to Pentecost. What we now call full Christian experience was possible only after the ascension and Pentecost, when the 'advocate from heaven' came to represent and act for the 'advocate in heaven'. Likewise, the experience of the new birth and new creation was possible only after the sin-bearing death of the Lamb of God and his resurrection. Likewise, the experience of cleansing was possible only 'through the Word' which the incarnate Logos brought from the Father (15.3; 12.48–50; 14.24; 17.14). In other words, in this chronological scheme we have to distinguish three decisive milestones in the transition period between the dispensations – the coming of the Word with the word, his lifting up on the cross, and his sending of the ἄλλος παράκλητος after his departure (14.25f.; 15.26; 16.7). As they passed each milestone the disciples entered into the fuller experience which had only then become possible; until Jesus' resurrection it was not possible for them to experience the recreative breath of God; until Pentecost it was not possible for them to experience the Spirit of Pentecost; their experience throughout this transition phase was limited to what was possible at that point.

In 14.17 ἔστιν is probably the original text, as being the more difficult reading (NEB, JB, TEV). The three verbs either reflect the time at which John wrote (Barrett, *Gospel* 387), or else the present tenses have a future reference, as in 13.6, 27, 33; 14.3; 15.27; 20.17; 21.23 (Bernard 546; Lagrange 384; Sanders and Mastin 328; see Moule, *Idiom Book* 7). In view of 7.39, 14.16, 20, 23, Jesus' words (all three verbs) could not be true of the disciples until after the sending of the Spirit; nor does there seem to be any significant theological distinction at this point between the Spirit's remaining with them and his being in them.

This all simply means that it is impossible to regard the experience of the apostles throughout this period as a possible pattern, far less the norm, for experience today. With Pentecost the transition phase came to an end; the old stage of salvation-history was wholly past and the new stage wholly in operation. Henceforth entry into the blessings of the new dispensation is immediate, whereas for the apostles it was 'staggered'. A set of experiences whose order and depth was determined by an utterly unique and unrepeatable set of events (those from Bethlehem to Pentecost) cannot be the pattern for the regular experience of conversion and Christian growth after Pentecost. Only if Jesus were to live, die, rise and ascend again and again, could the experience of the apostles be described as normative for later Christianity, since their experience was determined by their relation to the historical ministry of Jesus. If a norm is desired for the gift of the Spirit we have it not in John 20.22 or Acts 2.4, but in Acts 2.38.[14]

In short, John certainly shows that it may not be possible to equate Spirit-baptism with regeneration, *but only in the case of the apostles*. His theological message at this point indicates (and Luke and Paul certainly show) that from Pentecost onwards he who believes receives the Spirit in his cleansing, regenerating, baptismal power, bringing the forgiveness and life of the new dispensation. With the transition period ended, the theological emphasis of John is no longer complicated by a necessary chronological disjointedness, and the theological unity of the Spirit's life-giving and empowering ministry becomes a chronological unity as well.

[14] See ch. IX. Cf. J. R. W. Stott, *The Baptism and Fullness of the Holy Spirit* (1964) 11; R. Pache, *The Person and Work of the Holy Spirit* (ET 1956) 38–40, 72. Among Pentecostals, Stiles recognizes the 'dispensational' character of the Spirit's coming, and makes this point very forcefully (65f.).

# XV

# THE SPIRIT AND BAPTISM IN JOHN'S GOSPEL

DOES John give us to understand that the Spirit is mediated through the sacrament of baptism? One automatically thinks of 3.5, and the affirmative answer really stands or falls with this passage. The chief arguments for seeing a baptismal reference in 3.5 are as follows:

(*a*) the sacramentalism of John: together with 6.51c–58, 3.5 is regarded as the most explicit of the sacramental references.[1]

(*b*) In view of the almost thematic repetition of 'water' in the early chapters of John, it is often said that 3.5 is the Evangelist's description of Christian baptism in contrast to John's (and perhaps also Jewish purification rites).[2]

(*c*) The reason most frequently given is that the Christian reader of 3.5 could not fail to think of the rite of initiation into the Church.[3]

Before we deal with these arguments, two preliminary points must be considered.

(i) As the foundation for the sacramentalist understanding of John generally (and 3.5 in particular), ch. 6 must be given some attention.[4] By using this discourse John wishes to make two

---

[1] Schnackenburg, *Johannesevangelium* 383; Brown, *New Testament Essays* (1965) 77; Beasley-Murray 229f. For the range of opinions on the question of John's sacramentalism, see Brown, *Essays* 52–56.

[2] Dodd, *Interpretation* 312; see also 309–11; Brown, *Essays* 94; *Gospel* 155; Barrett, *Gospel* 174; Clark 27; D. R. Griffiths in *Christian Baptism* (ed. Gilmore) 156.

[3] See e.g. W. L. Knox, *Some Hellenistic Elements in Primitive Christianity* (1943) 91; Brown, *Essays* 93f.

[4] 'All question marks which may be put at my explanation of other passages should be concentrated on the claim that the author saw in this study as such a connection with the Eucharist . . .' (Cullmann, *Worship* 94f.).

points. First, belief must be centred on a Jesus who really became flesh and really died;[5] it is the reality of the incarnation and the necessity of the Incarnate One's death if men are to receive eternal life, which is emphasized throughout, and especially in 6.51c–58;[6] 6.35 makes it clear that the eating and drinking is another way of coming to and believing εἰς Ἰησοῦν.

Second, eternal life comes through the Spirit given by the Son of Man in his exaltation. This comes out most plainly in the key verses 27 and 63.[7] In v. 27, 'the food which endures to eternal life' is obviously at least very similar to the 'springs of water welling up to eternal life' (4.14), that is, the Spirit.[8] The future (δώσει) refers to the gift of the breath of life in 20.22. And the ἐσφράγισεν must refer to God's attestation of the Son by the anointing with the Spirit at Jordan.[9] The parallel with 1.33 is especially noticeable, for in both the qualification for baptizing in the Spirit/giving the heavenly food is the anointing with the Spirit. Verses 62–3 explain to the scandalized hearers that Jesus is not talking about a physical eating of the Son of Man in his human state, but about the great life-giving events which are the climax of his ministry. Jesus in his humanity as flesh and blood is no help to them, for help comes through the Spirit given by the incarnate Christ in his ascension.[10]

6.32, 35 and 45 may also be significant here, since 'the use of the term ἀληθινός sufficiently indicates that the food of eternal life belongs to the order of ἀλήθεια and therefore of πνεῦμα' (Dodd 341), since the only real parallel to v. 35's note of ἔρχεσθαι-πιστεύειν is 7.37–39, and since the citation of Isa. 54.13 is very close in thought to the great new covenant promises of Jer. 31.34 and Ezek. 36.27, which Paul for one saw

[5] Strachan 192; cf. Bernard 213f. 'The theme of the discourse is . . . unbelief and faith' (Hoskyns 288) – a view confirmed by the repetition of the theme in v. 29, 35, 36, 40, 47, 64, 69. Cf. Strathmann 121.

[6] A. Schlatter, *Das Evangelium nach Johannes* (1953) 115; Barrett, *Gospel* 236, 246; Dodd 339; Lightfoot 162; B. Gärtner, *John 6 and the Jewish Passover* (1959) 23f.; R. V. G. Tasker, *The Gospel According to St John* (1960) 95. For the sacrificial connotations of the phrase 'flesh and blood' see Jeremias, *Eucharistic Words* 221f., nn. 10, 11.

[7] Verse 27: as in the earlier discourses (3.3; 4.10; 5.19), Jesus' opening words sound out the theme which characterizes the succeeding verses; and 'v. 63 is the clue that the reader must hold fast in attempting to understand the discourse' (Dodd 341).

[8] For the parallels between chs. 4 and 6 see Hoskyns 292.

[9] Barrett, *Gospel* 238; cf. Marsh 295.

[10] Cf. Barrett, *Gospel* 249, 251; Dodd 341f. That ἀναβαίνοντα is used in the same way as ὑψόω here is generally recognized (e.g. Bultmann, *Johannes* 341; Lightfoot 163, 167).

fulfilled in the gift of the Spirit (II Cor. 3.3, 6; I Thess. 4.8 – note how 4.9 also echoes Isa. 54.13). Moreover, with the thought of Jesus' death we are at once into that complex event of death-resurrection-ascension-gift of the Spirit which John holds as an indivisible unity. The thoughtful reader will thus recognize that the assimilation of the life-giving food, which results from Jesus' sacrificial death and whose eating results in eternal life, must refer to the spiritual union of the believer with his Lord which follows Jesus' departure (14.20, 23; 15.1–8 – note the theme of reciprocal indwelling in 6.56; 14.20; 15.4f.), and which is effected by the sending of the other Paraclete.

Any interest in the Lord's Supper is incidental. John's chief purpose is to combat docetism, and he does so by heavily underscoring the offensiveness of the incarnation (σάρξ, τρώγειν). It is just possible that he is using the language of an alternative version of the words of institution at the Last Supper. But if so, then we should note that John's chief use for it is to describe not the effect of the sacrament as such, but the union of the ascended Jesus with his believing followers through the Spirit.[11] Any reference to the sacrament itself reveals not an exaltation of the sacrament as a means of receiving the Spirit and life of Christ, but rather a fairly blunt warning against any such false literalism. The eucharistic flesh avails nothing; life comes through the Spirit and words of Jesus.[12]

This confirms what we might have inferred anyway from John's silence about the Last Supper and about Jesus' baptism – namely, that John is concerned lest too much attention be given to the outward rite, and lest the Spirit be thought of as joined in some way to the physical elements, so that the Spirit, and the life he brings, could only be given through or in connection with these elements. In the discourse of ch. 6 John wishes above all to emphasize that Jesus himself is the source and sustenance of eternal life; he alone, truly incarnate, in his whole person, gives life.[13] Only, it is the incarnate Jesus *as given up to death,* who is the

[11] So Strathmann 123; and see Howard, *IB* 8 573. Note how Ignatius uses the same eucharistic language in similar metaphorical ways: *Trall.* 8.1; *Philad.* 5.1; *Rom.* 7.2f. (on which see J. B. Lightfoot, *Apostolic Fathers* II Vol. II [1855]; also on *Eph.* 5.2).

[12] Howard, *IB* 8 575; cf. Schweizer in *Neotestamentica* (1963) 389–91, and especially 395f.; also *TWNT* VI 439f.; VII 140f. For a fuller treatment of this passage see my forthcoming article in *NTS*.

[13] σάρξ καὶ αἷμα = the whole man (Brown, *Gospel* 282), the whole incarnate life (Barrett, *Gospel* 247), man as distinct from God (P. Borgen, *Bread from Heaven* [1965] 181, 189) = 'me' (v. 57); cf. 11.25; 14.6.

bread of life; however essential was the incarnation to the work of redemption, for John it is not merely Jesus descended who gives life, merely as σάρξ, but rather as also ascended, when he gives himself through and in the Spirit.[14] It is in the believing reception of the Spirit of Christ that we eat the flesh and drink the blood of the incarnate and crucified Christ.

In ch. 6 the Evangelist seems to be envisaging an initial and unrepeatable contact and act of union with Christ by faith, through which life is conveyed to man, rather than a repeated coming, believing and eating (Barrett, *Gospel* 243; Sanders and Mastin 190). 6.51c, 62f. make it clear that this entry into life-giving union with Christ can only result from his death, and is effected once-for-all by the Spirit given by Jesus on his ascending 'where he was before'. In the last analysis the emphasis in ch. 6 lies on the unitary act of redemption in Christ's death, resurrection, ascension and gift of the Spirit (cf. Strathmann 121).

(ii) 'Water' is frequently mentioned in the Fourth Gospel, and 3.5 must be set in the context of John's overall use of the concept – a necessary task too often overlooked by exegetes. From a survey of the relevant references – 1.26, 31, 33; 2.1–11 (4.46); 3.5; 3.22–26; 4.7–15; 5.2–9; 7.37–39; 9.7, 11; 13.1–16; 19.34 – the following important facts emerge.

First, John uses 'water' in two distinct ways – by way of contrast and by way of equation. In chs. 1, 2, 3, and 5, water is that which represents the old dispensation (in its preparatoriness, its poverty, its mere externality, and its inability to help), in *contrast* to that which Jesus gives in the new dispensation (represented by the gift of the Spirit, by wine and by healing).

On ch. 1, see p. 19 above. On ch. 3, see pp. 19ff. above. Most commentators recognize that the water in ch. 2 represents the poverty of the old dispensation in contrast to the richness of the new. Or are we to take it that John intends to contrast Christian baptism unfavourably with the Lord's Supper?!

If symbolism is intended in ch. 5, it is the contrast between the Torah which promised life to men, but which in fact did nothing for them, and the life-giving word of Jesus (Dodd 319; Lightfoot 149; Brown, *Gospel* 211; Marsh 249f.; also Sanders and Mastin 161). It is incredible that Cullmann should find a baptismal reference here (*Worship* 85–87), since the whole point of the story is that the water of the pool did not heal

[14] Cf. Schlatter, *Johannes* 114–19.

the man and did not even contribute to his healing. The healing was accomplished solely by the word of Jesus (cf. 15.3). Is ch. 5 perhaps something of a warning against a sacramentalist attitude to baptism, which fastens its hope in a looked-for automatic efficacy of the water-rite, rather than in Jesus and his word (cf. Bieder 271f.)?

In chs. 4, 7, and 19, water is a *metaphor* for the Spirit given by the glorified Jesus in his ascension (in contrast to the merely physical water of the old dispensation in Jacob's well and at the Feast of Tabernacles[?]).

That the water of which Jesus speaks in ch. 4 is the Spirit in his life-giving operation is indicated by several considerations, of which the following are the most important: (i) he describes it as ἡ δωρεὰ τοῦ θεοῦ. Since for Luke and quite probably Heb. 6.4 δωρεά = the Holy Spirit, and since Paul is very familiar with this sense (see p. 123 above), the implication is that ἡ δωρεὰ τοῦ θεοῦ was a more or less standard expression for the Holy Spirit in early Christianity. (ii) Both 'the gift of the Spirit' and ὕδωρ ζῶν were used in Judaism to describe the Torah (Strack-Billerbeck II 433f.; Barrett, *Gospel* 195); we are back in the contrast between the old order (characterized by law) and the new (characterized by the Spirit), as 4.12–14, 23f. confirm (cf. Rom. 7.6; II Cor. 3.6). John seems to have taken over the standard equation of Wisdom with the waters of the OT and identified Wisdom not with the Torah but with the Holy Spirit (Knox, *Hellenistic Elements* 64; cf. Brown, *Gospel* 178f.; Schnackenburg 467). (iii) The closeness of thought between 4.14b and 6.63a; 7.38f. (iv) In using ἅλλομαι (4.14), which is nowhere else used of water, John may have been thinking of the Spirit's action in Judg. 14.6, 19; 15.14; I Sam. 10.10 – the only occasions when ἅλλομαι translates ṣālēaḥ. (v) Water which is drunk and which becomes in him who drinks it 'a spring of water welling up to eternal life' can hardly be referred to baptism (contra Schweitzer 355f.; Cullmann, *Worship* 80–84; A. G. H. Corell, *Consummatum Est* [ET 1958] 60; Brown, *Gospel* 179f.). Cf. 7.37–39.

In 19.34, the primary reference is anti-docetic (see Beasley-Murray's excellent treatment – 224–6). There is probably a further imagery in mind: while the blood affirms the reality of his death, the water symbolizes the outpouring of the Spirit (Beasley-Murray 225f.; Dodd 349 n. 2; Barrett, *Gospel* 462f.; Sanders and Mastin 412; Clark 28; Thüsing 172; Betz 167f.; Braun III 168; Barth, *Taufe* 167f.). This may seem grotesque to us, but it is the picture of 7.38 which John has in mind (note that the emphasis on belief in 7.38f. is matched by ἵνα καὶ ὑμεῖς πιστεύητε – 19.35; according to Brown, *Gospel* 323, most authors agree on the connection between 7.38 and 19.34). John's point is not that the sacraments derive from the death of Christ (contra Schweitzer 358; Cullmann, *Worship* 114f.; Corell 75) – the blood is mentioned before the water (Schweizer in *Neotestamentica* 381; Strathmann 242; Barth, *Taufe* 416) – but that the Spirit and the life of the Spirit comes directly from the Crucified as a result of his glorification (so Barth, *Dogmatik* IV/4 137f.). We must not give the sacraments the importance or function of the Spirit.

In chs. 9 and 13, the water has no independent significance; the symbolism focuses on the source of healing and the act of cleansing.

With most recent commentators I believe that John means us to understand Jesus himself as ὁ ἀπεσταλμένος (9.7). The pool of Siloam represents Jesus, *not* baptism. *He* is the source of the water which heals, as he is the source of the water which revitalizes (4.14; 7.37f.). John probably intends no symbolism to be read into the water, since he does not mention it. Similarly in ch. 13, the water is only part of the stage-equipment for the central action, like the basin and the towel. The foot-washing itself is a σημεῖον representing Christ's death and the spiritual cleansing which it brings. Peter asks for the impossible, a more complete cleansing, and is rebuked in v. 10, where the shorter reading is original and which is best seen as a polemic against Gnostic claims to a fuller salvation. See my forthcoming article in *ZNW*.

In short, John uses water either as an *example* of what belongs to τὰ κάτω, or to *symbolize* what belongs to τὰ ἄνω.

Second, water for John usually symbolizes something other than itself (even in chs. 9 and 13 where the actions in which it is involved symbolize spiritual illumination and spiritual cleansing). The two exceptions are chs. 1 and 3, where the water refers to water-baptism. But in these cases the water signifies water-baptism as a merely external rite belonging to the order of Jewish purifications and only preparatory for the baptism of the Messiah – the baptism in the Spirit.

Third, the evangelist records only two other water-references on the lips of Jesus (in chs. 4 and 7). On both of these occasions water is used as a metaphor of the Spirit in his life-giving operation.

In the light of these facts we must re-assess the three arguments used to support the view that 3.5 is a baptismal reference.

(*a*) 'The sacramentalism of John' is a misnomer. John is not really interested in the sacraments in his Gospel. This does not mean that he is an anti-sacramentalist; but it certainly excludes the view that much of his symbolism was directed towards the sacraments. We may say that his symbolism points to and portrays the same basic facts of the eternal life won and bestowed by Jesus which the sacraments point to and portray. But that is quite different from saying that his symbols portray the sacraments themselves and indicate that the eternal life is received through the sacraments. This we cannot say. What our survey has shown is that John's symbolism always centres on Jesus, and on Jesus as the mediator of eschatological salvation – that is to say, on Jesus in his salvation-effecting action at the climax of his ministry in his glorification and exaltation, above all in his giving of the Spirit; for it is through the Spirit that the eternal life is bestowed on his followers. The only really plausible reference to a sacrament (in ch. 6), far from presenting the Lord's Supper as a channel through which eternal life is received, on the contrary, specifically dismisses this suggestion, and rather indicates that sacramental language can fittingly be used to describe the life-giving operation of the Spirit in the believer, *only so long as it is not interpreted literally* (that is, of a literal eating and drinking). This greatly lessens the probability of a sacramental reference in 3.5, and any suggestion that water-baptism is the channel through which the life-giving Spirit is mediated is almost totally excluded.

(*b*) The argument drawn from the context of the Nicodemus episode is greatly weakened. In the immediate context, water stands on the far side of the contrast between the old and new dispensations – as an example of what belongs to τὰ κάτω – as that with which the gift of the Spirit is contrasted. But the water reference in 3.5 is of a different order: in 3.5 water is co-ordinate, not contrasted, with the Spirit. It is more likely therefore to belong to that other set of water references which symbolize something other than water, which symbolize that which belongs to τὰ ἄνω. Moreover, in the parallel episode in ch. 4 we have an example of that other Johannine use of water – as a symbol of the life-giving operation of the Spirit (4.14). If there is any significance in the fact that these water references, together with 7.38, are the only ones which appear on the lips of Jesus, and that on each occasion there is a triple link between Spirit, water and life, it would suggest that the water of 3.5 likewise symbolizes the life-giving operation of the Spirit.

(*c*) The argument that no Christian reader could fail to see

Christian baptism, though powerful, must give precedence to the argument drawn from John's theology. Besides assuming that we know when the Gospel was written, and the sacramental understanding of the readers to whom it was addressed, it assumes also that it was John's intention to fit his writing into the context of that understanding and not to challenge or alter it in any radical way. But the Gospel itself hardly gives these assumptions credibility.[15] On the contrary, John seems to be challenging any sacramentalism which he assumes on the part of his readers.

On the other hand, we may not simply list 3.5 along with the other water-Spirit references, for in 3.5 water and Spirit are neither contrasted nor equated, but rather co-ordinated; both together are means of effecting the birth ἄνωθεν. More important, in the other water passages the water with which the Spirit is contrasted and/or equated has a point of reference in the passage which lies outside the contrast and equation (the water of John's baptism, the water of Jacob's well, the water of Tabernacles, the water from Jesus' side). Why then does Jesus speak of water in 3.5,[16] when the idea of birth ἄνωθεν itself does not require it (as the other verses show)? What is the initial point of reference of the water in 3.5 ? The most likely answer is that the author intended his readers to understand the water initially in terms of John's baptism, since in the other relevant passages of the first three chapters the water spoke directly of the old dispensation's rites of purification, particularly John's baptism ἐν ὕδατι.[17]

If this is so, the reader would then understand 3.5 to mean that Christian conversion-initiation is more than Johannine baptism ἐν ὕδατι: it consists either of (Christian) baptism in water and the gift of the Spirit in close connection,[18] or of a cleansing by the Spirit, a cleansing symbolized by John's baptism ἐν ὕδατι.[19]

---

[15] Apart from anything else, vv. 9f. may imply that the themes of vv. 1–8 are to be understood in terms which Nicodemus could have understood.

[16] Bultmann's excision of ὕδατος καί (*Johannes* 98 n. 2; followed by Lohse, *NTS* 7 (1960–61); Dinkler, *RGG*[3] VI (1962) 635; Marxsen, *Introduction* 256; Braun III 86; N. Micklem, *Behold the Man: A Study of the Fourth Gospel* [1969] 83) is wholly unwarranted.

[17] See White 253f.; cf. Marsh 178.

[18] Cf. Zahn, referred to by Bauer 35; Rawlinson 10f.; I. de la Potterie, cited in Schnackenburg 383 n. 3.

[19] The alternatives are by no means mutually exclusive. But that the mention of water implies reading 'baptism in' for 'birth from' has yet to be demonstrated for any passage in the NT. See on Titus 3.5; I Peter 1.23.

This seems to be confirmed by the language in the episode itself.

(i) Birth ἐξ ὕδατος καὶ πνεύματος is equivalent to birth ἄνωθεν (vv. 3, 7), in contrast to birth ἐκ τῆς γῆς. As John is ὁ ὢν ἐκ τῆς γῆς in contrast to ὁ ἄνωθεν ἐρχόμενος (3.31), John's baptism ἐν ὕδατι is to be contrasted with birth from water and Spirit. In view of 1.33 and 3.8, it is evident that the Spirit is the decisive element in the contrast. This would permit either of the two interpretations suggested above, but the same verses rule out the possibility of interpreting 3.5 in terms of the so-called baptism-in-water-and-Spirit.[20] The NT knows of no such baptism. It is more likely that water means water-baptism and Spirit means Spirit-baptism, and that birth from above involves *both* baptisms in very close connection.

Clark suggests that in 3.5 'the Evangelist looks back to the baptism of Jesus himself, when water and Spirit were conjoined' (27 – probably following Cullmann, *Worship* 76). But this line of reasoning is left suspended in mid-air since it has no point of attachment at its far end: had John intended such an association he could hardly have failed to describe Jesus' baptism and the way in which it conjoined water and Spirit. See p. 33 above.

(ii) Birth ἐξ ὕδατος καὶ πνεύματος is birth ἐκ τοῦ πνεύματος in contrast to birth ἐκ τῆς σαρκός (v. 6). It stands wholly within the realm of τὰ ἄνω, and wholly outside the realm of τὰ κάτω.[21] It is something impossible to man (v. 4) – something that man cannot engineer, or contrive, or achieve. It is wholly Spirit-given. And it is given mysteriously, so that the coming of the Spirit cannot be pinned down to a precise time and precise mode, and the effect of his coming cannot be measured; rather, one just becomes aware of his presence in the believer (v. 8).[22] This hardly squares with the view that John thought of the Spirit as given through Christian baptism, let alone through the water of Christian baptism.[23]

(iii) ὕδωρ καὶ πνεῦμα cannot be regarded as independent and unrelated elements in the birth ἄνωθεν; far less can we speak of two

[20] Contra Bauer 35; Barrett, *Gospel* 174; Flemington 87; Wilkens 138.

[21] Cf. Hoskyns 213, 215; Barrett, *Gospel* 175; Lightfoot 116.

[22] Schweizer points out that it is not the Spirit but the bearer of the Spirit who is described in v. 8 (*TWNT* VI 439). More precisely, v. 8 describes the one born of the Spirit *in respect to his birth* ἐκ πνεύματος.

[23] Cf. some valuable comments by Strathmann 68. Contra especially E. F. Scott, *The Fourth Gospel*[2] (1908); Macgregor 72; Brown, *Gospel* CXIV; Schweitzer 359; Cullmann, *Worship* 76; Clark 28.

births.[24] The phrase is a hendiadys, and the single preposition governing both words indicates that ὕδωρ καὶ πνεῦμα forms a single concept[25] – water-and-Spirit. This implies either that Christian conversion-initiation is a (theological) unity of which both water-baptism and Spirit-baptism are integral parts (in which case the verse does not say how they are related), or that the water is a symbol of the life-giving power of the Spirit as in 4.14 and 7.38. The latter is perhaps more likely in view of the fact that the OT finds water a fitting symbol of God's activity in quickening men to life (e.g. Isa. 55.1–3; Jer. 2.13; 17.13; Zech. 14.8; Ezek. 47.9), and one not infrequently linked in Jewish thought with the eschatological re-creation and renewal effected by the gift of the Spirit (Isa. 32.15–17; 44.3–5; Ezek. 36.25–27; 39.29; Joel 2.28; see also Jub. 1.23; Test. Jud. 24.3; 1QS 4.20f.).[26] It should not go unnoticed that the closest parallels to the water and Spirit correlation of John 3.5 are to be found in Ezek. 36.25–27 and 1QS 4.20–22.[27] The further we set John's Gospel into the context of Palestinian Judaism, as expressed particularly in the Qumran sect, the more weight will we have to give to this use of 'water' *with* 'Spirit' to symbolize renewal by Spirit. Nor should we forget that John's baptism seems to have been for the Baptist himself a symbol of the eschatological purging effected through the Spirit. As it is the Spirit-of-truth (πνεῦμα καὶ ἀλήθεια) who makes spiritual worship possible (4.23f.), so it is the water-of-the-Spirit (ὕδωρ καὶ πνεῦμα) which effects birth ἄνωθεν.

The other way of taking the hendiadys, water-which-is-(also)-Spirit (Dodd 312), as though the Spirit operates through the water of baptism (see the authors cited in n. 23 above), or the water is made potent by the Spirit (E. K. Lee, *The Religious Thought of St John* [1950] 189), is hardly acceptable in view of the considerations marshalled in these paragraphs.

(iv) The further conversation indicates that the birth ἄνωθεν, ἐκ πνεύματος is to be equated with the eternal life which results from

[24] As does, e.g., Hoskyns 215.
[25] A fairly typical feature of the Johannine style. See also 4.23f.; 6.63; Dodd 314 n. 2, 341f.; Brown, *Gospel* 130, 297. Schnackenburg 471 n. 3 refers also to 1.14, 17; 14.6; I John 3.18; II John 3.
[26] Cf. Barth, *Taufe* 445, 449; S. H. Hooke, NTS 9 (1962–63) 375.
[27] Cf. F. M. Cross, *The Ancient Library of Qumran and Modern Biblical Studies* (1958) 155.

the Son of Man being lifted up and which comes to man through faith (vv. 13–15). We are thus led forward to 20.22 where the play on πνεῦμα is very similar to that in 3.8. Birth from above is the gift of the Spirit by the ascended Lord to those who believe in him; and in 20.22 that birth is effected in complete independence of water.[28]

It may be that John is also doing here what he did in 6.51–56 – taking up sacramental language for its symbolical value with the aim of correcting a false sacramentalism[29] – Christian baptism being the initial point of reference for the 'water'. By including the words ὕδατος καί he acknowledges the importance of water-baptism and its close connection with the gift of the Spirit in conversion-initiation. But for him its importance lies in its relation to and symbolism of the Spirit's renewing work.

It is, of course, a feature of John's style that Jesus uses words which cause misunderstanding, so that he can go on to correct that misunderstanding and to draw out their true meaning (see e.g. Lightfoot 131). It is quite likely that in 3.5 and 6.51–56 he is doing the same sort of thing. Bultmann, commenting on ἄνωθεν, notes that the twofold meaning of John's language consists 'in that he uses concepts and statements which in their regular sense refer to earthly matters, but in their actual sense to divine' (*Johannes* 95 n. 2).

It is important to remember that in 3.3–8 John is talking of regeneration ἐκ πνεύματος, to which 'water' is somehow intimately related, not of baptism, to which we must relate the Spirit. Had John regarded the water (meaning water-baptism) as important in itself and essential to the thought of re-birth, he would surely have mentioned it again and given it more prominence. The fact that he does not, the fact that he only mentions water as part of a single concept with Spirit, and the fact that he goes on to stress that the birth ἐξ ὕδατος καὶ πνεύματος is a birth effected by the Spirit and belongs wholly within the sphere of πνεῦμα, and wholly outside the sphere of σάρξ, implies that he is saying something like this to his readers, whether disciples of the Baptist who still over-valued John's baptism, or Christians who over-valued the Christian sacrament: The water which you value is only a symbol of the

---

[28] See also p. 175. On the place of faith see Strathmann 68; Beasley-Murray 230f. There may well be a link intended between 1.12, 1.33f. and 3.5. Cf. also de la Potterie (see n. 18 above).

[29] Cf. Barth, *Dogmatik* IV/4 133.

quickening power of the Spirit; water-baptism is of no avail, it is the Spirit who gives life.

John's writings reflect a later stage when the magical-sacramental views of the mystery cults would be exerting a dangerous influence on many Christians.[30] This danger he seeks to counter by his silence on the two great sacramental rites in Jesus' ministry, by his correction of literalistic sacramentalism and emphasis that the sacramental elements are essentially symbols, and by his insistence on focusing attention on the life-giving activity of the Spirit which is the climax and result of Christ's exaltation in death, resurrection and ascension.

If Brown is correct in his conjecture that one of the purposes of the Fourth Gospel was to bridge the gap between the Church of John's day and 'the already distant Jesus' (*NTS* 13 [1966–67] 128), then we should note that far from localizing Jesus' presence in the sacraments, John seems to be warning against the attitude which finds solace for the delay of the parousia in the sacraments. John therefore ignores the sacraments and points directly to the Spirit. Jesus is present with his disciples in the Spirit and through the Word.

The Fourth Gospel, we might say, was the last plea of first-generation Christianity for a true balance in its devotional and sacramental life, before the development of institutional, hierarchical and sacral Christianity began to tip that balance more and more out of the true, until, within a relatively few generations, for the great majority of Christians, worship in Spirit and truth was submerged beneath a growing mass of ritual and ceremony.

[30] Howard, *Christianity* 149; Macgregor, *NTS* 9 (1962–63) 118.

# XVI

## THE SPIRIT AND THE WORD IN THE
## LETTERS OF JOHN

THE author of the Fourth Gospel may have believed that the
apostles' Spirit-baptism was distinct from and subsequent to their
regeneration, and also that water-baptism played a key part in the
birth ἄνωθεν. Do Pentecostals and sacramentalists find any further
support for their views in his other writings (assuming that we
owe the Johannine epistles to his pen)?[1] The passages which
demand attention are I John 2.20, 27; 3.9; and 5.6–12.

### I John 2.20, 27; 3.9

We take these passages together since χρίσμα and σπέρμα are
obviously closely related; most would agree that they refer to the
same thing – either the Word or the Spirit, or the Spirit with the
Word. The suggested meanings for χρίσμα are broader; they can
be summed up under two heads:

(*a*) where the reference is to something other than the Spirit:
(i) a sacramental rite either of baptism or anointing;[2] (ii) the Word,
the Gospel;[3]

(*b*) where the reference is to the Spirit: (i) the Spirit alone,[4] and

---

[1] See Kümmel 310–12, 315.

[2] J. Chaine, *Les Épîtres Catholiques*[2] (1939) 170; Wilckens 107; Dix, *Laying
on of Hands* 10f.; Marsh 201; J. Ysebaert, *Greek Baptismal Terminology* (1962)
186, 263; cf. Thornton, *Mystery* 22, 45; Lowther Clarke 12. H. Windisch and
H. Preisker give three alternatives which include these two views (*Die
katholischen Briefe*[3] [HNT 1951] 117); they think both χρίσμα and σπέρμα derive
from a sacramental-magical view (119).

[3] C. H. Dodd, *The Johannine Epistles* (Moffatt 1946) 62–64; Beasley-Murray
234–6; Dinkler, *RGG*[3] VI 635; Braun III 172.

[4] R. Law, *The Tests of Life* (1909) 352; A. Schlatter, *Erläuterungen* 9 Teil
45f.; Delling, *Taufe* 107f.; J. R. W. Stott, *The Epistles of John* (1964) 106, 109f.,
114; TEV. Windisch's third possibility is Spirit-baptism.

even as distinct from conversion-initiation;[5] (ii) the Spirit as given in baptism,[6] or in some more complex rite.[7]

The range of meanings suggested for σπέρμα is more limited: either the Word,[8] or the Spirit alone,[9] or the Spirit as specifically given in or through baptism.[10]

The first alternative we may dismiss at once. χρίσμα is certainly used metaphorically, and neither literally nor of a magical rite. Besides a ritual anointing with oil being impossible to prove and 'altogether unlikely' for NT times, the decisive fact is that the χρίσμα abides *in* them, and has the personal function of teaching them (v. 27).[11]

The second alternative – χρίσμα = teaching, the Word of God – is much more weighty.[12] John often speaks of receiving (λαμβάνειν) the testimony (μαρτυρία – John 3.11, 32, 33; 5.34; I John 5.9), the commandment (ἐντολή – John 10.18; II John 4), or the words (ῥήματα – John 12.48; 17.8). Even more significant is the way he can speak of this divine teaching abiding (μένειν), or being (εἶναι) in them.[13] On the other hand, John speaks in a similar way of receiving the Spirit (John 7.39; 14.17; 20.22), and of the Spirit and the divine presence in the disciples (14.17, 20; 15.4; I John 3.9, 24; 4.12, 13, 15, 16).

Dodd cites Ign. *Eph.* 17.1, where Ignatius equates the ointment (μύρον) poured on the Lord's head (Matt. 26; Mark 14) with 'God's knowledge, which is Jesus Christ'. But compare Clement of Alexandria, who in commenting on the parallel incident in Luke and John takes the

[5] Most Pentecostals.

[6] A. E. Brooke, *Johannine Epistles* (ICC 1912) 55f.; Lampe, *Seal* 61, 81; Davies 161; G. Johnston in *Peake* 907b; R. Bultmann, *Die drei Johannesbriefe* (1967) 42f. J. Schneider, *Die Briefe des Jakobus, Petrus, Judas und Johannes*⁹ (NTD 1961) is not so certain (157).

[7] B. F. Westcott, *The Epistles of St John* (1883) 73; Chase 59; W. Nauck, *Die Tradition und der Charakter des ersten Johannesbrief* (1957) 94–98.

[8] Dodd 77f.; Braun III 117f.

[9] Büchsel, *TDNT* I 671, 672 n. 37.

[10] Windisch-Preisker 122f.; R. Schnackenburg, *Die Johannesbriefe*² (1963) 176, 191; Davies 99.

[11] Dodd 59; Beasley-Murray 233f.; Schnackenburg 161; J. Michl in *Festschrift für Max Meinertz* (1951) 143 n. 15. See also p. 134 above.

[12] However, it is dismissed by Windisch-Preisker 117; Michl 143f.; Nauck 94; Schnackenburg 134.

[13] ῥήματα: John 15.7; ὁ λόγος: John 5.38; I John 1.10; 2.14; ἡ ἀλήθεια: I John 1.8; 2.4; II John 2; ἐντολή: I John 2.8; ἡ μαρτυρία: 5.10; most noticeable is the close parallelism between 2.27 and 2.24 – see Beasley-Murray 234.

ointment to be a symbol τῆς εὐωδίας τοῦ χρίσματος ἁγίου πνεύματος (*Paedagogus* II.8.61.3).

The answer may well be that·John in speaking of χρίσμα is not thinking clearly of one or other, but of both.[14] Yet, while it is probably a mistake to distinguish sharply between the two, we must give the Spirit first place: the χρίσμα is the Spirit – albeit the Spirit working in conjunction with, or even through the Word.

First, the χρίσμα teaches you about everything. Now, for John, the function of teacher is always a personal one.[15] This contrasts with the very impersonal language of 2.24 – ὑμεῖς ὃ ἠκούσατε ἀπ᾽ ἀρχῆς, ἐν ὑμῖν μενέτω; whereas it compares very favourably with the role of the Spirit in 3.24 and 4.13. The role of the teaching is passive, the role of teacher (χρίσμα) and the Spirit is active. Moreover, the διδάσκει ὑμᾶς περὶ πάντων (2.27) may well be a deliberate echo of John 14.26 – ὑμᾶς διδάξει πάντα.

Second, it is very difficult to avoid the conclusion that by σπέρμα John means the Spirit, especially when he uses it in talking about divine begetting. This rules out Dodd's parallel with the parable of the sower (where the metaphor is agricultural not personal) and makes certain the parallel with John 3.3–8. It is the Spirit who effects the divine birth, the Spirit who is the divine seed.

The parallels with James 1.18 (ἀπεκύησεν ἡμᾶς λόγῳ ἀληθείας) and I Peter 1.23 (ἀναγεγεννημένοι ἐκ σπορᾶς . . . ἀφθάρτου διὰ λόγου ζῶντος θεοῦ καὶ μένοντος) are hardly as close. Moreover, the σπορά is *distinct from* the λόγος, and it could well be that we should identify the σπορά with the Spirit (γεγεννημένον ἐκ τοῦ πνεύματος – John 3.6). This would confirm my suggestion that the Spirit works through the Word (διὰ τοῦ λόγου). Certainly it does not provide support for the view that σπέρμα = λόγος.

Third, as to the connection between the Spirit and the teaching, we should note the following points: (i) it is the Spirit of God who is behind and prompts the correct confession (4.2); (ii) the Spirit is the truth (5.6) – hence the comment that the χρίσμα is true (2.27);

---

[14] So Bultmann, *Theology* II 88; de la Potterie in Schnackenburg 152; cf. A. N. Wilder, *IB* 12 (1957) 245f.; T. W. Manson, *JTS* 48 (1947) 29. On σπέρμα Schulz speaks of 'the Spirit revealing himself in God's Word' (*TWNT* VII 545); cf. Westcott 108. Nauck thinks a decision between the two (Spirit or Word) is not possible (64).

[15] Apart from the taunt to the blind man (John 9.34), only the Father (8.28) and the Spirit (14.26) are called teachers other than Jesus (6.59; 7.14, 28, 35; 8.[2], 20; 18.20).

(iii) the Spirit was promised as one who would bear witness concerning Jesus (John 15.26), and is described as τὸ μαρτυροῦν (I John 5.6) – hence Christians have in themselves ἡ μαρτυρία (5.11); (iv) compare also 4.4 and 5.4 where victory is ascribed both to ὁ ἐν ὑμῖν and to ἡ πίστις ἡμῶν; (v) nor should we forget the close link between the ῥήματα and the Spirit in John 6.63, and the relation between the παράκλητος and the παράκλησις of the Christian community.

While Barrett's attempt to give παράκλητος the sense of 'the Spirit of Christian paraclesis' is hardly to be accepted — the legal terminology of John 15.26; 16.8–11, and the sense of I John 2.1 make NEB's 'Advocate' preferable – the idea of the Spirit working through the Word to make it effective would be wholly Johannine (cf. Barrett, *JTS* 1 [1950] 12–15; *Gospel* 385f.; Schweizer, *TWNT* VI 440–42; Bultmann, *Johannes* 432, 442, 444, also 140; Richardson 112–15; Käsemann, *RGG*³ II 1277f.; Schlier 236–8). The Johannine emphasis on the Word (λόγος – 5.24, 38; 8.31f., 37, 43, 51f.; 12.48; 17.14, 17; I John 1.10; 2.5, 7, 14; ῥήματα – 3.34; 6.68; 12.47f.) reminds us of the important role Paul gives to preaching.

We may say with some confidence, therefore, that the χρῖσμα and the σπέρμα refer to the Spirit, but the Spirit using the proclamation and teaching of the Gospel, so that to respond to the one is to receive the other.

But should we define this activity of the Spirit more closely and tie it down to some particular ceremony? Or rather, does *John* intend that we should do so, or presuppose such a context? Or, on the other hand, should we divorce this talk of the Spirit completely from conversion-initiation, as Pentecostals would wish?

The answer to all these questions is the same – No! In a letter in which baptism is conspicuous by its absence, we have no grounds whatsoever for saying that John is thinking of an activity of the Spirit at baptism.[16] As Schnackenburg points out on 2.20, John does not reflect on the way in which they first received the Spirit; his concern is with the continuing, abiding power of the Spirit (cf. 3.9 – μένει). Moreover, the probability that the thought here is of the Spirit operating in conjunction with the Word makes a reference to a baptismal confession less likely.[17] John has in mind

[16] Contra Windisch-Preisker 123; Nauck 96.
[17] Contra Beasley-Murray 235.

the Gospel which is responded to rather than the response itself. We seem to be back with Paul here, with the focus on that time when the Gospel was proclaimed and the Spirit used it in his work of renewal, so that to believe (in) the Word was to receive the Spirit (cf. John 7.39; I John 5.1, 10). The decisive elements in conversion-initiation on the divine side (the phrase is always γεγεννῆσθαι ἐκ τοῦ θεοῦ) appear once again to be the Spirit and the Word. Of baptism there is no thought.[18]

On the other hand, it is impossible to go along with a Pentecostal view of these passages – namely that the anointing is a baptism in the Spirit subsequent to conversion. First, if we take σπέρμα = the Holy Spirit, then since the divine σπέρμα is the agent of regeneration, we can hardly say other than that regeneration is the σπέρμα (Spirit) coming to abide in the initiate.

Second, it is quite likely that both χρίσμα and σπέρμα are Gnostic words, and almost certain that 2.20, 27 are aimed at Gnostic teachers.[19] And, as Dodd remarks, 'It is a safe assumption that these early heretics, like their successors, the "Gnostics" of the second century, laid claim to a superior gnosis, or knowledge of divine things, of which they deemed the ordinary Christians incapable' (53). With this claim we may compare the Pentecostal teaching on the baptism in the Spirit; for though they are hardly Gnostics, in that they believe *all* Christians could and should have this greater and deeper experience of God, yet, *in fact*, since *in their eyes* only a minority of Christians have had this experience, the practical outworking of the doctrine is the same: only they have had this 'second blessing', and all other Christians are less well equipped for service and much poorer in spiritual experience. It is precisely against such esoteric and factious teaching that John directs his polemic. *All* Christians have knowledge,[20] because all have been anointed with the Holy Spirit. There are not a number of Christians who are still awaiting this anointing. Even the *possibility* that there could be unanointed Christians would have been out

[18] See also p. 133 above. Faith, though quite prominent, is always thought of as a present continuing belief in Jesus (3.23; 4.16; 5.1, 5, 10, 13). Similarly ὁμολόγειν in 2.23 and 4.2 (contra Nauck 86).

[19] Dodd 60f., 77; cf. Schnackenburg 154.

[20] πάντες is more difficult and better attested than πάντα, and the change from πάντες to πάντα is more easily accounted for than its reverse. As Schnackenburg points out, the emphasis falls on the οἴδατε not its object. The πάντες is best seen as a counter to the Gnostic claim to have special knowledge over against the less enlightened Christians.

of the question for John, since it would have meant conceding a crucial point to the heretics. The anointing with the χρίσμα of Christ is not to be distinguished from the regeneration through the σπέρμα of God; all who are born of the Spirit are *ipso facto* anointed with the Spirit.

Third, we have seen how closely the Spirit is related to the teaching. But the teaching which abides in them is what they have heard 'from the beginning' (2.24; cf. 2.7; 3.11; II John 6). The reception of the Spirit who abides in them (2.27) is hardly to be distinguished from the reception of this teaching. In other words, the Spirit was received, like the teaching, at and as the beginning of their Christian lives.

### I John 5.6–12

Does John have the Christian sacraments in mind here? The majority of exegetes would probably answer with a strong affirmative so far as v. 8 is concerned. Verse 6, it is generally agreed, refers to the once-for-all historical events in Jesus' life – the ἐλθών requires this – his baptism and his death, the former being the inauguration of his ministry and the latter its climax. As most agree it is probably correct to infer from v. 6b that John is attacking those who affirmed Jesus Christ's baptism but denied his passion: hence, John firmly asserts that Jesus Christ, the Son of God, came not by the water only, but by the water *and* by the blood. This certainly gives a better understanding of these words than the explanation which sees in v. 6b a reference to the Christian sacraments.

Windisch and Wilder sharply distinguish the two prepositions διά and ἐν, giving the latter the sense of 'with': that is, he has brought water and blood, namely the two sacraments (so Goguel 317; cf. Schweitzer 358f.). But the switch from διά to ἐν is probably no more than a stylistic variation (Brooke 135; Schweizer in *Neotestamentica* 375; Beasley-Murray 237 n. 2; Schnackenburg 259; Barth, *Taufe* 399, who refers to Rom. 6.4 (διά) and Col. 2.12 (ἐν); cf. Blass-Debrunner-Funk 233(3) with 219(4)), and the ἐλθών undoubtedly governs v. 6b as well (cf. Windisch-Preisker 132; Schnackenburg 258f.). That two different events are involved, and not simply Christ's baptism (cf. Flemington 89f.) or 19.34 (e.g. Thüsing 165–74; JB), is indicated by the separation of δι' ὕδατος καὶ αἵματος into two separate phrases – οὐκ ἐν τῷ ὕδατι μόνον, ἀλλ' ἐν τῷ ὕδατι καὶ ἐν τῷ αἵματι (Brooke 135).

Many believe, however, that with v. 7 the focus changes from past history to present experience: viz to the Christian sacraments. The principal argument is that whereas in v. 6 the water and the blood were historical factors, to the reality of which the Spirit testified, now in vv. 7f. the water and the blood have become joint witnesses with the Spirit in the present experience of the Church. From being past events, the objects of the Spirit's witness, they become themselves present witnesses with the Spirit.[21] Confirmation is found in the parallel with Ignatius: particularly *Smyrn.* 7.1: 'They hold aloof from the Eucharist . . . because they refuse to admit that the Eucharist is the flesh of our Saviour Jesus Christ, which suffered for our sins . . .' The Lord's Supper carried such a clear message about the reality of Christ's death that those who denied the latter could not bring themselves to partake of the former (at least in company with their orthodox fellows).[22] Thus, it is maintained that for both Ignatius and John, 'the eucharist was considered a testing-point of one's attitude towards the humanity of Jesus'.[23] Once again I find myself unconvinced.

(i) It is a fact that αἷμα by itself is never used in the NT as a designation of the Lord's Supper.[24] And, for all the much vaunted parallels, the same is true of Ignatius. He refers to the eucharist by the single term 'bread' (*Eph.* 5.2; 20.2), and by the dual terms 'flesh and blood' (*Philad.* 4); but when he uses σάρξ alone he is almost always speaking of the incarnate Jesus (*Eph.* 7.2; 20.2; *Magn.* 1.2; 13.2; *Philad.* 5.1; *Smyrn.* 1.2; 3.1; *Polyc.* 5.2 – *Smyrn.* 7.1 is the only exception). And he never uses αἷμα alone except in reference to Christ's passion (*Eph.* 1.1; *Philad.* inscrp; *Smyrn.* 1.1; 6.1). In *Smyrn.*, 'flesh and blood' refers not to the eucharist but to the incarnate Jesus (3.2 (Armenian version); 12.2).[25] Moreover, the only two other references to αἷμα in I John (1.7; 5.6) undoubtedly

---

[21] Schnackenburg 261; Schweizer in *Neotestamentica* 377; Bultmann, *Johannesbriefe* 83f.; cf. Dodd 130f.; Nauck 147f.

[22] Schnackenburg 262; Schweizer in *Neotestamentica* 377f.

[23] O. S. Brooks, *JBL* 82 (1963) 296; cf. Nauck 150f.

[24] Brooke 132; Beasley-Murray 240. Nauck thinks that this is a point in favour of the view that the reference is to baptism alone – the Spirit being the gift of baptism, the water the element of baptism, and the blood the ground of baptism (149).

[25] That 12.2 refers to the eucharist is possible (Schnackenburg 263), but it is more likely to be a final emphatic rebuttal of the false doctrine of the docetists, especially in view of the context and of the strong antidocetic polemic which has run through the first seven chapters of the letter.

refer to Christ's death, and whereas in 5.6 it is seen as a past event, in 1.7 its cleansing power is part of the present continuing experience of the Christian community.

Any connection between John 19.34 and I John 5.8 supports the view that in the latter John is thinking of the death of the incarnate Jesus, rather than of the sacraments (see Dodd 129f.; Beasley-Murray 241).

(ii) More important is the question whether in fact the water and blood references have changed.[26] In the first place, to say that the water and the blood are the objects of the Spirit's witness in v.6 is not quite correct. The Spirit bears witness to the Son of God, to Jesus Christ, to him who came by water and blood – not merely to two events of his earthly life. The Spirit thus testifies that the earthly Jesus was the Christ, the Son of God. This is the very point which John has been emphasizing in the preceding paragraph (5.1, 5), and it is this thought which he takes up and continues into vv. 6f.: This Son of God is he who came by water and blood, Jesus Christ . . . The water and the blood are emphasized, not because they as such are the objects of the Spirit's witness, but because the events which they designate were the focus of the dispute with the docetists – the key points of the whole incarnate life of the One to whom the Spirit bears witness (his promised role – John 15.26; 16.9, 14).[27] Then, having thus identified Jesus Christ, the Son of God with the one who came by water and blood, John takes up these two events and, because they span the whole of Jesus' ministry, calls them as witnesses to the reality of the incarnation, beside the key witness, the Spirit.

In the second place, it does not follow that the change in tense (ἐλθών v. 6; εἰσιν οἱ μαρτυροῦντες v. 7) rules out a reference to the historical events. Having failed to take into account the preceding context of vv. 6–8, the sacramentalists have also failed to take into account the verses which follow.

Schnackenburg makes v. 9 begin a new train of thought (263), but the αὕτη ἐστὶν ἡ μαρτυρία τοῦ θεοῦ can only refer back to vv. 7f. Schnackenburg's attempt to show that the formula always points forward (264) breaks down, since all the parallels he cites have the

---

[26] Brooke 137, Barth, *Taufe* 405, Beasley-Murray 241, Schneider, *Briefe* 183, say No.

[27] Note how close the thought is between John 16.9 and I John 5.1, 5, 10.

explanation following immediately (usually of the form αὕτη δε ἐστὶν X ὅτι or ἵνα), and they all stand at the head of a new sentence and never in a subordinate clause. Whereas in v. 9 the ὅτι αὕτη ἐστίν . . . with no explanation given inevitably points back to what went before. That John has simply departed from his usual custom is further implied by the fact that he has done the same in v. 6, following μαρτυρέω with ὅτι = because, rather than ὅτι = that – so un-Johannine a conjunction that Manson thought it sufficient ground to prefer the Vulgate reading (he suspects the original was ὅτι ἐστὶν ἡ ἀλήθεια) that *Christ* is the truth (27).

Verse 9 clearly indicates that this threefold witness is the witness of God, and it is the testimony which he bore (μεμαρτύρηκεν) (cf. John 5.31–39).[28] The tense here and in v. 10 is rather striking, since it indicates that there is *both a past and present* element in this witness. Verse 10 confirms this: he who believes in the Son of God *has* (ἔχει) the testimony *in himself* . . . the testimony that God *has borne* (μεμαρτύρηκεν) to his Son. We see further how past and present are held in tension in vv. 11f., when this testimony is defined:[29] 'that God gave (ἔδωκεν) us eternal life, and this life is in his Son. He who has the Son has life: he who has not the Son of God has not life.' The ἔδωκεν refers to the historical ministry of Christ;[30] v. 12 to the possession of the Spirit of the Son.[31] We have, therefore, on the one hand, the historical events which testify to the Son of God and to the eternal life which is in him. This is God's testimony, and it is valid now as when he first gave it (μεμαρτύρηκεν). And, on the other hand, and hard to distinguish finally from the former, is the inner testimony, the indwelling Spirit who testifies to Jesus Christ, God's Son both in his incarnate life (4.2; 5.7f.) and in his abiding in Christians (3.24; 4.13; 5.11f.).

This brings us back to the χρίσμα and the σπέρμα, and to the happy balance John maintains between the objective givenness of the Christian message and the subjective experience of the indwelling Spirit of Christ. As in 2.27, so here, John is thinking both of the Christian message and of the Spirit who worked in conjunction

---

[28] Dodd 131f.; Beasley-Murray 241; cf. Law 124.
[29] Contra Schnackenburg 266. It is incorrect to say that the formula of John 3.19; 17.3 (I John 4.10 is different) does not introduce a definition.
[30] Brooke 140.
[31] Cf. 4.4; 'he who is in you' is the Spirit of Christ, as against 'he who is in the world', viz. the spirit of antichrist (4.3); see also 3.24; 4.13, and cf. 5.12 with John 6.63; 20.22.

with it. Or, to put it in terms of the present argument, he was thinking of the faith of those born of God's Spirit (5.4) – the faith that Jesus is the Son of God (5.5). This faith was a belief about Jesus Christ who became flesh and was both baptized and died (5.6). With many the hearing of that message was matched by the witness of the Spirit to their consciences as to its truth (5.7). Those who believed entered into a spiritual relationship of life with Jesus through the Spirit (5.10f.). In this relationship they were kept from error by remaining faithful to the *continuing* witness of the message first delivered (2.24, 27; 5.8), and by responding to the *continuing* teaching and witness of the Spirit (2.27; 5.8). It was through the indwelling Spirit and the indwelling gospel that they were able to overcome the world (4.4; 5.4f.).

The ἐν αὐτῷ of 5.10 would rule out the sacramental reference if nothing else did – whereas it accords too well with 2.14, 24; II John 2 for ἡ μαρτυρία to be anything other than the Christian message.

In short, the water and the blood refer no more to the sacraments in 5.8 than they did in 5.6. Rather they designate the key events in the incarnate ministry of Jesus. As such they join with the Spirit in bearing witness to the reality of that incarnate ministry – but that witness, whether we take it as a whole (the Spirit working in conjunction with the message) or in its parts (Spirit and message), is not a once-for-all witness, but a continuing witness, one that abides in all who believe that Jesus is the Christ, the Son of God.

To sum up briefly. Even if Pentecostals were justified in arguing from John that the *apostles'* Spirit-baptism was a post-regeneration experience, I John emphatically rejects any suggestion that the anointing of the Spirit is an experience which some Christians may not possess. And even if John 3.5 can justly be understood to indicate the important role of water-baptism in regeneration, most probably as being the occasion and context of the Spirit's life-giving descent and entrance into a life, I John certainly gives the sacramentalist no further scope, since it does not even mention the Christian rite. Our study of John's writings generally has rather confirmed that for John as well as for Luke and Paul the Spirit and the Word are co-ordinate factors and the decisive instruments of God's saving purpose.

# PART FIVE

# XVII

## THE SPIRIT AND BAPTISM IN HEBREWS

W E have now examined the three principal NT theologians – Luke, Paul and John – and we have seen that they are in remarkable agreement as to the centrality of the gift of the Spirit in conversion-initiation. The importance they have ascribed to water-baptism has varied according to the variety of situations addressed: John's theology at this point has been least easy to clarify, but Luke and Paul have clearly seen it as the vital, perhaps necessary, expression of the faith to which God gives the Spirit. We turn now to the few passages which remain to be studied – in Hebrews and I Peter.

*Heb. 6.1–6*

Apart from Acts 8 and 19 no other passage has provided such strong support for those who hold a high doctrine of Confirmation. On the face of it, it would seem natural to see in 6.2a a reference to two rites performed at initiation – Christian water-baptism, and laying on of hands. Nor can one complain when Acts 8 and 19 are called in to illuminate the relation between these two rites. The deduction then lies to hand that the second rite has to do with the gift of the Spirit. Its place in a list of first principles and elementary instruction to enquirers or converts implies that it was a rite of no little significance and importance. Was it then merely an act which corresponds to a welcoming handshake today, as Lampe suggests?[1] Was the διδαχή not much more likely to be an explanation concerning the gift of the Spirit? As Leeming asks, 'What other instruction could have been given about the laying on of hands in connection with baptism?'[2] It is then possible to

---

[1] *Seal* 77f.; cf. p. 87 n. 9 above.
[2] 218; see also Thornton, *Mystery* 170; Neunheuser 43f.; cf. Chase 45.

call in vv. 4f. and to argue that while φωτισθέντας refers to baptism,[3] the μετόχους γενηθέντας πνεύματος ἁγίου refers to the gift of the Spirit in Confirmation.[4] Pentecostals have not made much of the passage, but presumably they would be happy either to adapt this exposition to their own tastes, or to say of the two rites in 6.2a, with T. H. Robinson, 'Both concern a second stage in the spiritual history of the Christian, the reception of the Holy Spirit.'[5]

(i) Taking first the list of foundation elements (6.1f.), we are immediately faced with the difficult βαπτισμοί. Many explanations of this puzzling plural have been offered.[6] But if we accept that this letter was written to Christians,[7] vv. 1f. must contain basic teaching given to new Christians or to those enquiring about the Christian faith.

The difficult phrase τὸν τῆς ἀρχῆς τοῦ Χριστοῦ λόγον most probably means something like 'the rudiments of Christianity' (NEB), 'elementary teaching about Christ', or perhaps even 'the original teaching given by Christ' (so J. C. Adams, *NTS* 13 [1966–67] 378–85). Kosmala's 'teaching about the beginning of the messianic life' will hardly do in view of the meaning of Χριστός elsewhere in the epistle.

Most probably those addressed are converts from Judaism, the initial preaching to them having taken up what was valid in their old belief. This is the best explanation of the non-(specifically)-Christian list of six points: they describe an area of overlap between Judaism and Christianity in terms common to both; they are the

---

[3] So A. Nairne, *The Epistle to the Hebrews* (1917) lxxxiv; Cullmann, *Baptism* 15; Church of Scotland, *Biblical Doctrine* 43; Richardson 348; Mollat 83; M. E. Boismard in *BNT* 222; H. Strathmann, *Der Brief an die Hebräer*[8] (NTD 1963) 104; H. W. Montefiore, *The Epistle to the Hebrews* (1964) 108; E. Käsemann, *Das wandernde Gottesvolk* (1938) 119.

[4] Chase 46; Lowther Clarke 10; Thornton, who also refers γευσαμένους τῆς δωρεᾶς τῆς ἐπουρανίου to baptism (*Mystery* 169f.).

[5] T. H. Robinson, *The Epistle to the Hebrews* (Moffatt 1933) 72.

[6] See e.g. C. Spicq, *L'Épître aux Hébreux* II (1953) 148.

[7] H. Kosmala, *Hebräer – Essener – Christen* (1959) has argued that the writer is not addressing Christians but Jews – Jews whose beliefs were very similar to those of the Essenes and who could not yet be called Christians (but see also Bruce, *NTS* 9 [1962–63] 217–32). In particular, Kosmala argues that the six points of 6.1f. are identical with the basic views of the Essenes (31–38). It has often been noted that none of the six elements of instruction are particularly Christian, as distinct from Jewish (there is no mention of Christ or of the Holy Spirit – see e.g. E. C. Wickham, *The Epistle to the Hebrews* [1910] 39; Nairne 66; O. Michel, *Der Brief an die Hebräer*[12] [1966] 238 n. 4; F. F. Bruce, *The Epistle to the Hebrews* [1964] 112).

points at which the Christian evangel to Jews would begin, the points which the evangelist would then elaborate in specifically Christian terms. βαπτισμοί must then at least include a reference to Christian baptism, a conclusion confirmed by the close link here between βαπτισμοί and laying on of hands (cf. Acts 8.19).

This would rule out the interpretation of βαπτισμοί in terms of water-baptism and Spirit-baptism (Baker 6; Harper, *Fire* 15f.; also allowed as a possibility by Marsh 189). The latter was not an element of Jewish teaching and it is most improbable that the letter was written to disciples of the Baptist. Bruce's suggestion that βαπτισμοί may refer to a pre-baptismal bath, 'a legacy from Roman Judaism' (116) is hardly convincing. That βαπτισμός is used instead of the usual βάπτισμα is hardly decisive against the reference to Christian baptism in view of the strongly supported reading of βαπτισμῷ in Col. 2.12. On Adams' view (see p. 206), βαπτισμοί would probably refer to Christ's instruction on the relation of John's baptism to that of his own disciples (383). But if such διδαχὴ βαπτισμῶν was preserved (a questionable assumption – in Acts 1.5; 11.16 the two baptisms are John's water-baptism and Christ's Spirit-baptism), it would be regarded as part of the justification for continuing the practice of water-baptism and so part of the basic teaching about Christian baptism. However, if we relate διδαχὴ βαπτισμῶν to the only teaching on baptism which is attributed to Jesus (apart from Acts 1.5; 11.16) we must look to Matt. 28.19 (Mark 16.16) where the reference is to Christian baptism as such.

As to the relation between baptism and the laying on of hands, the very unusual use of τε (instead of καί) suggests that what is envisaged is a single ceremony,[8] like that in Acts 19, the single rite of initiation. A separation into two distinct rites can therefore hardly be advocated on the basis of this passage.

The relation between 6.1 and 6.2 is also fairly clear. It is best to read διδαχήν with the great majority of commentators, and to take the 'instruction about cleansing rites and the laying on of hands, about the resurrection of the dead and eternal judgment', in apposition to 'the foundation of repentance and faith'. That is to say, the laying of the foundation consists in the giving of instruction; the foundation is laid by instructing about . . .[9] This has an important corollary, for it means that repentance and faith

---

[8] τε indicates a closer relationship than καί (Spicq 148).

[9] So Bruce 112; J. Moffatt, *Epistle to the Hebrews* (ICC 1924) 74; Michel 238, even though he prefers to read διδαχῆς; NEB.

were here brought about, partly at least, through instruction about the Christian's beginning and the world's end. So far as baptism is concerned it seems that instruction about it had to be given before repentance and faith could be truly established. Repentance and faith did not (usually) come to a decisive climax apart from baptism.

The neatly balanced phrases in 6.1 show that repentance and faith were the negative and positive sides of conversion: the turning from and the turning to (Spicq 147; Michel 239; Strathmann 103; cf. Bultmann, *TWNT* VI 211f.). This spiritual frontier with both its renunciation of the old ways and commitment to Christ is well expressed in baptism.

Repentance and faith, we may say, were stirred up by the promise and warning of resurrection and judgment, and were brought to saving expression in the rite of initiation. If this is a fair conclusion, it confirms our earlier conclusions, that in the primitive Church baptism was primarily an expression of repentance and function of faith. Note also that 'baptism' is distinct from 'laying on of hands' and cannot be used as a title for the complete rite of initiation, let alone for the total event of conversion-initiation.

The close connection of baptism with repentance and faith on the one hand, and with laying on of hands on the other, means that this passage also tells against rather than for the Pentecostal. We have not yet discussed the role of the Spirit, but if Acts is any guide, the laying on of hands not only expressed more fully the community's acceptance of the initiate, but also helped the initiate to receive the Spirit. His repentance and faith came to its vital climax in this single rite of baptism-laying on of hands, and to this repentance and faith the Spirit was given.

(ii) The relation of the clauses in 6.4f. to one another is not certain, but the fact that the middle two are closely bound together by τε . . . καί,[10] and the repetition of γευσαμένους, suggests a structure on the following pattern:

$$\text{ἅπαξ φωτισθέντας γευσαμένους τε τῆς δωρεᾶς τῆς ἐπουρανίου}$$
$$\text{καὶ μετόχους γενηθέντας πνεύματος ἁγίου}$$
$$\text{καὶ καλὸν γευσαμένους θεοῦ ῥῆμα}$$
$$\text{δυνάμεις τε μέλλοντος αἰῶνος.}$$

[10] Blass-Debrunner-Funk 444.

That is to say, the subsequent clauses seem to be rhetorical elaborations and explanations of the initial experience described in ἅπαξ φωτισθέντας.[11] The once-for-all illumination consisted in, on the one hand, a tasting of the heavenly gift and coming to share in the Holy Spirit, and on the other, a tasting of the word of God and powers of the age to come.

Can we define these clauses more closely? The μετόχους γενηθέντας πνεύματος ἁγίου clearly speaks of the gift of the Spirit, which we have seen elsewhere to be the central element in and decisive mark of conversion-initiation. The preceding clause is probably a very near synonym. Not only are they bound together by τε . . . καί, but δωρεά we have seen elsewhere to be closely associated with the Spirit. We may paraphrase: 'not only did they come to experience the gift of salvation-justification which the Spirit brings, but they also received the gift which *is* the Spirit himself.'[12] Nor can we really separate the last clause from the Spirit. The δυνάμεις cannot be understood as other than mighty works effected by the Spirit (cf. 2.4), especially when they are defined as the 'powers of the age to come'. For throughout the NT the Spirit is characteristically the eschatological Spirit – the power of the age to come breaking into and operative in the present age – and the δυνάμεις are the manifestations of his δύναμις as the eschatological Spirit. Moreover, the two limbs of this clause are bound together once again by the unusual τε.[13]

We may therefore say that in the two γευσαμένους clauses we have described the conversion experience of the converts in both its inward and outward aspects: the ῥῆμα and the δυνάμεις being what they heard and saw, the δωρεά and the πνεῦμα ἅγιον being what they experienced in their hearts. These two γευσαμένους clauses describe more fully the experience denoted by ἅπαξ φωτισθέντας. The conversion-initiation experience (the once-for-allness of the event is shown by the aorists and the ἅπαξ) was an illumination of mind

11 So Moffatt 78; cf. Westcott, *The Epistle to the Hebrews* (1889) 147; Michel 241 n. 1; Schweizer, *TWNT* VI 444 n. 784.

12 H. Windisch, *Der Hebräerbrief* (HNT 1931) 50, and Schweizer, *TWNT* VI 444 n. 784, take δωρεά = πνεῦμα; cf. Montefiore 109; Michel 242. Wickham 41, and Strathmann 104, take the two clauses together as equivalent to 'the heavenly gift of the Holy Spirit'. The suggestion that δωρεά refers to the Lord's Supper (Bruce, *Hebrews* 120f.; Michel 242) is hardly to be entertained (Westcott 148; Spicq 150; Beasley-Murray 246; Montefiore 109).

13 Note again the close connection between the Word and the Spirit as the divine instruments of conversion.

and heart brought about by experience of the Gospel's power (cf. 4.12) and the power of the Spirit, the Spirit's gift and the gift of the Spirit. That φωτισθέντας = βαπτισθέντας is wholly improbable.[14] It means rather the saving illumination brought by the Spirit through the Gospel.[15]

(iii) How then do we relate vv. 1f. to vv. 4f.? That the two are closely connected there can be no doubt .The instruction preparatory to baptism, helping to bring about repentance and faith as it does, cannot be very different from the preaching of the Word (cf. 10.26). And if baptism is the decisive moment and act of commitment, it cannot be far removed from the entry into the once-for-all illumination and experience of the Spirit. The precise relation between all these different elements in conversion-initiation may be seen when we realize that we have here again the different parts played by the different participants in conversion-initiation: there is the preaching of the evangelist which culminates in the initiate's acceptance into the community by the rite of baptism and laying on of hands; there is the individual's act of repentance and faith which cannot be separated from his experience of receiving the Word and becoming a partaker of the Spirit; and there is the divine act of illumination (φωτισθέντας – 6.4; 10.32), in which the Spirit is given with his heavenly gift in all his power.

If indeed vv. 1f. deal with the area of overlap between Jewish and Christian teaching, it implies that the decisive differentia of Christianity must be looked for rather in vv. 4f. This would confirm our earlier findings: that the essence of NT Christianity is an experience (γεύεσθαι) – an experience of the Holy Spirit. Without that experience the Christian's religion is little different from that of the Jews; it is by going back on that experience (10.29) that they commit apostasy; it is by going on from that experience that they reach maturity.

10.29: τὸ πνεῦμα τῆς χάριτος – 'the Holy Spirit, who offers himself to man in free grace' (Michel 353), or, 'the Holy Spirit through whom God communicates his grace and favour' (Montefiore 179). If Zech. 12.10 is in mind here (πνεῦμα χάριτος LXX – so Windisch 97; Michel

---

[14] See especially Delling, *Taufe* 103 and n. 375.
[15] See Windisch 50; Käsemann 119 n. 7; Spicq 150; Beasley-Murray 245f., who refers to II Tim. 1.10; II Cor. 4.4–6; Eph. 1.18; and II Esd. 14.22ff., where a petition for the Holy Spirit results in the gift of enlightenment. See also p. 133 above.

353; Strathmann 135; Schweizer, *TWNT* VI 444f.), the writer is thinking of the Spirit as poured out in the end time. That this is the salvation effecting act (contra Schweizer 445) is implied not only by its association with 'the blood of the covenant' (see p. 213 below), but also by the parallel with 6.4–6: if the spurning the Son and profaning his blood = the crucifying the Son (6.6), then the outraging of the Spirit corresponds to the apostasy from the enlightenment etc. of 6.4f.

It is true that the Spirit does not have the same prominence in Hebrews as in Paul (presumably because of the prominence given to Christ – Westcott 331); yet 2.4 is not so very different from Rom. 15.19 etc., nor 10.29 from Eph. 4.30; and the understanding of Christian conversion in 6.4f. is hardly different from Paul's. It is perhaps significant that the OT passages specifically referred to the Spirit speak respectively of the inadequacy of the old dispensation (9.8), of the coming of the new covenant with its forgiveness and the law written within (10.15–18), and of the need for perseverance once begun in the Christian way (3.7–15).

The corollary to this is that baptism alone means nothing for Christianity. It is only when it is related to the experience of God's illumination, God's salvation and God's Spirit that it becomes the rite of Christian initiation. In short, submission to the rite of baptism and laying on of hands brings the initiate's repentance and faith to that climax and decision in which and through which he is illuminated and enters into the saving experience of God's Spirit; so that there is no room here either for a rite or a gift of the Spirit distinct from and subsequent to conversion-initiation.

## Heb. 10.22

It is generally agreed that the λελουσμένοι τὸ σῶμα ὕδατι καθαρῷ refers to Christian water-baptism; the chief dispute is over its relation to the preceding clause. On the one hand are those who argue that there is merely rhetorical parallelism, so that τὰς καρδίας and τὸ σῶμα could be interchanged without altering the sense in any way;[16] on the other hand are those who distinguish the two clauses as giving the conjunction in conversion-initiation of the inward and spiritual cleansing with its outward and visible symbol.[17]

---

[16] Bultmann, *Theology* I 137; Michel 346f.; Oepke, *TDNT* IV 304; Spicq 317; Beasley-Murray 249f.; cf. Mollat 68; Tremel 201f.

[17] Wickham 85; Windisch 93; Flemington 98; Strathmann 133f.; Bruce, *Hebrews* 250f.; cf. Delling, *Taufe* 103; Bieder 149f.

To my mind the latter is much truer to the thought of Hebrews than the former.

For one thing, the heart and the body *together* (*not* each individually, as Beasley-Murray seems to think)[18] represent the entire personality, the whole man.[19] Moreover, there are more types of Hebrew parallelism than synonymous parallelism;[20] in particular, there is what we might call 'complementary parallelism', a type, I suppose, of the more widely recognized 'synthetic parallelism': to pick an example at random, Job 29.5:

> When the Almighty was yet with me,
> when my children were about me.

Taking these two facts together it becomes apparent that the heart is best seen anthropologically, as the inward, hidden aspect of man, while the body is the outward, visible aspect of man. As these two complement each other, so there are two complementary aspects of Christian conversion-initiation: the outward and the inward – the sprinkling of the heart and the washing of the body.

For another thing, this inward, spiritual and outward, material antithesis is wholly in line with the sharp contrast the author has already made in 9.13f.: there is a cleansing which merely operates on the flesh, and a cleansing which reaches the conscience, and these two are not the same. As we have seen, this sort of distinction was by no means uncommon in the ancient world.[21]

It will no doubt be pointed out in objection that this puts Christian baptism on the same level as the Jewish rites and ceremonies and that this would be abhorrent to the man who wrote 8.13–10.10.[22] But this objection cannot be sustained, for the fact remains that Christianity is not a ritual-less religion, and that in the ritual of water-baptism it has a ceremony which closely resembles Jewish lustrations. Indeed, if Christian baptism is at all in view in 6.2, it follows that for the writer Christian baptism ranks with and is no

[18] Beasley-Murray 249.
[19] Moffatt 145.
[20] See e.g. O. Eissfeldt, *The Old Testament, An Introduction* (ET 1965) 57f.
[21] See Josephus, *Ant.* 18, 117, where βαπτισμός is used for John's baptism; Philo, *De Plantatione* 162, and the other Philo passages cited by Oepke, *TDNT* IV 302; 1QS 3.4–9, which also speaks of the inability of the 'water for impurity' to cleanse from sin; in Paul see Rom. 2.28f., and cf. I Cor. 7.34. See also Aesch. fr. 32 in Nairne 101; and pp. 15f. above.
[22] Cf. Kuss, *Auslegung* I 143; Montefiore 174f.

different from Jewish βαπτισμοί (9.10)[23] in that its cleansing reaches no further than the body. Yet, at the same time, it is superior to those older rites in that it belongs to the new covenant; it is accompanied by the reality which it symbolizes, as they were not and could not be; moreover, it helps to bring about that inner cleansing in that it is the vehicle of the repentance and faith which receives the inner cleansing. In other words, Christian baptism is both one with the Jewish lustrations in its merely external operation, and different in that it belongs to the fulfilment and reality of which these other lustrations were only shadows.

It would appear that in the Day of Atonement ceremony of Lev. 16, especially vv. 6, 16, and the red heifer ritual of Num. 19, especially vv. 9, 17f., the author of Hebrews has seen the OT shadow of the two sides of Christian conversion-initiation; he has already pointed to this shadow in 9.13; and now in 10.22 he points to the reality thus foreshadowed: the blood of Christ which is so much better than the blood of goats and bulls, and the pure water of Christian baptism which is so much better than 'water for impurity' fouled with the heifer's ashes.[24]

This then is why the writer has retained a ceremony which was handed down to him by the first Christians, not because it accomplished an inner cleansing where the OT ablutions touched only the outside of a man – only the blood of Christ could do that – but because it was the vehicle of repentance and faith and was accompanied by the inward cleansing, even though it itself cleansed only the body.

That the blood and only the blood of Jesus is the decisive factor in the purification of the Christian which enables him to draw near (that which above all else shows the superiority of Christianity over the religion of the OT – see 7.19, 25; 10.1, 19–22; 11.6; 12.18, 22) is clearly the view of the writer (see 9.12–14; 10.19, 29; 12.24; 13.12, 20). Cf. I John 1.7; Rev. 1.5; 7.14.

The close complementary nature of the two cleansings (of heart and body) remind us that we cannot separate Christian baptism from conversion. It is related to the cleansing of the heart as the

---

[23] Apart from 6.2 βαπτισμοί is used only for Jewish ceremonial washings in its two other NT occurrences (Mark 7.4; Heb. 9.10). The experience of 6.4f. corresponds to the inner purification of the heart in 10.22, while the βαπτισμοί of 6.2 obviously corresponds to the outward washing of the body in 10.22.

[24] Cf. Moffatt 144; Strathmann 134.

body is related to the heart. It is the outward embodiment of the spiritual transformation which is taking place inside a man. It would simply not occur to the writer, or to early Christians generally, that the two could be separate. The popular idea that conversion precedes baptism, and that baptism is a confession of a commitment made some time previously is not to be found in the NT.[25] Baptism is the act of faith, part of the total cleansing which enables the convert to draw near and to enter the Holy of Holies by the way opened up for him by Jesus (vv. 11–22).

[25] Contra Robinson, who seems to distinguish conversion from baptism (144) as he did earlier (72); Bieder, who seems to refer the cleansing of the heart to the effect of preaching 'in the time of preparation before baptism' (148).

# XVIII

## CONVERSION-INITIATION IN PETER

IN recent years I Peter has been the subject of much scrutiny,[1] with the debate centring on the question: To what extent has a baptismal sermon or liturgy, or echoes of a baptismal ceremony, been incorporated into I Peter? The debate is peripheral to our study,[2] and for us the really important issue is, What is the author's understanding of baptism? To answer this question we naturally turn to the one indisputable reference to baptism in I Peter – 3.21. Although it follows one of the most notorious cruces of interpretation in the whole NT, the obscurity of 3.19 fortunately does not affect us much.

### I Peter 3.21

Part of the difficulty in this passage lies in the fact that vv. 19–21 appear to be inserted into a more established confessional framework (vv. 18, 22).[3] The reason for this insertion is to point the parallel between the salvation of Noah through the waters of the Flood, and the salvation of Christians through the waters of baptism (otherwise there would be no adequate reason for the insertion). 3.19 is only the first part of the transitional sequence of subordinate clauses by means of which Peter swings attention away from Christ's death to Christian baptism. It is this realization, that

[1] See the literature cited by R. P. Martin, *Vox Evangelica* (1962) 29–42; and Kümmel's *Introduction*. Other writings include Beasley-Murray 251–8; Delling, *Taufe* 83–6; W. J. Dalton, *Christ's Proclamation to the Spirits: A Study of I Peter 3.18–4.6* (1965) 62–71; and J. N. D. Kelly, *The Epistles of Peter and of Jude* (1969).

[2] I take I Peter to be a genuine letter which uniformly looks back to the single event of conversion-initiation (see especially Moule, *NTS* 3 [1956–57] 1–11; T. C. G. Thornton, *JTS* 12 [1961] 14–26; Kümmel 295f.; Dalton 65–71; Kelly 15–25).

[3] Beasley-Murray 258; see further Dalton 87–102; Kelly 151f.

the thought is driving single-mindedly towards baptism, which gives us the clue to some of the problems which face us. Peter has seen that the parallel between Noah's salvation and the Christian's salvation lies not simply in the fewness and number of those saved,[4] but in the fact that water features both times. It is true that the analogy is far from complete (properly speaking Noah was saved *from* the waters of destruction, but valid typology does not require exact parallelism in all its details);[5] but this is precisely why Peter uses the preposition διά – its ambiguity is what enables him to draw the analogy between the water of the Flood and that of baptism.

The local sense is the only really suitable sense for the story of Noah; but the instrumental sense is more appropriate for baptism – διεσώθησαν δι' ὕδατος = ὃ . . . σώζει βάπτισμα. His use of διά means that Peter can fit the antitype neatly on to the type and ignore the fact that Noah was really saved from the water. In this I agree with Reicke, *The Disobedient Spirits and Christian Baptism* (1946) 141–3; *Peter* 113; C. E. B. Cranfield, *The First Epistle of Peter* (1950) 86; F. W. Beare, *The First Epistle of Peter* (1947) 147f.; J. Moffatt, *The General Epistles Peter, James and Judas* (Moffatt 1928) 142; E. G. Selwyn, *The First Epistle of St Peter*[2] (1946) 202; Dalton 209f.; Kelly 159.

Moreover, it is the *water* 'which saves you now in its antitype, namely baptism'.

Despite the cumbersome nature of two nouns in apposition to ὃ, I prefer this to the explanations of Selwyn 203, and Cranfield 87, who take ἀντίτυπον in apposition to ὑμᾶς, and of Reicke, *Baptism* 145f., and Buse 178f., who refer ἀντίτυπον to *Noah's* salvation through water and translate 'which "antitypical" baptism now saves you'. The former is possible, but less likely since attention is focused on the mode of salvation. The latter is to be rejected: Peter is not describing Noah's salvation through water as a baptism (ἀντίτυπος can mean both the prefiguring shadow and the fulfilling reality – Arndt and Gingrich); far less is he saying that Noah's salvation is what saves his readers now (see further Beasley-Murray 260); and the sense is as cumbersome and as difficult grammatically as the more usual interpretation (as Reicke

---

[4] See B. Reicke, *The Epistles of James, Peter and Jude* (Anchor Bible 1964) 112f.; Dalton 207f.

[5] Cf. Kuss 146. Prof. Moule reads rather too much allegorical significance out of the type when he emphasizes the idea of drowning at this point (*Phenomenon* 74); cf. F. L. Cross, *I Peter – A Paschal Liturgy* (1954) 29.

recognizes – 146). We need not be surprised at the cumbersome nature of the clause: the thought has moved so swiftly and the parallel is so difficult and so compressed that the easiest way out was to put the two nouns in apposition. See also Kelly 160.

Beasley-Murray objects to making ὕδατος the antecedent of ὅ, on the grounds that 'it involves regarding the water as the means of salvation, which . . . is difficult to harmonize with the immediately following words "*not* the removal of dirt from the flesh but . . ." ' (259). On the contrary, it is simply because ὕδατος is the antecedent of ὅ that Peter feels it necessary to add the qualifying and corrective clause. If the whole preceding clause (that is, salvation through water) is the antecedent, we are left with a tautology – 'salvation through water now saves' – and to save the sense we have to resort to that last expedient of a weak hypothesis, viz. emendation of the text (here of ὅ to ᾧ).[6] It is much simpler and better to say that Peter regards water as characterizing Christian baptism, so that in a real sense the water of Christian baptism, which corresponds to the water of the Flood, 'now saves you'. In what precise sense Peter immediately goes on to explain.

The Christian water-rite saves, but, adds Peter, I am not talking about the action of the water. Baptism *is* 'the washing away of bodily pollution', but that operation of the water has nothing to do with the salvation effected. I am talking about the συνειδήσεως ἀγαθῆς ἐπερώτημα made to God. Baptism is the expression of that, and *as such* it saves. The Greek phrase is puzzling, and when so much depends on it for our understanding of baptism our inability to catch its precise meaning is frustrating. Opinion in recent years has been almost equally divided between two meanings: a pledge proceeding from or to maintain a clear conscience or right attitude (JB, TEV), and an appeal or prayer to God for a clear conscience (RSV, NEB). Fortunately it is not essential to choose between these alternatives, for the former characterizes baptism as an expression of commitment, while the latter characterizes it as an expression of repentance. ἐπερώτημα may even indicate a specific moment in the ritual of initiation – the act of confession[7] or moment of (silent) prayer immediately prior to the immersion; but it is

---

[6] So Beasley-Murray 260, following Erasmus, Hort and Beare 148. Only a few minuscules (the earliest cited is from the eleventh century) can be called in to support this theory of a primitive textual corruption.

[7] Cf. Selwyn 205; Moule, *Worship* 51; and Rom. 10.9–10.

more likely that Peter is here denoting the actual water-rite itself as the pledge or prayer, the ἐπερώτημα being in apposition to the βάπτισμα: water-baptism saves in that it is the ἐπερώτημα of a good conscience. Moreover, it saves δι' ἀναστάσεως 'Ιησοῦ Χριστοῦ. That is to say, the prayer or pledge of baptism is efficacious of salvation simply because it is addressed to the risen one, is based on his resurrection, and results in a sharing of that new life from the dead (cf. 1.3).

R. E. Nixon in *Studia Evangelica* IV (ed. F. L. Cross 1968) 437–41, tries to argue that βάπτισμα here = the Christian's baptism of suffering. But it is difficult to describe suffering as a pledge from man to God. This clause also rules out the suggestion of Unger, *Bib.Sac.* 101 (1944) 496f., and L. S. Chafer, *Bib.Sac.* 109 (1952) 215, that βάπτισμα here refers to Spirit-baptism. On the contrary, this passage confirms that βάπτισμα always means the water-rite as such.

We should note for the meaning of baptism that the contrast in the parenthesis is not what many would expect: Peter does not contrast an outward cleansing with an inward cleansing or speak of baptism as God's means of cleansing the heart. Some feel this lack so deeply that they attempt to read it into the sense or even to twist the thought.[8] So accustomed have some commentators become to the view that baptism is something which God effects, a channel of divine grace touching the whole man without and within, that they refuse to believe that Peter could be saying anything different here.[9] But what Peter says is quite unambiguous at this point: baptism saves, not in its washing away the filth of the flesh, but by expressing man's repentance and/or faith to God. By the negative he does not deny that baptism is a rite which touches the body;[10] but he does deny that it is the outward cleansing which saves (that is, οὐ . . . qualifies not βάπτισμα alone but the phrase σώζει βάπτισμα). This is why he says οὐ, and not οὐ μόνον. By the positive statement he affirms that baptism is essentially the expression and vehicle of man's faith, not of God's inner working grace. The antithesis is not at all surprising to those who have followed

[8] Reicke, *Baptism* 187; Schneider, *Briefe* 85; K. H. Schelkle, *Die Petrusbriefe, der Judasbrief* (1961) 109; Delling, *Taufe* 87f.; and those cited in nn. 9, 11–13 below.
[9] See e.g. Kuss 144 n. 95, 147; S. I. Buse in *Christian Baptism* (ed. Gilmore) 177.
[10] Schlatter, *Erläuterungen* 9 Teil 57f.

the whole exposition so far; it is surprising only to those who have failed to grasp that baptism is the means by which men come to God rather than that by which God comes to men.

Dalton (followed by Kelly 161f.) is unnecessarily sceptical about referring σαρκὸς ἀπόθεσις ῥύπου to the material effect of the baptismal water on the body, and proposes as an alternative the much more difficult and improbable hypothesis that the phrase refers to circumcision (215–24). In a context where the train of thought has forced the author to use the word 'water' to characterize baptism it is natural for him to correct the resulting theological imbalance by defining baptism (and the role of water therein) more closely.

For Peter, then, baptism has two aspects: it is a water-rite which cleanses the body, and it is an expression of man's ἐπερώτημα to God. It can also be said to save, so long as we realize that it is only the second aspect which is relevant here. It is not the water or its cleansing operation which effects salvation; the water-rite as water-rite effects nothing more than the washing of the body. When he says that baptism saves, Peter means baptism in so far and only in so far as it is the expression of commitment and repentance. There is *nothing* here of baptism as 'an inward and spiritual grace . . . cleansing the soul',[11] nothing here of baptism creating a good conscience,[12] nothing here of baptism creating 'the possibility (by cleansing the believer of his sins) of "calling upon God" '.[13] Baptism's role in salvation is to serve as the vehicle of man's ἐπερώτημα εἰς θεόν, not of God's χάρις εἰς ἄνθρωπον. This conclusion becomes of fundamental importance when we realize that I Peter 3.21 is the nearest approach to a definition of baptism that the NT affords.

In short, it is not what baptism does to a man, nor something which God is supposed to do to a man through baptism, but what man does with baptism and how he uses it, which is decisive for his salvation, so far as baptism is concerned. We must add this final qualification since, of course, the finally decisive thing in salvation is God's operation on man. What we cannot say from I Peter 3.21 is that 'baptism' describes or effects that divine operation. This has important consequences for the other 'baptismal' passages in I Peter, to which we now turn.

[11] C. Bigg, *St Peter and St Jude*[2] (ICC 1902) 165.
[12] Schnackenburg, *Baptism* 9.    [13] Bultmann, *Theology* I 136.

*I Peter 1.2*

These words bring together the two sides of conversion: man's obedience and the divine cleansing. The thought is of the new covenant in the Spirit, in which the ὑπακοή of the believer and the ῥαντισμός of Christ's blood correspond to the obedience and sprinkling which established the old covenant (Ex. 24.7f.). The thought moves solely in the realm of a spiritual cleansing; the act of ὑπακοή is probably thought of as expressed in baptism (cf. 3.21), but the sprinkling of Christ's blood is the sprinkling of the heart, precisely equivalent to the inward and spiritual healing by Christ's wounds of 2.24. There is no reference to a baptismal rite of sprinkling,[14] far less any suggestion that the baptismal water contained the blessing of Christ's atoning blood.[15] What stands in the forefront of the author's mind is the thought of consecration – the action of the consecrating Spirit who unites the consecration of man with the consecration of Christ's sprinkled blood to set man apart unto God, and in this way establishes the new covenant relation between God and man.

*I Peter 1.22*

Here we have the same combination of ideas: cleansing and obedience. Once again the cleansing is moral and spiritual (τὰς ψυχὰς ὑμῶν ἡγνικότες), as also in James 4.8 and I John 3.3,[16] and there is no reference to baptism.[17] Note further that this purification is not something effected by God, but, as in the other Catholic epistles, is something which men do. I Peter tells us how: by obedience to the truth. In I Peter this probably refers to the once-for-all act of obedience at conversion-initiation (ἡγνικότες – perfect); in fact it may well refer to baptism – their response of faith to the gospel, their acceptance of the challenge and invitation made therein, and their commitment to the One thus proclaimed.[18] This again compares well with 3.21, so that ὑπακοή here is not very different from ἐπερώτημα there. At all events it confirms that baptism, if in

---

[14] Contra Beare 51.

[15] Contra Reicke, *Peter* 77, 85.

[16] Hort 87; Bigg 122; Moffatt 109; Hauck, *TDNT* I 123; Windisch-Preisker 57; Selwyn 149; Schelkle 52.

[17] Contra Beare 83; Buse 176; Cranfield 41; Reicke, *Peter* 86. This applies also to the καθαρισμὸς τῶν ἁμαρτιῶν of II Peter 1.9; cf. Heb. 1.3; I John 1.7, 9 (contra Käsemann, *Essays* 193; Schneider, *Baptism* 29; Moule, *Phenomenon* 73).

[18] Cf. Beare 84; Reicke, *Peter* 86; Kelly 79.

mind here, is for Peter essentially man's act of obedience, not God's act of purification, and that it is the *obedience* which results in purification, not the baptismal rite, but the obedience even when expressed in baptism.

## I Peter 1.3, 23

So far we have seen how Peter puts great emphasis on the act of man in conversion-initiation (ὑπακοή, ἐπερώτημα, see also 2.25); here he focuses attention exclusively on the work of God. As elsewhere in the NT, the supremely decisive factor in conversion is the action of God in creating or remaking anew (cf. e.g. John 3.3–8; II Cor. 5.17; Titus 3.5; James 1.18). The divine instrument of regeneration is the Word (λόγος), which Peter goes on to equate with the particular proclamation (ῥῆμα) of the gospel which came to his readers (cf. James 1.18, 21).

Here again there is no thought of baptism;[19] the thought is of conversion rather than of initiation in so far as these are distinct.[20] Whereas in 3.21 baptism is man's instrument of response to God, in 1.23 the Word is God's instrument in effecting new birth in man. It would be folly to drive a wedge between these as though they were separate events, for the former is linked with purification and salvation (1.22; 3.21), and to the latter is attached regeneration. We are here once again within that complex event conversion-initiation whose unity cannot be broken.

Titus 3.5 is sometimes called in to support the reference to baptism here (e.g., Delling, *Taufe* 84), but that which most suggests the thought of baptism in Titus 3.5 is quite lacking in I Peter 1.3, 23. A closer parallel is James 1.18, and baptism is not in view there at all, as Delling admits (84 n. 288; cf. M. Dibelius and H. Greeven, *Der Brief des Jakobus*[11] [1964] 136).

We are therefore in full accord with Peter when he insists that baptism be seen as the means by which man comes to God rather than the means by which God comes to man. God comes to man through the Word of preaching, and the meeting takes place ἐν ἁγιασμῷ πνεύματος.

What of the Spirit and the relevance of I Peter to Pentecostal doctrine? It is true that he is not given the same prominence as in Paul; but we should note how closely 1.2 compares with II Thess.

[19] See Dalton 69.  [20] Cf. Selwyn 123.

2.13 and I Cor. 6.11, and 1.12 with such Pauline passages as I Cor. 2.4. Moreover, 1.12 may be an allusion to Pentecost (ἀποσταλέντι ἀπ' οὐρανοῦ),[21] and may perhaps also indicate that the preaching of the gospel referred to here resulted in religious revival, in which many were converted and the Spirit wrought wonders through the preachers and his power and presence were experienced and manifested in a very palpable manner.[22] In the light of 1.12 we should probably think of the regenerative power of the Word in 1.23 as being due to the Spirit.[23] Peter may well intend to distinguish between the σπορά (ἐκ) and the λόγος (διά) and to equate the former with the Spirit, as I John does with the synonym σπέρμα.[24] And though he quotes the LXX of Isa. 40.6–8 he may have in mind that Isa. 40.7 speaks of the *rūaḥ* – the flesh and its beauty wither and fade because the *rūaḥ* of the Lord blows upon it; but it is not so with the Word of the Lord: when God breathes his *rūaḥ* upon it, far from withering and fading it abides for ever and becomes a creative force bringing life to all who hear (cf. 1.12, 23). Finally, 4.14 indicates that the Christian knows the constant presence of the Spirit with him – it is this which enables him to rejoice despite his sufferings. Notice especially that both the sufferings (v. 13) and the Spirit are Christ's (v. 14 being an allusion to Isa. 11.2), and that the relation between Christ's glory yet to be revealed (v. 13) and the Spirit of glory (v. 14) suggests Paul's talk of the Spirit as the ἀρραβών and ἀπαρχή of glory, the glory of the End-time.[25] This implies that the Spirit comes to rest upon a man, to 'en-Christ' him, at and as the beginning of his Christian life, giving that initial share in Christ's exalted glory which enables the Christian to endure to the end. At all events we can say firmly that the Pentecostal doctrine of the baptism in the Spirit has no foothold in I Peter, and that, on the contrary, I Peter is sufficiently close to Paul on this point to confirm our complete rejection of this doctrine.

---

[21] Hort 61; Bigg 111; Moffatt 102; Windisch-Preisker 55.

[22] Preisker 152; Schelkle 42; cf. Selwyn 138, 267.

[23] Note the weakly attested variant for 1.22: . . . ἀληθείας διὰ πνεύματος.

[24] Most, however, equate σπορά and λόγος, often with reference to Christ's parable of the sower. This would certainly accord with the following quotation: the imperishable seed being contrasted with the grass that withers.

[25] Beare has some grounds for distinguishing the thought here from the more developed and more distinctively Pauline idea of the Spirit indwelling the heart (36). But we should not press the point, since the idea of 'resting on' may simply be due to the allusion to Isa. 11.2. On the parallel between 4.14 and II Cor. 3.17f. see Selwyn 224.

James has nothing of relevance to our study. In 4.5 the πνεῦμα is best understood as the human spirit, as the context suggests (see further Dibelius 266–8; B. S. Easton, *IB* 12 [1957] 56). It is possible, though unlikely, that James thinks of the Spirit when he speaks of the regenerative power of the Word making converts the ἀπαρχή of his κτίσματα (1.18 – cf. Dibelius 136), and of receiving the ἔμφυτος λόγος which has power (δύναμις) tό save their souls (1.21). C. L. Mitton, *The Epistle of James* (1966) compares Gal. 5.22, 'where the Holy Spirit is thought of as a seed, deeply planted, and bearing rich fruit in Christ-like qualities' (65). In general, however, in James the thought of Wisdom has largely taken the place which other NT writers give to the Spirit (Büchsel 463).

Our study of Hebrews and I Peter has therefore confirmed our earlier conclusions. The essence of NT Christianity was an experience of receiving the Spirit – an experience closely connected with hearing the Word, a reception manifested in eschatological power (Heb. 6.4f.; cf. 2.4; I Peter 1.12, 23; 4.14; James 1.18, 21). But Hebrews and I Peter are most remarkable for their striking confirmation that NT Christianity as a whole understood water-baptism as an expression of faith and repentance (Heb. 6.2), of ὑπακοή and ἐπερώτημα (I Peter 1.2, 22; 3.21), and confined its cleansing effect to the physical body (Heb. 10.22; I Peter 3.21).

# XIX

## CONCLUSION

In this study we have noticed that there are three or four elements and three parties involved in Christian conversion-initiation. Each of these elements and parties could be said to be the characteristic emphasis of each of the three main streams of Christianity. Catholics emphasize the role of the Church and of water-baptism (and laying on of hands); Protestants emphasize the role of the individual and of preaching and faith; Pentecostals emphasize the role of Jesus Christ as Baptizer in the Spirit and of Spirit-baptism.

The Catholic doctrine was a natural development over the centuries. When the Spirit became less the subject of experience and more the object of faith, and direct inspiration became suspect as a result of the Montanist excesses (and the finalizing of the Canon), it was natural that the one very tangible and public element of conversion-initiation should become more and more the focus of attention.[1] Water-baptism could be regulated, whereas faith and the Spirit can not. Here controls could be set up and order maintained. The Spirit became more and more confined to 'the Church', until in all but name 'the Church' stood above the Spirit. To all intents and purposes the Spirit became the property of the Church, with the gift of the Spirit tied to and determined by a ritual act, and authority to bestow the Spirit confined to the bishop.[2] Over the centuries this sacramental doctrine became more and more magical, and conversion-initiation, far from merely focusing on water-baptism became wholly identified with it, with Confirmation in the West a much delayed 'second half'.

Against this extreme sacramentalism and sacerdotalism Protes-

[1] Cf. Robinson, *Spirit* 48, 155, 172.
[2] See Swete, cited by H. Watkin-Jones, *The Holy Spirit in the Mediaeval Church* (1922) 343; Scott, *Spirit* 244f.; cf. E. E. Aubrey, *JTS* 41 (1940) 7f.

tants reacted, and in their reaction the emphasis was shifted from water-baptism to preaching and personal faith, with authority centred in the Bible rather than in the Church. With many this came to mean putting all the weight on faith, and on faith as distinct from and prior to water-baptism; faith was exalted together with the role of preaching, and the role of water-baptism was played down. The Spirit, however, did not return to prominence, largely owing to Protestant suspicion and hatred of the Anabaptists. He was the begetter of faith and of all good, and the reality of his manifestations in the apostolic age was accepted, but little was said about the gift of the Spirit as such, and the charismata were thought to have ceased with the apostles.[3] In scholastic Protestantism the Spirit became in effect subordinate to the Bible, and the latter replaced the sacraments as the principal means of grace and inspiration. Where Catholics fastened on to the objectivity of the sacraments, Protestants fastened on to the objectivity of the Bible.[4] Though the Spirit was regarded as the principal participant in the work of salvation, he was still hardly to be experienced apart from the Bible.[5] 'The Bible only is the religion of Protestants', and conversion is essentially justification by faith alone.

Like earlier 'enthusiasts' Pentecostals have reacted against both these extremes. Against the mechanical sacramentalism of extreme Catholicism and the dead biblicist orthodoxy of extreme Protestantism they have shifted the focus of attention to the *experience* of the Spirit. Our examination of the NT evidence has shown that they were wholly justified in this. That the Spirit, and particularly the gift of the Spirit, was a *fact of experience* in the lives of the earliest Christians has been too obvious to require elaboration (eg., Acts 2.4; 4.31; 9.31; 10.44–46; 13.52; 19.6; Rom. 5.5; 8.1–16; I Cor. 12.7, 13; II Cor. 3.6; 5.5; Gal. 4.6; 5.16–18, 25; I Thess. 1.5f.; Titus 3.6; John 3.8; 4.14; 7.38f.; 16.7 – the presence of the Spirit was to be better than the presence of Jesus). It is a sad commentary

[3] See e.g. J. Buchanan, *The Office and Work of the Holy Spirit* (1843) 87ff., 203ff., 243f., 250ff.; Smeaton 47ff., 140ff., 198ff., 208ff.; Kuyper 182, 283–427; Palmer 77ff., 123ff., 145; also B. B. Warfield, *Miracles Yesterday and Today* (1918) 21ff.

[4] Cf. Brunner, *Truth as Encounter* (ET 1964) 77f.

[5] See H. Watkin-Jones, *The Holy Spirit from Arminius to Wesley* (1929) 170f.; G. F. Nuttall, *The Holy Spirit in Puritan Faith and Experience* (1946) 23f., 31–33; and cf. the recent statements of B. Ramm, *The Witness of the Spirit* (1959) 64, and J. I. Packer, *'Fundamentalism' and the Word of God* (1958) 119. See also Hendry 72–95.

on the poverty of our own immediate experience of the Spirit[6] that when we come across language in which the NT writers refer directly to the gift of the Spirit and to their experience of it, either we automatically refer it to the sacraments and can only give it meaning when we do so (I Cor. 6.11; 12.13; II Cor. 1.21f.; Eph. 1.13f.; Titus 3.5–7; John 3.5; 6.51–58, 63; I John 2.20, 27; 5.6–8; Heb. 6.4), or else we discount the experience described as too subjective and mystical in favour of a faith which is essentially an affirmation of biblical propositions, or else we in effect psychologize the Spirit out of existence.

The Pentecostal attempt to restore the NT emphasis at this point is much to be praised, but it has had two unfortunate aspects. First, the Pentecostal has followed the Catholic in his separation of Spirit-baptism, from the event of conversion-initiation (represented in water-baptism), and has made the gift of the Spirit an experience which follows after conversion. This is quite contrary to the NT teaching. According to Luke and Paul baptism in the Spirit was not something subsequent to and distinct from becoming a Christian; nor, it must be added, was it something which only an apostle (or bishop) could hope to bring about, or something which happened only once or twice in apostolic days. The gift of the Spirit may not be separated in any way from conversion, whether to be set before conversion as its presupposition, or after conversion as a merely empowering, confirmatory or charismatic gift. The gift of the Spirit (that is, Spirit-baptism) is a distinct element within conversion-initiation, indeed, in the NT, the most significant element and focal point of conversion-initiation. It is the gift of saving grace by which one enters into Christian experience and life, into the new covenant, into the Church. It is, in the last analysis, that which makes a man a Christian (e.g., Mark 1.8; Acts 11.16f.; Rom. 8.9f.; I Cor. 12.13; II Cor. 3.6; Gal. 3.3; Titus 3.6f.; John 3.3–8; 20.22; I John 3.9; Heb. 6.4). It is true that when the Spirit thus entered a life in the earliest days of the Church he regularly manifested his coming by charismata and his presence by power (to witness), but these were corollaries to his main purpose – the 'christing' of the one who had taken the step of faith (πιστεύσας).

The second mistake of the Pentecostal is that he has followed the Protestant in his separation of faith from water-baptism. Con-

[6] See A. R. Vidler, *Christian Belief* (1950) 56; and cf. Newbigin 91; L. M. Starkey, *The Work of the Holy Spirit: A Study in Wesleyan Theology* (1962) 143.

version is for him Spirit-engendered faith reaching out to 'receive
or accept Jesus', so that a man is a Christian before his water-
baptism and the latter is little more than a confession of a past
commitment. This may well accord with present Baptist practice,
but it is not the NT pattern. The NT writers would to a man reject
any separation of the decisive movement of faith (πιστεῦσαι) from
baptism, either by way of putting the act of faith prior to baptism,
thereby reducing baptism to a mere symbol, or by way of putting
it after baptism, thereby exalting baptism to an instrument of
divine power which operates on a person without his knowledge
or consent. Baptism properly performed is for the NT essentially
the act of faith and repentance – the actualization of saving faith
without which, usually, commitment to Jesus as Lord does not
come to its necessary expression. As the Spirit is the vehicle of
saving grace, so baptism is the vehicle of saving faith.[7]

By thus asserting the prominence and centrality of the gift of
the Spirit in conversion-initiation we have been able to give water-
baptism its proper NT role, neither more nor less – viz. as the
expression of the faith to which God gives the Spirit. The initial
refusal to use 'baptism' as a shorthand description of conversion-
initiation has been amply justified. βάπτισμα or βαπτισμός in the NT
means the water-rite pure and simple, whose cleansing efficacy
reaches no further than the body (Matt. 3.7; Mark 7.4; Luke 3.3;
John 3.25; Eph. 4.5; Heb. 6.2; 9.10; 10.22; I Peter 3.21; also Rom.
6.4; Col. 2.12; it is used once metaphorically – Mark 10.38f. =
Luke 12.50). βαπτίζειν, βαπτίζεσθαι means either to baptize literally
(in water) or to baptize metaphorically (in Spirit into Christ, in
suffering into death), but it never embraces both meanings simultaneously (Matt. 3.11; Mark 1.8; 10.38f.; Luke 3.16; 12.50; John
1.33; Acts 1.5; 10.47; 11.16; Rom. 6.3; I Cor. 10.2; 12.13; Gal.
3.27). The NT writers would never say, for example, that the 'sign
(of baptism) is or effects what it signifies'. Spirit-baptism and water-
baptism remain distinct and even antithetical, the latter being a
preparation for the former and the means by which the believer
actually reaches out in faith to receive the former. Again, Oepke's
talk of baptism as 'the action of God or Christ'[8] is correct only if

[7] Cf. Barth, *Dogmatik* IV/4, who abandons his earlier 'sacramental' understanding of baptism, and, like his son, defines Christian baptism in terms of the
human decision which corresponds to the divine turning to man, and as man's
prayer to God, the human answer to the divine work. See also p. 94 above.
[8] Oepke, *TDNT* I 540.

he means Spirit-baptism. It is incorrect if he means water-baptism. In the NT there is no third alternative.

I must confess to being completely unmoved by any appeal to 'the sacramental principle', or 'incarnational basis to sacramental teaching' (e.g. Wotherspoon, *Sacraments* 1–30). We have seen clearly enough that Hebraic thought and NT writers like Luke, Paul and the author of Hebrews knew well how to distinguish and contrast inward and outward, spiritual and physical. It is true, of course, that God came to men in and through physical, material, human flesh in Jesus, but it is perilous to draw from this a general principle which can be applied forthwith to the sacraments. Rather our study of the relevant NT passages shows that for those authors the divine instrument in the divine-human encounter is the Spirit and, or through, the Word, while the corresponding human instrument is faith and, or through, baptism.

If the NT is to be our rule, therefore, the rite of water-baptism may not be given the central role in conversion-initiation. It symbolizes the spiritual cleansing which the Spirit brings and the finality of the break with the old life; it is a stimulus to faith and enables commitment to come to necessary expression; it is the rite of acceptance by the local Christians or congregation as representative of the world-wide Church; but otherwise it is not a channel of grace, and neither the gift of the Spirit nor any of the spiritual blessings which he brings may be inferred from or ascribed to it. A recall to the beginnings of the Christian life in the NT is almost always a recall not to baptism, but to the gift of the Spirit, or to the spiritual transformation his coming effected.

In short, in the beginning, no Christian was unbaptized, but not all those baptized were *ipso facto* Christians. No Christian was without the Spirit, for only those who had (received) the Spirit were *ipso facto* Christians. The NT teaching at this point may be expressed epigrammatically thus:

Faith demands baptism as its expression;
Baptism demands faith for its validity.
The gift of the Spirit presupposes faith as its condition;
Faith is shown to be genuine only by the gift of the Spirit.

The importance of this conclusion for Christianity as a whole should not be underestimated in a day of radical questioning, when many Christians are searching within the Bible, their traditions and themselves in an attempt to grasp the root and living heart of the Christian faith stripped bare of all its accretions and non-essentials, in a day when the question is being asked with increasing frequency and particularly by Christians themselves: What is a Christian? What is the distinguishing hallmark of the Christian? Our study has given us the NT answer to this question with some precision; with remarkable consistency the answer came: That man is a Christian who has received the gift of the Holy Spirit by committing himself to the risen Jesus as Lord, and who lives accordingly.

If this is an accurate assessment of NT Christianity, and the apostolic tradition and teaching has any normative significance for us today, then it in turn inevitably raises several other large and important questions for present-day Christianity at both denominational and ecumenical level. For example: Are modern theologies of conversion-initiation adequate? Do Churches really understand the respective roles of Spirit, faith and baptism, or give them satisfactory expression in their various liturgies and practices of initiation? Can infant baptism any longer be justified by the prevenient grace argument so popular today? Has modern evangelism held forth the promise of the Spirit explicitly enough? Such questions can only be asked, since to answer them goes beyond the scope of the present study.

But there is an even more basic question which our conclusions raise, and one which must be answered before these other questions can be fully dealt with: Accepting that the gift of the Spirit is what makes a man a Christian, how do he and others know if and when he has received the Spirit? In what ways does the Spirit manifest his coming and his presence? What indications are there that the Spirit is active in a congregation or in a situation? Clearly these are questions of first importance at all points of Christian life and activity. And in case it should be thought that I have been less than just to the Pentecostals let me simply add in reference to these questions that Pentecostal teaching on spiritual gifts, including glossolalia, while still unbalanced, is much more soundly based on the NT than is generally recognized. But here and now I can only point out the relevance of these issues, since to discuss the manifestations of the Spirit is a subject in itself. If God wills I shall in due course take up this subject since it is a necessary sequel to the present study.

# INDEX OF MODERN AUTHORS AND WORKS

(*Italics* indicate that a new title appears for the first time)

# INDEX OF BIBLICAL REFERENCES

## OLD TESTAMENT

237

# NEW TESTAMENT

(*Italics* indicate some discussion of the passage)

## OTHER JEWISH AND EARLY CHRISTIAN WRITINGS